FALSE ALARM

The Computerization of Eight Social Welfare Organizations

JOHN M. GANDY
LORNE TEPPERMAN

Wilfrid Laurier University Press

Canadian Cataloguing in Publication Data
Gandy, John M.
    False alarm : the computerization of eight social welfare
organizations

Includes bibliographical references and index.
ISBN 0-88920-987-1

1. Social service – Data processing.   2. Social
work administration – Data processing.   3. Social
service – Employees – Effect of automation on.
I. Tepperman, Lorne, 1943-   .   II. Title.

HV29.2.G36 1990   361'.0028'5   C90-093121-3

Copyright © 1990
Wilfrid Laurier University Press
Waterloo, Ontario, Canada
N2L 3C5

Cover design by *Leslie Macredie*

Printed in Canada

False Alarm: The Computerization of Eight Social Welfare Organizations has been produced from a manuscript supplied in electronic form by the authors.

CONTENTS

LIST OF DIAGRAMS AND TABLES

Acknowledgements

Many individuals and institutions have contributed to the success of our research and the production of this report.

We are especially grateful to the staff and Boards of the eight social welfare organizations we studied in this research. Their cooperation meant investing considerable time and energy in our project. They were kind enough to fit our needs into already busy and demanding schedules, and we thank them for it.

Our research staff — Duncan Matheson, Susan Scott, Marne Hunt and Jacqueline Latter — assisted us in developing data collection instruments, collecting the data, and analysing the data from specific organizations they had studied. We appreciate their contribution. Organizing and facilitating their work was office manager Jennifer Jarman and her successor Carol Irving, both of whom carried out their tasks exceptionally well and with good humour.

Additional early contributions were made by Alison Harold-Steckley and Lucy Lach, who helped with the literature review; and Rhonda Lenten, who conducted a score of interviews in one of the larger organizations.

Once the data were collected, William Crosson consulted on statistical questions and programmed our computer runs. Special thanks go to Angela Djao who spent part of her sabbatical year working with us to analyse the data. Our report benefited considerably from her insights which prodded us to explore new aspects of the data.

Important integrative and editorial work was carried out by Steve Stunell and Alan Wain. They helped us pull together the mass of separate analyses into a form that could be worked on, added to, and brought to some conclusions.

Innumerable drafts of the manuscript were prepared by Heather White; she showed considerable patience in coping with an unusual number of changes in our thinking and writing.

Although they are not responsible for what we have done with their suggestions, we would like to thank those colleagues who read and commented on one or more drafts of the manuscript: Professors Jack Richardson (Sociology, McMaster University), Lorna Marsden (Sociology, University of Toronto), Jim Gripton (Social Welfare, University of Calgary), C.C. (Kelly) Gotlieb (Computer Science, University of Toronto) and Ms Susan Fawcett (Sociology, University of Toronto).

Finally and most important, we want to thank the Social Sciences and Humanities Research Council of Canada. Our research was made possible by grants from its Human Context of Science and Technology Strategic Grants Program. We hope that the finished work will justify their confidence and the support they have provided since we first approached them with our idea nearly five years ago. This book has been published with the help of a grant from the Social Science Federation of Canada, using funds provided by the Social Sciences and Humanities Research Council of Canada.

J.G.
L.T.

Preface

The growing use of computers is one of the most important technological developments since the Second World War. The computer has made it possible to store and retrieve data very quickly, greatly facilitating the administration of human service and social control organizations. But for the most part, administrators and managers have failed to consider the effects of this technology on their organizations, staff, clients, or external environment. Lenk (1980) and Mowshowitz (1976) both found that users of computer technology have applied it without considering its social impact, for example.

The need for research on the social impact of information processing has been a recurrent theme in the organizational literature (Kling, 1980; Attewell and Rule, 1984). The present research examines a sector of society in which the use of computerized information is relatively new. We believe that answering the most pressing organizational questions on computerization will help others reduce the tension between the computerized system and those affected by the system.

Computerized information systems can be destructive or constructive for organizations and staff. However, the impact of a system cannot be predicted from its logical design alone: one must analyze how well the design fits the needs, interests, and existing practices of those who are likely to use it. This is the approach we have taken in studying the impact of the introduction of this technology on social welfare organizations and their staff.

We selected social welfare organizations as the setting for our research for several reasons. First, the programs of these agencies are based on values that many believe are put at risk by computerization: namely, the values of confidentiality, self-determination, privacy, autonomy, discretion, initiative, and professionalism. Second, the clientele of social welfare agencies are highly vulnerable to centralization and changes in the power between the individual and the organization. Third, in social welfare agencies, personal autonomy and the exercise of ethical choice are more significant issues than in other types of organization. Finally, in recent years government, private funding bodies, and the Canadian public have demanded greater accountability from social welfare organizations. Increasingly, agencies are expected to generate and use data that are reliable, well organized, and easily retrievable. Computer technology has already shown its value in generating high quality data for the information systems of business organizations. Recently, many Canadian social welfare organizations have introduced computerized information systems in the hopes of gaining similar benefits.

However, we have been unable to locate good research on the effectiveness of these new systems. The present research is an empirical in-depth examination of computer use in social welfare organizations. It has been designed to test the predictions of social welfare specialists and others regarding the impact of computerization on these organizations and those staffing them.

The introduction of a computerized information system significantly changes organizations responsible for collecting and storing data. Secondary effects are often independent of the technology, however, as the U.S. Office of Technology has pointed out: "Because much more information can be obtained, handled, processed and distributed so much faster, old problems are not merely exacerbated but new ones created" (Office of Technology Assessment, 1981, p. 7). Because the technology has impacts well beyond the social welfare organization using it, a potential exists for changing or modifying the values central to the provision of social services and to the larger society. As Mowshowitz notes: "use of computers for statistical purposes and for monitoring individual behaviour may improve some . . . services, but there is the very real possibility of extensions of legitimate power which limit individual freedom" (1976, p. 273).

As in other organizations, the control over social welfare workers is critical. In addition, social welfare organizations exercise social control over clients. The nature and quality of information has important consequences for the life chances of all who use the services of social welfare organizations, whether voluntarily or not.

In the foreseeable future, computers will be used more widely by social welfare agencies. Computerized information systems may increase accountability and improve management practices in social welfare agencies. However, the differential use of computerized information systems by social welfare organizations will not be explained solely on rational grounds, i.e. in terms of the potential of the technology for increasing effectiveness. Some problems associated with computer use are common to all organizations. Others are peculiar to social welfare agencies. In either event, computer use will change the way information is viewed and used in social welfare agencies.

We have identified three major problems that characterize the present state of knowledge and empirical research on computerization and social welfare organizations.

First, there is a shortage of careful empirical research on social service organizations that have adopted and used computers. Little work of any quality has been published. On the other hand, quite a lot of speculative and prescriptive work has appeared. The reader is sometimes hard pressed to distinguish between the two: empirical research tends to shade off into prescription, and prescriptive research tends to put forward solutions as though they were based on empirical data. Hence confusion arises as to the status of the evidence one is examining.

Second, the published empirical work provides an inconsistent picture of the reasons organizations computerize and the consequences of this decision. The inconsistency may be due to differences in the types of organizations studied; or to trends over time, with computer adoption and implementation becoming easier with time. Or the inconsistency may simply reflect variations in the quality of the research.

Finally, much discrepancy exists between the "findings" and predictions of the normative or speculative work, and the findings of more conventionally empirical work. In general, the early prescriptive work published up to about 1980 offers a dire picture of the dangers of computerization. This negative image is simply not borne out by the empirical work completed since 1980. Again, it is not immediately clear whether the prescriptive work was wrong and the empirical work right; the prescriptive work was right in the long run and the empirical work, right in the short run; or whether some other combination of explanations is needed.

Chapter 1

The Institutional and Social Context
of Computing in Social Welfare
Organizations

Most of the research on computing in organizations in the last decade has examined the success or failure of information systems, or tested and developed new, innovative uses for computer technology. This thrust is consistent with the belief of many computer scientists, who have carried out this research, that computer technology will help organizations, both private and public, achieve their goals more effectively and efficiently. Those proceeding from this perspective often assume agreement on the social goals of computing (Kling, 1980c, p. 63; Danziger and Kramer, 1986, p. 1).

A second but smaller group of researchers has undertaken research on the social character and consequences of the use of computer technology in organizations. These researchers proceed from the premise that there is no consensus on the social goals of computing. They are more concerned with the consequences of computer technology for the staff and customers or clients of organizations, and view social equity as a more important value than efficiency.

Kling (1980c) calls this second group of researchers, into whose camp the present authors fall, "segmented institutionalists." Empirical research by this group of scholars has examined the impact of computer technology in public and private organizations. However, very little of their research has been conducted in human service organizations.

Surveys of the findings of this research make it very clear that a great many variables determine the impact of computing on organizations; nonetheless, these variables are available for study. Moreover, earlier research shows the importance of understanding the social and institutional worlds in which the computer technology is utilized. One observer states that this places a heavy burden on the researcher to "develop keen accounts of the technologies in use and of the basic social processes that organized the institutional, occupational and social worlds in which technology is employed" (Kling, 1980c, p. 104).

In addition to the research literature on computer use in organizations,

1

we reviewed the literature on the use of computer technology in human service organizations. Most of this literature is speculative, not based on empirical data. However, as with the more general research on computers in organizations, it provides insights about the social and institutional worlds of social welfare organizations that are central to this research.

This chapter will review the research and literature that we found most useful in the design of our own research and, specifically, in selecting the variables we studied most intensively. It will also discuss the organizational imperatives, needs, values, and external pressures that have been identified as determining the use and impact of computer technology in social welfare organizations.

The Use of Computerized Information Systems in Social Welfare Organizations: An Overview

Social welfare organizations are typically characterized as people-sensitive institutions grounded in intuitive, unsystematic decision-making procedures (Davis and Allen, 1979). Yet they are not wholly intuitive and unsystematic. Anthony (1965) and Wilensky (1967) point to a reciprocal relationship between the structure of an organization and the kinds of problems the organization must solve. The organizational structure and processes reflect both the philosophy of the organization and the need to perform specific functions well.

Each information system must be understood as part of the organization that uses it (Weirich, 1980). Different types of organization and levels of organizational activity demand different data bases and processing procedures. Social welfare organizations range in size from large, bureaucratic, government-administered centres to small privately-owned or government branch service agencies. Their respective information systems vary accordingly: large agencies tend to have management-oriented computer systems in accounting, services and client data; medium agencies, to have management-oriented computer systems located outside the organization in a computer bureau. Small agencies often share computer time with a main office (Schoech and Schkade, 1981). As well, strategic planning, management and operational control levels of activity demand different types of information, requiring different hardware and software applications (Gorry and Morton, 1971). Some uses of computers by social welfare organizations include:

1. storing general client data;
2. automating case management, which involves tracking the client from the initial entry period and recording the plan of action, units of service delivered and client's progress;

3. determining client eligibility for financial and social service;
4. comparing intake data on new clients and previous clients with a high-risk profile;
5. reporting general statistics;
6. accounting, payroll, maintenance operations;
7. listing cases per program, by their opening and closing dates, to indicate length of treatment;
8. recording number of cases per geographic area, to determine service needs;
9. monitoring number of hours of client contact required for guidance in certain programs.

(Sources: Schoech and Arangio [1979], Schoech and Schkade [1980b], and Fein [1975].)

Essentially three organizational levels of activity are found in a social welfare organization: strategic, management and operational/tactical. The strategic level is mainly administrative. Here the objectives, goals and policies of the organization are conceptualized. Resources required to achieve these objectives are also specified. The information required at this level is obtained from sources external to the organization (Gorry and Morton, 1971).

The second level, managerial, is less conceptual and more concrete. Organizational resources must be obtained and used efficiently to accomplish organizational goals. Policies must be successfully implemented through planning and monitoring. These ends are accomplished by functional cooperation and interpersonal interaction (Mason and Mitroff, 1973).

Finally, operational/tactical activity involves efficient operationalization of the organization's tasks and services as they were conceived at the strategic level. This requires monitoring and maintaining services by obtaining information from within the organization (Holland, 1977).

Primary information transactions occur at the worker/client level. The service worker is thought to be the primary information user; further, the information generated here activates organizational functioning. Information needed varies according to level of activity and the respective functions associated with each level, i.e., strategic planning, management and operational control. Types of decisions the information must support also depend on the level of organizational activity. For example, decisions at the top management level are complex and risky. Top decision-makers are constrained by policy guidelines, legislation, regulation, grant guidelines and advisory committees. Decisions by middle management are less complex and more predictable. Finally, decision makers at the lowest organizational level are subject to multiple subordination (professional, organizational, client group, environmental); their decisions, therefore, differ qualitatively from those taken at the other two levels (Schoech and Schkade, 1980a, 1981; Cohen *et al.,* 1979).

The type of information needed varies from level to level, and from organization to organization, depending on the specialized activities of each. Another source of variance is the type and degree of influence exerted by the external environment. Gruber (1974) identified "social pressures" that change the nature of social welfare organizations: they include monitoring and evaluation of social programs; new technologies; new kinds of decisional analysis (e.g., simulation and modelling; social forecasting); and rationalization of the budgetary process. Although often arising outside the boundaries of the organizations, these processes influence agencies through government regulations and standards, and through third-party demands for service or accountability (Lowe and Sugarman, 1978).

A major problem with information support systems is the inconsistent quality and reliability of case records in social welfare organizations (Schoech and Schkade, 1980a). Standardization is lacking largely because "there never has been a commonly accepted language that describes the client's problem, the action taken by the worker, and the result or outcome of having taken the action" (Quinn, 1976). Since processes and outcomes vary so much, managers have no standard against which to assess performance (Cohen *et al.,* 1979).

Use of Computer Generated Data in Performance Assessment

Performance assessment involves defining goals and objectives, standardizing organizational processes, and quantifying output. Techniques used in input-output analyses are largely derived from business management and the industrial model of production (Karger, 1986). There, input is managed so that the outcome will be in the desired amount and of maximum quality. "This new managerial view is extending its hegemony in education, health planning and social services" (Gruber, 1974). Yet the product of non-profit service delivery systems is far less amenable to specification than that of profit-oriented systems (Ehlers *et al.,* 1976; Karger, 1986). Quantifiable variables may include process costs, amount of staff time used in direct and indirect services, and number of clients served per unit time, or per program. The danger lies in making quantity measures more important than the quality of service provided (Noah, 1978).

Performance assessment is highly related to accountability. Data on agency and worker activity summarize organizational activities and can be used for internal and external reporting; however they are not sufficient for performance assessment, which requires an active attempt by agency administrators and managers to establish goals and objectives, standardize procedures, and quantify output measures. Failure to conduct such assessments is often seen as resistance to change (Reid, 1974).

Information Needs of Social Welfare Organizations

Lewis (1978) notes that the culture of social welfare organizations differs from that of business organizations. "Selective inefficiency" may be necessary here in the interests of ethical practice or agency survival. Williams (1983, p. 14) is more specific, questioning whether, in a computerized system, individual clients will continue to develop relationships with identifiable, individual social workers. He feels it is important to determine what elements of self-direction, autonomy and authority the social worker will retain, as these are crucial to work maturation and personal identity.

Given the confusion about goals, one approach to effective computer use might be to give priority to developing valid and reliable indicators of program output. However, a critic of information systems in non-profit agencies cautions that perhaps "professional work is too complex and diffuse in its impact to be easily accounted for and naive attempts to account for outcome might undermine the credibility and integrity of the work itself" (Herzlinger, 1977, p. 87).

Certain characteristics of human service agencies give rise to unique information needs: these organizations process people, who are simultaneously their input, raw material and product; they lack determinate and effective technologies; and they have ambiguous, often contradictory goals which must accommodate the multiple expectations and conflicting demands of a pluralistic society (Sarri and Hasenfeld, 1978).

Human service agencies also differ from business agencies in that equally complex decision-making takes place at the bottom and top of the organization (Schoech and Schkade, 1980b). Further, in the private sector, management measures success in terms of financial profit. In human services, this profit motive is usually missing. Thus, the output of non-profit service delivery systems is less amenable to specification and evaluation (Noah, 1978). As a result, much can be learned from problems already solved in privately-run organizations, but care must be taken when transferring technology and its social organization from one field to another.

Most human service agencies currently use the microcomputer, if any computer at all. The microcomputer-based information system can automate agency functions such as bookkeeping, client profiles, staff time and effort, needs assessment, information and referral, client tracking and scheduling, and program evaluation (Schoech, 1979). Unlike mainframe computers, microcomputers short circuit "hassles over access and control," or transform the issues from inter-agency conflicts into intra-agency conflicts.

Although Sharron (1984) predicts that a new generation of mini- and microcomputers will probably sweep through the social services in the next decade, we are persuaded by the conclusions of Danziger and Kraemer (1986) that changes in the nature and impacts of computing in organizations

have been incremental and this is unlikely to change. On this point, Glastonbury (1986, p. 11) has observed that social welfare organizations "shuffled
rather slowly into computing over the last decade." There is little reason to
believe that this pattern will change with the introduction of mini- and microcomputers.

Computerization — A Threat to the Values, Ideology and Professionalism of Social Work?

A point frequently made in the literature is that computerization of information systems threatens the value base of social work, traditional ways of
delivering service, and relations between clients and staff. Some fears about
the impact of this technology grow out of the organizational impact of computer technology in other sectors. Other fears are harder to explain and suggest computerization is like a Rorschach test, bringing out hidden, diffuse
fears about formal organization *per se* (Turkle, 1980).

Some resistance to a new technology like the computer may flow not
from a real likelihood of loss, but from an unwillingness to retrain and learn
new skills. Perceived gains and losses are not only rooted in the unique experiences of individuals; they are socially structured. That is to say, they are
widely shared by groups of people and often supported by some group-
enhancing ideology, a world-view that dignifies the group and its activities.
Professional socialization, as delivered to students in medical, law, social
work or nursing schools, for example, shapes the perceptions of professional
practitioners-to-be, often for life. One concern of the present study is to study
the effect of such professional socialization on the willingness of social
workers to adopt and profit from computers. The literature on social work
education uniformly argues that professional socialization will stand in the
way of computer utilization.

Some of the controversy about computers in social welfare organizations arises out of the conflict one conventionally finds between line and professional staff in large organizations. This conflict derives from conflicting
loyalties and priorities. The staff person's loyalty is owed first to the client,
second to the profession, and a distant third to the organization. Professional
activity is tailored to honour one's loyalties in that order. Sometimes organizations are successful in "re-socializing" professionals, so that loyalty to
their profession is placed third after loyalty to their organization. In organizations which are relatively profession-dominated, or non-bureaucratized,
adopting computers requires first resolving conflicting views about the purpose of the organization and the purpose of using the new technology.

The role of professional socialization in all this is unclear. Many claim
the professional social welfare ideology opposes computers because they dis-
turb the unique relationship between client and worker. That such an ideol-

ogy exists is amply documented. Indeed, it goes hand in hand with a generalized hostility toward research or data analysis of any kind. Gripton comments: "Social work's opposition to computers is similar to that of other professionals whose services are mediated through extensive face-to-face interactions with clients" (Gripton, n.d., p. 1).

The computer has been described as dehumanizing, extra-human, anti-human, alienating, depersonalizing and mechanistic (Abels, 1972; Sullivan, 1980; Gruber, 1974; Gripton, n.d.; Welbourn, 1980). This description reflects the social work profession's commitment to humanistic values. One observer predicted the technological mandate to increase efficiency and productivity would transform social workers from competent professionals to machine-like components, depriving them of their dignity and worth, de-skilling them and devaluing the social work profession. To meet these dangers it has been proposed that efficiency be redefined in human terms; planning be based on the needs of workers and extend from a humanistic framework; and an evaluative technology be developed which can be used universally (Karger, 1986).

A consensus in the literature suggests computerized information systems may encroach on the judgement or "artistry" of the professional staff (Zuboff, 1982). Computerization also tends to overestimate the reliability, validity and significance of quantifiable data, and this may be dysfunctional (Danziger, 1985). More specifically, staff in social welfare organizations fear that computerization will objectify and depersonalize interaction between them and their clients (Goodfriend, 1979; Geiss and Viswanathan, 1986; Butterfield, 1986). In health agencies with computerized information systems, staff felt the computer eroded human compassion (Trute *et al.*, 1982). In the social welfare literature computers are often seen as having the potential for reducing the discretionary powers of staff, particularly professionals in "people-oriented" organizations (Levi, 1985).

Professional staff in social welfare organizations are also concerned about changes in the work environment. These include fears about the necessity of learning new skills, roles and role relationships (Blacklock, 1982). Also, "The application of computers to other than routine information processing threatens loss of professional power, status and prestige" (Gripton, n.d., p. 1).

Confidentiality of client records is said to be very important to professionally trained social workers who fear that information about clients might be used for non-professional or political reasons (Boyd *et al.,* 1978; Hill, 1974; Staff Association of the Children's Aid Society of Metropolitan Toronto, 1978). Computerization provides new opportunities to compromise the privacy of records because of easier access to files (Reamer, 1986). One author (Holbrook, 1986) points out that dependent populations such as welfare recipients, who have the most to fear from computer technology, are usually least aware of their rights regarding public records.

Major areas of concern are control of access to stored information, specification of confidentiality requirements for those receiving the information, and controls on the disclosure of non-essential personal data (Noah, 1978; Goodfriend, 1979; Butterfield, 1986; Barker, 1986). A researcher reminds us that "the computer's capacity for information storage, access and transfer of data at relatively low costs makes investigating client records easier, faster and more thorough than ever before. The data that will be misused is also increased" (Birmingham, 1981, p. 23). A further dimension of the confidentiality issue is pointed out by Glastonbury (1985, p. 92), who warns that

> the computer will take the personal social services into an entirely different league, with huge transfers of private data, by accident, illicit behaviour or conscious decision. If the social worker is to be part of a network of data-gathering, a contributor to data banks, then it will no longer be possible to talk intimately and privately to clients. The relationship will therefore be affected and will become more formal and guarded. It will be harder to provide good assessments, and the trusting and cooperative relationship which is at the root of effective counselling will be wiped out (Glastonbury, 1985, p. 92).

The literature leaves one confused as to whether these expressions of concern are merely "ideological" — that is, discussions of problems that practising social workers "ought" to be concerned about — or actual concerns of social workers confronted with computerization. Moreover, whether the concerns are ideological or actually held by practising social workers, does computerization actually create the problems the literature suggests it will? The literature at hand does not provide an answer to this question.

Pressure for Increased Accountability

The growing pressure for increased efficiency is part of a more general social pressure — namely, for accountability (Boden, 1982). However, Glastonbury (1985, p. 28) suggests the history of computer uses in social service departments indicates "pressure and opportunity played a large part, with careful design and reflection often some way behind." Davis and Allen (1979) accurately point out that large amounts of money are no longer readily appropriated to human service organizations to be used as they see fit. Funding bodies are demanding more detailed financial and service delivery information, so they can compare organizations that provide similar services to similar clients (Butterfield, 1986).

This pressure for increased accountability originates outside the human service agency. First, public funds and their purchasing power have dwindled because of inflation and recession (Karger, 1986). Scarcity is forcing agencies to be more scrupulous in their budgeting and spending (Cohen *et al.,* 1979). Second, the general public increasingly demands to know how their tax dollars are spent (Weirich, 1980). Third, many different groups claim some authority over the agency: they include funding sources, legislative bodies, client groups, boards of directors, accrediting bodies and unions (Weissman, 1983). These political struggles limit and shape the agency's internal activities.

Weissman (1983), who studied the relationship between accountability and service effectiveness, contends it is curvilinear, not linear. A maximum point exists at which the most effective service coincides with a certain degree of accountability. Any additional demands for accountability reduce the effectiveness of service provision. Efforts to increase accountability beyond that point may also have harmful repercussions for personnel. Reinforcing demands to provide more service while disregarding the quality of service reinforces wrong behaviour (Noah, 1978). Winters agrees that the demands by government and others for greater accountability and improved management will increase the agency's use of computers; however, the organizational "cost" of this increased computer use should not be minimized.

The literature leaves unclear whether pressures for increased accountability are the real driving force behind computerization and whether computerization serves to reduce that pressure by real or perceived improvements in "accounting."

Constraints on the Development of Measures of Efficiency and Effectiveness of Social Welfare Services

With ambiguous goals, social welfare organizations have difficulty developing outcome measures of service efficiency and effectiveness (Nutter, 1983; Quinn, 1973; Reid, 1974). Some think social welfare programs produce outcomes that are too subtle to be measured. Newman and Turem (1978, p. 321) have observed that ". . . the social work profession does not define goals in terms of output but rather input (for example, casework hours, number of persons served)." Defining goals in terms of input has meant that most agencies cannot meet demands for increased accountability. In addition, input factors differ from the private sector. For example, business accounting packages are designed around sales revenues, whereas human service accounting systems must be designed around grants, contracts and donations (Sircar *et al.,*1983).

Defining quantifiable units of service is also difficult. Among the problems of measuring the amount and type of service are: a diversity of service definitions; lack of standardized service delivery; and "soft services" that involve relationships and counselling (Nutter, 1983; Schoech, 1982; Quinn,

1973). Cohen *et al.* (1979) also caution that in emphasizing quantity in assessment, quality of services and service outcomes is often neglected or downgraded.

Problems related to the nature of the information itself are also potentially disruptive. Is it possible that the human services, in attempting to computerize, are trying to achieve the unachievable? Perhaps, as Tepperman (1984) suggests, some data are simply not "codable." If "codable," what information is "relevant" and what information should be excluded? These questions are hardest to answer in social service organizations.

Some observers believe the style and content of management in social welfare organizations is insufficiently specific and rigorous for translation into computer instructions (Schoech and Schkade, 1981). Of course many administrators were former professional staff, who "carry with them the culture and attitudes of the professional, including strong resistance to quantitative measures of their organization's activity" (Herzlinger, 1977, p. 84).

Computers, which have thus far been applied to structured objective analyses, are limited in their ability to analyse the unstructured situations which often confront managers and administrators (Gorry and Morton, 1971). Computer use at the worker-client level may be efficient for collecting information. However, advanced data collection and classification can become an end in itself, at the expense of understanding unique client configurations (Weirich, 1980).

Computer applications have thus far been limited to well-defined, well-structured problems (Mason and Mitroff, 1973). Decision-making at the administrative, managerial and even operational levels, however, is often unstructured, spontaneous, intuitive, and not "data based." Decisions stemming from intuition or indeterminate knowledge bases often rely more on experience, judgement, attitudes and predisposition than on data (Vogel, 1986, p. 77).

Shortcomings of the information systems in social welfare organizations currently reflect innate characteristics of both the organizations and the information structure. Information systems continue to evolve as technology becomes increasingly necessary to human services. However, as the changing human service agency has incorporated new technology, the technology itself has placed new demands on the organization.

The introduction of computers has led to some clarification of organizational goals, decision criteria and organizational relationships. Developing an information and evaluation system forces the organization to better define itself and its procedures. Goals and procedures have to be clarified; and programs and services have to be reexamined as goals are better defined (Fein, 1975; Quinn, 1976). Each organizational unit then assesses its goals in relation to overall organizational goals (Yadav, 1983). After the objectives and goals are clearly identified, administrators and managers can use information to intervene where undesirable trends are spotted (Davis and Allen, 1979). A practical illustration of goal-oriented behaviour is provided by Fein (1975, p. 22):

> Goal-orientation was brought into the system on the case-activity card, since workers had to indicate the purpose for each interview and the outcome in relation to purpose. This was initiated to encourage more purposeful, goal-oriented use of therapy time.

What the literature leaves unclear is the question of whether social service organizations are able to solve these problems of goal definition, information collection, and measurement of organizational output. Nor is it clear whether computers simply provide an opportunity and challenge to solve these problems, or actively make their solution both more necessary and more difficult. .

Computer Technology — A Threat to the Existing Power Structure and Staff Relationships?

"Power" is defined as the ability of an individual or group to influence the direction of another individual or group. The source of power, within our framework, is information. Those with control over this resource may have their authority, status, visibility and career affected (Mason and Mitroff, 1973). An 'information elite' may withhold or use knowledge to further their interests (Weirich, 1980; Bell, 1973). Further, Karger (1986, p. 124) comments as follows on the possible impact of technology on power relations in social service organizations:

> When a sophisticated technology is introduced into a program that does not pay sufficient attention to the organization and mission of social work, and when that technology is mastered by only a few, severe dislocation and stratification is encouraged in the workplace. In particular, social service technocrats who can master the new technologies come to dominate social workers who cannot compete in the technological arena. Thus, the pre-existing relations of power within the workplace become transformed into a stratified system of power relationships as the new technocrats are treated as the most important members of the social.

Many believe a computerized information system centralizes power within and among organizations (Zuboff, 1982). This leads to a greater isolation of administrators from middle management and front line staff; increased routinization of task performance; the failure of front line staff to exercise initiative; and growing alienation among junior staff.

Power is exercised through the interplay of two or more individuals or interest groups contesting the control of data, with the aim of controlling employee behaviour (Noah, 1978). Control is achieved by witholding valuable information and using it as a bargaining tool, or by using the information to monitor or assess the work already performed (Glastonbury, 1985; Holbrook, 1986).

Does using computerized information systems serve to maintain the existing power structure or does it introduce new patterns of control and coalition formation? Tepperman (1984) and Kraemer and Dutton (1979) hold the former position. Information elites seek to preserve and expand, not share, their power. If these elites are under managerial control, introducing computer-based systems should reinforce managerial power. Danziger (1985) agrees information systems reinforce existing power distributions, and Noah takes a more definitive position: "Information systems are, in effect, intended to bring employees' behaviour under the control of data even though the contingencies established by the design of the information system are often unanticipated" (Noah, 1978, p. 107).

Computerized information systems in social welfare organizations are apparently most useful to senior management and least useful to direct service staff and middle managers (Hoshino, 1982; Nutter, 1983; Trute *et al.*, 1982; Glastonbury, 1985; and Zuboff, 1982). Computer systems in social welfare settings were generally designed for routine administrative tasks (Boyd, Hylton and Price, 1978). Kling (1980) reports computing is viewed as a salient technology by managers, data analysts, and clerks who use it regularly; but for others, computing has little utility. However, no computerized information system determines administrative decisions: rather, it merely generates information that will assist in decision-making (Davis and Allen, 1979; Noah, 1978). However, as Vogel points out, it may be of limited assistance:

> Human Service managers . . . operate in a world with a variety of constituencies and hence a variety of objective criteria, no one of which can consistently be ranked above all others. This raises serious questions about the applicability of the "rational actor" model — descriptively or prescriptively. Alternate choices often include costs or benefits are extensively difficult to estimate — qualitatively as well as quantitatively (Vogel, 1985, p. 74).

Evidence also suggests that computerized information does not increase managerial power as much as it might. Dery (1977) studied four computerized welfare information systems in California to determine if these systems yielded comparatively more and better information for management decisions than other systems. They did not. Evidently their failure resulted from poor data, inappropriate techniques for computer implementation, and staff resistance. Dery concludes that when the demand for computer use comes from outside, the system responds less to the needs of management for useful information.

Moreover few managers have used computerized information systems arbitrarily to extend their control (Kling, 1980). Nevertheless, a study of computerization in child welfare organizations in a large U.S. city revealed staff felt the pressure for greater accountability resulted in more control by managers who used mandated time frames monitored by computer. Staff thought these controls hindered their ability to "perform good casework practice, while at the same time making sound casework judgments and decisions" (Brady, 1983).

Some staff fear computerization will change the existing supervisory practices. On this, one scholar comments: "Information technology can potentially depersonalize supervision, alter social communities and often means that technology absorbs much of the judgment that routine jobs used to entail" (Zuboff, 1982, p. 96).

Brady (1983) found computerization was changing the relationship of front line staff with their supervisors. Staff disliked the amount of time used in the supervisory conference to review statistical data to determine whether accountability requirements had been met. Staff often regard the use of computer data for performance evaluation as a threat to their autonomy (Niece *et al.*, 1983; Holbrook, 1986). One observer has noted: "Some computer workload monitoring systems reduce the discretion of subordinates, particularly among those who previously enjoyed relative freedom from supervision because they . . . did tasks where normal collection of performance data was not feasible" (Danziger, 1985, p. 15).

It is unclear from the literature, then, whether computerization increases real managerial control, or merely potential, perceived, or feared control. There is much literature pointing in each of these directions. As before, we are confused as to whether this is an issue social workers "ought" to worry about or really do worry about; and in either event, whether the fears are justified.

Staff Resistance To Computerization

The greatest potential for staff resistance to computerization is at the operational level of the organization; according to the literature provision must be made to prevent it. Fein (1975) recommends reducing the threat to the individual by emphasizing the importance of overall program success. On the other hand, successful computerization may require social workers to "overcome their traditional resistance to serious evaluation of their own work and to leap the 'skill barrier' to become 'computer literate'" (Sharron, 1984).

Even managers in human service agencies sometimes resist the computer. Schoech reports that:

Sabotage by management can also become a problem. The ability of an information system to document management deficiencies has created situations in which, to save itself, management has labelled the system as a costly failure and quickly removed it (Schoech, 1982, p. 193).

Quinn (1973) studied the extent and intensity of staff resistance to the introduction of computers in an experimental project aimed at improving the integration of several social service agencies. He argues staff resistance can be explained by looking at the "complex of stabilized interaction patterns among staff" that constitute the "latent structure" of the organization. These interaction patterns centre on three areas of role performance — face management or identity, information or communication, and power or status — that are established by implicit contracts between individual staff members. He hypothesizes that introducing a computerized information system disrupts established patterns of communication and power. This theoretical perspective, useful in analyzing the implementation of information systems, may underestimate the full impact of the organizational context, treating the agency as a closed system; thus, its conclusions are useful, but incomplete.

Failure to input information or use the output, and even outright sabotage, are defensive responses to the imposition of technology (Dickson and Simmons, 1970). Staff members may see the system as a threat to previously established stability. However, a recent survey of automation in Canada reported little evidence that staff resistance was an obstacle to technological innovation (Betcherman and McMullen, 1986).

Another explanation for staff resistance "stems from social workers' interests and temperaments and the failure of their training to equip them to evaluate their own work." Furthermore, "computerization has been perceived by social workers as a preoccupation of senior management" (Sharron, 1984).

Although optimal computer use demands accuracy and consistency in data recording, a recent study of computer use by social workers concluded that "Many social workers loathe everything connected with statistics, figures and technology" (deGraff, 1987, p. 15). It is therefore not surprising that inaccuracy is perceived as a problem in many organizations that have implemented computerized systems (Hoshino, 1981; Dermer, 1977, Bowers and Bowers, 1978). In discussing worker response to a new system, one director observed that demands of computer technology for accuracy, meeting tight deadlines, and scheduling access only aggravate the problem of rigidity, "a problem that has always plagued social workers" (Rubin, 1976, p. 44). A related issue is the resistance of social workers to the additional paperwork required.

This resistance may also reflect an aversion to collecting detailed data which question the adequacy of their performance (Reid, 1974). Social workers' resistance may be expressed through three types of behaviour — aggression, avoidance and projection (Sullivan, 1980; Dickson and Simmons, 1970). However, Thies (1975) found that attitudes are more significantly influenced by current experiences than by long-standing preconceptions; negative initial attitudes can be modified through favourable experiences.

In summary, what the literature leaves unclear is the extent and focus of staff resistance in social service organizations, and the actions an organization might take to avoid or overcome resistance. Combined with the earlier dire predictions, is the literature predicting resistance, describing resistance, or urging it?

Factors Associated with Success or Failure in Implementing a Computerized Information System

The successful implementation of a computer system depends on many factors which must be defined, understood, and controlled throughout the implementation process. However, many processes in social welfare organizations depend on some combination of information, experience, intuition, and an ability to relate similar situations or events; here, computer utilization falls short of corresponding human capabilities (Kates, 1982). Many computer software packages are quantitative rather than qualitative analytic tools. With computers, social welfare organizations can assess what is happening; but they cannot tell why (Sharron, 1984).

The assumption that decision-making will improve if more information is available may be seriously misconceived. Information overload often hinders decision-making (Vogel, 1985; Cohen *et al.*, 1979; Hoos, 1972; Ackoff, 1967; Brooker, 1965). Few managers, for example, have great informational needs. Rather, they need new methods to understand and process the information already available (Pounds, 1969).

Understanding an organization's information needs, although crucial to successfully implementing a computerized information system, is not the only consideration. In addition, more practical, day-to-day aspects of the organization play a significant role in determining the success or failure of a system. Schoech and Schkade (1980b, p. 24) believe:

> The agency that is most successful in designing and implementing data processing (DP) will already be functioning well since it can take the time and risks associated with changes required in implementing such a system ... similarly financing must be adequate for the smooth and orderly development of the system ... structurally, an agency must have well-defined and formalized goals, procedures, and systems ... must collect data that reflect its basic decisions and guide its basic control mechanisms towards its goal.

Wilson (1966) concurs with the first point, but suggests a failing agency also needs to change. "A failing agency must change or face extinction, while a successful agency can best withstand pressures and risks associated with a major change."

Sircar *et al.* (1983, p. 61) also caution against needless expenditures of time and effort in attempting to define and standardize service in agencies undergoing rapid redefinition and change at the policy and funding levels. For whom, then, will computerization prove successful?

Ein-Dor and Seger's (1978) typology for predicting the success of a Management Information System (hereinafter referred to as an MIS) is divided into three variable groups: uncontrollable (variables 1 to 4), partially controllable (variables 5 to 7), and fully controllable (variables 8 to 9). They claim that MIS projects are less likely to succeed in:

1. Smaller as opposed to larger organizations;
2. Decentralized organizations;
3. Organizations making decisions in a shorter time frame;
4. Organizations with a highly limited supply of requisite resources in the external environment;
5. Organizations with insufficient resources budgeted for system design and implementation;
6. Less mature organizations;
7. Organizations with unrealistic expectations and negative attitudes toward computerization;
8. Organizations where the executive to whom the MIS chief must report is of a low rank;
9. Organizations where no steering committee is involved in computerization.

Successful implementation of computerized information systems can also be traced back to a key decision-maker or backer. The involvement and commitment of top decision-makers throughout the several years needed to design, implement, debug, and reap the benefits of the system are seen by many as crucial (Bowers and Bowers, 1978; Cobb, 1976; Schoech and Schkade, 1980b; Schoech, 1979).

Planning, design, and implementation require costly expertise and technology. Costly machines or machine time, special forms and various other supplies force the organization to accept great short-term expenses in return for possible long-run benefits (Weirich, 1980).

An important predictor of success is the technical adequacy of the system for that organization (Gorry and Morton, 1971). The output format should be brief and tailored to the needs of the user. The design or layout of coding forms should also be meaningful to the person recording the data

(Cohen *et al.,* 1979; Lowe and Sugarman, 1978).

Part of the adjustment process occurs within the organizational environment. As the new information system is increasingly used, old ways of doing things may no longer be effective (Noah, 1978). Therefore "environmental arrangements controlling the behaviour of individuals may drastically change." However, Schoech and Schkade (1980) suggest the opposite: "as an organization moves toward maturity, data processing adjusts to accommodate the user, the organization and the decision-maker, rather than vice versa." The resolution lies somewhere between these two extremes. The decision to implement and use an information system demands, first, that the organizational environment be adjusted. The technology must be accommodated spatially.

This, in turn, affects the workers; previously established standards must now be adjusted to accommodate reorganized communication patterns. Information flow may change to allow for new procedures and new positions created by computerization. Neither is the information system itself a given: constant adjustments must be made to reflect the changing environment.

Some authors argue social service agencies encounter problems in implementing computer technology precisely when they attempt to use computers too much like business organizations (deGraff, 1987; Schoech and Schkade, 1981; Poertner and Rapp, 1980; Lewis, 1979). These managers often find themselves having too much information, too little of which would really help in making decisions (Holland, 1977).

In social agencies where the information system has been computerized, two contrasting patterns are common. Some managers form unrealistic expectations of the value of the computer in management decision-making, particularly when they have not been involved in designing the system (Dermer, 1977). Thus, when the system runs into problems they dismiss it as useless (Poertner and Rapp, 1980). Other managers abdicate their management responsibilities to computer specialists. This may lead to a lack of communication with front line staff, a conflict of values, misunderstandings, mistrust, and power struggles (Schoech and Arangio, 1979; Sullivan, 1980). Bowers and Bowers see this as a major problem:

> Many of the problems encountered in systems development seem to have resulted from too much authority being given to or taken by "systems people." This is caused in some cases by management ignorance or timidity and in others by lack of interest in the system (Bowers and Bowers, 1978, p. 42).

For this reason, all of the writing on the implementation of computer systems stresses the importance of involving management in all stages of the process.

The literature is full of admonitions about the importance of involving staff in plans for the design and implementation of computerization (Weissman, 1977; Schoech, 1982) to reduce what Mann (1986) calls "adoption trauma." Many social welfare organizations have made the same mistake that industry made in developing their systems with little or no involvement by support staff, who will enter data in the system, or direct service staff, who are potential users. One scholar who has done extensive research on the development of information systems regards relevant consultation with appropriate staff as "absolutely essential to securing the staff commitment that will result in effective operation of the system" (Trute *et al.*, 1982, pp. 11 to 12).

This view is also shared by Danziger and Kraemer (1986, p. 207). They concluded that one of the necessary, but not sufficient, conditions for increasing the usefulness of computer technology for staff in organizations is more responsive computer experts, and more attention paid to the felt needs of staff regarding the design and operation of the organization's computer-based information system.

Service delivery personnel, in particular, feel vulnerable to possible effects of the new information system, such as displacement and increased monitoring. As they are responsible for producing much of the information system's input, it is imperative that they cooperate. "Failure to deal with resistance at this level has led to the untimely demise of many information systems" (Holland, 1977, p. 11).

Computer experts should meet with representative personnel at the administrative, managerial and operational levels. Administrators and managers should define their information needs for decision-making, and learn the uses and the technical limitations of operational informational systems (Cohen *et al.*, 1979).

Service personnel should become more knowledgeable and experienced in using computers (Schoech and Arangio, 1979). Quinn (1976) believes field staff trained to work with both technicians and other human service personnel would improve communication and prevent a misinterpretation of design capabilities and needs.

Cohen *et al.* (1979) caution against several unexpected consequences of computerized information systems. Records move faster, but more of them come into existence. The increase in paperwork demands an increased clerical staff. Second, sophisticated hardware does not guarantee that valid data are collected. Efforts to ensure accuracy must be increased. However, a lack of consensus on the desired outcome of services becomes more obvious than ever, as data produced for extra-agency reports and for intra-agency evaluation have no standard against which to assess performance.

Other problems encountered in introducing computer technology into these organizations are insufficient commitment of money, time and effort, thus reducing a system's benefits (Schoech and Arangio, 1979). Also limiting the usefulness of a computerized information system in these organizations is their dependence on external organizations and their staff. Different attitudes toward sensitive information may result in some organizations withholding information from others who may break confidentiality rules (Sharron, 1984).

Does the literature offer a valid description of the "adoption trauma," or unsuccessful implementation process, or simply overdramatize one feared, possible scenario of many that might come to pass? Further, are the suggested means of preventing such problems likely to work in the event of a traumatic adoption? The literature offers too many proposed solutions, without indicating which are more important to consider and which less important.

Conclusion

In this chapter we have focused on the "micro" level of analysis. "Macro" issues associated with the computerization of information in human service agencies include topics such as the right of access to information (Flaherty, 1982; Kates, 1982; Mowshowitz, 1980a), the right to privacy (Schoech and Schkade, 1981; Flaherty, 1982; Black, 1982; Mowshowitz, 1980a; Weirich, 1980), freedom from surveillance (Niece *et al.*, 1982), and risks of unemployment due to computerization (Peitchinis, 1983; Kates, 1982; Mowshowitz, 1980b). These topics all bear close examination, but will not be examined in this volume.

"Micro" analysis has revealed the importance of considering many different variables when assessing the computerization of information systems. It has also identified many of the dimensions of the social and occupational worlds of social welfare organizations that impinge directly on the use and impact of computer technology. Our review of the literature — on selected dimensions of computing in organizations, and a more global review of computing in social welfare organizations — has indicated that there are many issues, problems, and outcomes that are generic in organizational settings when computer technology is used. However, there are also a number of different, if not unique, potential and anticipated issues, problems and outcomes that are seen as important parts of the social and occupational worlds of social welfare organizations. Both of these will be examined to explain present patterns of use and the impact of computer technology in one group of non-profit human services organizations whose output is service, both instrumental and affective.

But how many of these potential issues and problems really materialize and under what circumstances? We certainly need more and better empirical knowledge about this, to provide the awareness that is needed. Without awareness of the facts, the degree and kind of preventive action needed cannot be predicted. It is with this purpose in mind that we undertook the research that is reported below.

The relative lack of empirical research on computerization in human service organizations is surprising, given the concerns and anxieties in the literature reviewed here. This lack of research has led one scholar to conclude present observations on the relationship of computers to society represent no more than "persistent anxieties" (Mowshowitz, 1979). Although the main thrust of this literature is that continuing vigilance is needed to ensure that computer technology will not destroy human dignity and individual autonomy, optimism is expressed that ways can, and must, be found to use it to improve the computerized delivery of services.

Among the key questions and problems that remain unanswered or unresolved are the following: (1) Do social welfare organizations have information needs that, with our present level of knowledge, cannot be quantified without undermining the creditability and integrity of the services provided? (2) Does computerization threaten the value base of social work, the delivery of service and/or relations between clients and staff? If so, what can be done to minimize the impact? (3) Does a computerized information system challenge the existing power structure in the organizations? (4) What are the sources and extent of staff resistance to computerization in social welfare organizations? And (5) What characteristics of the organization or staff are predictors of the success, or lack of success, in the introduction of computer technology in social welfare organizations?

The next chapter will describe how we proceeded from a complex and rather confusing body of literature to design and execute the research.

Chapter 2

The Method of Research

Introduction

Our literature review found little empirical research on the impact of computerization on human service organizations. Most empirical studies merely described the use of computers and/or the responses of individuals to computerization, but did not discuss organizational change *per se*. Even so, few studies were systematic and empirical.

According to the literature, the introduction of computer technology leads to greater centralization of control. Such a shift affects both the social structure of the organization and the people it serves. On the other hand, the level of computer use in any organization is determined by the existing system: by the attitudes, values and expectations of people involved in, and affected by, the system. These forces are not independent of one another. In fact, they are constantly interacting to determine the character and impact of computer technology.

Computerized information systems reflect the needs of the organization, as perceived by internal administrators and influential persons in the external environment. Thus, following Zuboff (1982), we hold that the attributes and impact of an information system are shaped by the world view they reflect and impose, and the experience to which they give shape.

We are persuaded by Mowshowitz (1980b) that two persistent themes — equity and social control — should be central to any analysis of the human context of decisions about, and use of, computers. In particular, the concept of equity or fairness is central to social welfare. Notions of the individualization of clients, and the importance of professional discretion in social welfare, are consistent with this concept. From this standpoint, neither people nor their needs are equal. Decisions about the distribution of resources, access to services, and the delivery of services should reflect differences in power and influence in the organization and in the larger society.

But issues of efficiency are also important, since most organizations undertaking computerization claim that their goal is increased efficiency.

Efficiency implies a great many organizational changes that are somewhat easier to specify than the changes associated with equity and control. A comprehensive, efficient information system will make the best use of available resources in meeting the organization's needs for the quick re-evaluation of budget estimates; quick provision of financial information; quick management access to service statistics, in relation to stated goals; quick and accurate cost analysis of services; quick access to both current and terminated files; monitoring of case flow through treatment stages; continuous word-processing capability (where appropriate) to reduce secretarial typing and report writing time; up-to-date and complete information on the staff complement; statistical analyses, using standard software routines, of the data on client characteristics, treatments, and outcomes; a sufficiently complex and accurate information base on client characteristics, needs, and progress in treatment to be of use in decision-making; and fast turnaround and easy access to all information on clients by the front-line staff, perhaps through an interactive software.

Accordingly, we must study changes in the quality of the agency's information system as a consequence of computerization. Specifically, this means studying changes in the amount of information made available to direct service staff and to management; the kinds of information made available; the amount of information utilized by direct service staff and management: i.e., the numbers of uses and users, and the average frequency of use; the speed of information turnaround, between the time data are collected in raw form and returned in processed form to direct service staff and managment; the relevance of information provided for decision-making; and the perceived quality of information being made available.

Questions surrounding equity, social control and efficiency should all be examined in an empirical study of computerization. We begin this chapter by laying out the equity questions that need addressing, then the social control questions, and finally the efficiency questions.

Equity Concerns

The six questions we hoped to ask about shifts in equity following computerization concern potentially dangerous shifts in the quality and distribution of information, and the mechanisms available for resolving conflict.

First, do computers limit discourse, by limiting the amount or kinds of information that can be stored and analyzed by the organization? Stated otherwise, would objective assessors conclude that the quality of information available to the agency improves or worsens following computerization? This can best be answered by comparing pre-computerization (or low-technology) files with post-computerization (or high-technology) files, with impartial assessors rating randomly selected files.

Second, do computers give an unwarranted appearance of accuracy, objectivity and validity? Answering this question about information quality requires an external verification of the accuracy of the files. It is often claimed that computerized files are hard to correct and update. If so, older computer files ought to contain a higher proportion of out-of-date or wrong information than newer ones. Computerized data would be less accurate than non-computerized data that are equally old. This is verifiable by selecting a random sample of files and interviewing the described clients, on selected factual items of information, to determine the proportion of factual information in each file that is accurate.

Third, do computers capitalize on people's blind faith in science in order to claim unwarranted authority for organizational decisions? Our concern about the blind acceptance of computerized decisions derives not so much from the quality of decisions made, as from the basis upon which the organization defends its decisions. Through interviews with personnel and an observation of its procedures, and by examining official agency documents (e.g., executive meeting minutes, publications), one could reveal whether a shift towards greater authoritativeness in tone occurs following computerization.

Fourth, do computers fragment decision-making, thereby losing a holistic understanding of the problem, client and context? The decontextualizing of decisions can be studied by interviewing personnel (asking whether they perceive a problem), observing decision procedures, and drawing inferences about decision procedures from client files.

Fifth, does computerization reduce problem-solving interaction between decision-makers, in favour of isolation or person-machine interactions? If interaction and communication are reduced among decision-makers, a likely consequence is the loss of a shared, holistic appreciation of the problem-in-context. Thus, a good measurement of ongoing communication in the organization is critical, and can be obtained by (a) asking people whether they feel they have the kinds of information they need from others within the organization; and (b) asking people how often they communicate about cases under their care with named others in the organization, versus how often they previously communicated with them.

The question here is whether intra-agency communication networks become less connected (or integrated) than they once were, as a result of reliance upon the computer and person-machine interaction.

Sixth, does computerization reduce information usefulness by reorganizing the flow of communications? Conceivably, the connectedness of communication within the organization is not lessened so much as re-organized by computerization. This may result in the formation of information-sharing cliques that diminish the flow of valuable information about clients. This, in turn, may result in a loss of cooperation across hierarchical levels (i.e., between workers), or a loss of skill-teaching and clinical discussion between workers and specialist-experts (including those experts who program or access the computer).

Social Control Concerns

The questions we hoped to ask about social control were related to shifts in the distribution of power and its impact on decision-making.

First, do computers fragment responsibility for decisions within large organizations? In particular, do they distance decision-makers from the consequences of their decisions? Whether computers further remove clients from decision-makers can be evaluated by asking personnel their views on this matter; by observing decision-making procedures; and by examining agency records to see who has made the most important decisions, and who has had the most frequent contact with a given client.

Second, do they separate planning from execution, or headwork from handwork? That is, do they contribute to de-skilling? Whether computerization brings about de-skilling, for example in the form of reduced discretion at lower levels and more power at upper levels, or through more reliance on machine-generated recommendations, can be determined from the same sources as used immediately above.

Third, do computers allow or promote indiscreet use of personal information about clients? Whether confidentiality is violated is a question of the type, quantity, and purpose of communications about clients with persons outside the service organization. Such indiscretion should be ascertainable by examining the client file to see who (if anyone) has been given information about the client (assuming this is documented in the file); by asking personnel about their past behaviour in this regard, and whether they have heard of abuses; by observing decision-procedures; and by asking about communications outside the organization.

Fourth, does computerization equalize benefits among those connected with the organization — namely, funding agencies, management, workers, clerical staff, and clients? Who gains most from computerization? If service improves, the client gains. If the monitoring of worker performance increases, management gains. If expenditure of funds is better monitored, funding agencies gain. If more and better information about clients is made rapidly available to workers, workers gain.

Of course, all of these gains must be viewed in relation to costs. How much more information (or how many more hours a month generating information) is necessary to get each gain from computerization? How does the allocation of organizational hours change with computerization? How many more person-hours are given over to information-generating and data processing after computerization than before it, compared with client-serving hours? The tasks that are computerized also give a clue to who is likely to benefit. Where computerization is primarily management oriented, i.e., a management information system is installed, the worker and client are least likely to gain directly, if at all.

Aside from such direct measurements of the kinds of information computerized and the time various participants spend generating the data, there is also the question of who gets more information after computerization than before, and how recipients value the information they are getting — i.e.: Do they consider it useful? Do they use it? Do they sense an improvement in organizational functioning that benefits them personally, or their clients?

Finally, by examining client files, it should be possible to determine whether decision-making is faster after computerization than before — a change that is presumably in the client's interest; whether decisions are being made in more predictable ways; or organizational routines, in general, are better established. A similar establishment of routines may be discernible in management. For example, the timing of budget and personnel evaluations may become better established with computerization. One can assume that in any organization a predictable process is better than an unpredictable one.

Fifth, does computerization promote alienation and lower the self-esteem of staff and clients? Feelings of alienation and self-esteem can be studied by asking relevant questions in the interviews with selected staff and clients.

Sixth, do computers reduce discretion and judgement exercised by front-line staff in decision-making? The level of discretion and judgment exercised by front-line staff can be determined by interviews, questionnaires, a review of agency policies, and observation.

Seventh, do computers reduce initiative and personal responsibility of middle managment and front-line staff? Staff attitudes toward opportunities for the exercise of initiative and the personal responsibility taken for clients can be ascertained from questionnaires and interviews.

Finally, do computers increase bureaucratic surveillence of clients? The nature and extent of bureaucratic surveillence of clients can be determined by a review of agency policy and procedures, and interviews with clients.

Efficiency Concerns

To measure increased efficiency, we would need to measure the effects of improved information flow on the agency's delivery of social services. Better information flow is not an end in itself: it may lead to better service, but this is far from certain to happen. The opposite may occur if actions needed to bring about improved information flow significantly disrupt stable cooperation, cause worker demoralization, or excessively politicize the treatment process in a given agency.

As noted earlier, the assessment of changes in efficiency is complex and multifaceted. We hoped to determine the effect of computerization on the perceived efficiency of information systems in social service organizations; the kinds of activities, values and attitudes that allow a high level of computer utilization: i.e., utilization for casework or management, not simply for accounting purposes; the kinds of values and attitudes that allow computer use to improve organizational efficiency; the kinds of values and attitudes that allow continuing improvement.

The possibility of conflict resulting from organizational change cannot be neglected. We would have to study the kinds of inter-group conflict that are unleashed in the process of computerization, and the means by which conflicts are resolved; group and organizational thinking about computers and their use, and changes in collective values and attitudes over time. Finally, we would need to understand the causes of discrepancies between agency perceptions of system efficiency following computerization and the perceptions of outside observers; and the importance of shared ways of thinking for successful computerization, and the ways this sharing can be achieved.

To summarize to this point, we began our research in the hopes of getting comprehensive information, by various means, that would address many important questions about efficiency, equity and social control — all questions that had been raised or hinted at in the literature. But we were not able to succeed to the degree we had hoped for.

Restrictions on the Collection of these Data

As it turned out, we were only able to get a small proportion of all the information we had wanted. For this reason, some important questions went unanswered. Most especially, we obtained little firsthand information about the actual (as opposed to perceived) improvement in information quality and decision-making after computerization. Thus we are unable to say whether efficiency actually improved, stayed the same, or worsened. We can only report people's perceptions on this matter. We also learned little about the changes in treatment of clients, as we neither interviewed clients nor observed their treatment. We have only staff perceptions as to whether client treatment had changed, and if so, for the better or worse. We also learned little about patterns of communication among decision-makers, as no sociometric analysis was carried out as orginally intended.

There are a number of compelling reasons why we did not learn about these things. In some cases, for example, sociometric communication patterns, the data collection would have been too time-consuming given the other tasks to be done; and we were already placing heavy time demands on both our field workers and respondents. Some tasks had to give way. In addition, the data collection proved slower and more difficult, and started later, than we had originally intended. Continuing refinement of the questionnaire and interview schedules meant that we were late beginning this phase of data collection and could not risk further complication by introducing too many items, or items that might put off our respondents. It had already taken a longer time to get set up in our eight final organizations than we had anticipated: there was at least one false start — an organization that was found belatedly to fall outside our range of interest and needed replacement. In many cases, negotiation to enter an organization for study proved slow and complicated. Once inside, we often found these organizations were not at the stage of computerization we had been led to believe by responses in the initial survey.

Beyond this, at least three major problems confronted us. One was that clients had yielded little information of value in the pilot study we conducted, and many organizations were, in any event, reluctant to give us access to their clients. We simply had to let this go. Many organizations were also reluctant to have us assess the quality of their records in a direct, impartial way: there could be no objective rating of records as planned. This is not surprising in a field that is underfunded and always fearful that funding will be further reduced if any inadequacy is discovered. Finally, there was sensitivity in some cases to a no-holds-barred analysis of intra-agency conflict, and in some instances conflict had already been exacerbated by computerization. We were not invited to stir up the conflict by asking too pointed questions about its nature and extent.

There is no evidence that the motives for denying us data varied systematically: for example, by agency size, or according to type of organization. We got no sense that attempts were being made to deny us any particular kinds of information; simply, that top managers did not want us interfering with the organization's functioning.

Take an example: the issue of confidentiality. The literature is full of warnings that confidentiality is put at great risk by computerization. We had intended to study systematically what kinds of client data were communicated within and between social welfare organizations, and whether these communications constituted a violation of confidentiality. We were unable to do this for a variety of reasons, chiefly practical: e.g., shortage of time.

Whenever we asked about problems of confidentiality, most respondents denied there was a problem. This was a consistent finding. Moreover, few respondents even knew what their organization's policy on confidentiality might be: this was not an important issue in the organizations we studied. Accordingly, we concluded that the concerns in the literature about confidentiality were unwarranted.

Of course, other interpretations of the same data are possible. We relied largely on staff perceptions of reality: on their perception that confidentiality was not being violated within the organization. This leaves open the possibility that confidentiality was being violated or, more generally, that staff perceptions were misinformed, biased or outright lies. And, of course, there is the same motive to tell us lies (or half-truths) as there is to deny us data: namely, to prevent a negative evaluation and/or further probing.

On the other hand, during the course of the research our data collectors heard a great deal of negative comment about the organizations, their management and practices. The data collectors became familiar fixtures of the agencies they were studying. Initial anxiety about giving us information seems to have diminished, even disappeared with the passage of time. So there is no particular reason to believe that we did not get true perceptions from our respondents.

Neither is there reason to believe that all the respondents' perceptions were uninformed by reality, especially about issues where someone might have been expected to know something. Not only was confidentiality not a widespread concern, it was no one's concern. No one we spoke to seemed to think it was a problem. If data abuse actually was a problem, as the literature uniformly anticipated, one of our respondents would have thought so (and said so)!

Our failure to get all the data we wanted more likely reflects a general rigidity, or vulnerability in these organizations: the inability to take risks. The same risk-averseness that made it difficult for these agencies to fully cooperate with our research — from which they, as well as others, might have learned a great deal — may have hindered their ability to fully adopt the technology we were studying. Just as they could not spare staff time or risk disruption to probe certain aspects of their functioning in relation to our research, they could not stop to learn all that they needed to know about computerization. The result was, generally, a slow, painful and incomplete adoption of the new technology.

None of the foregoing is meant to take away from the magnificent cooperation we received from the eight agencies we studied. They were simply up to their ears in work and were willing to be studied so long as we did not interrupt them more than was absolutely necessary. Once we appreciated that this point of view was endemic, not particular to the agencies we had approached, we settled for what we could get in the way of data. As it is, we collected a great deal of useful information; it is simply not all we had planned to collect.

We learned a lot about who was using computerized information, how people felt about computerization, and who was losing and gaining power or control by this technological change. Considering the state of the literature at the time we began, this is no mean feat. If we are far from where we had hoped to be by the end of the project, we are also far from where we began. The shortcomings of our study are, of course, regrettable but a fact of life. At this point, it is important only for the reader to distinguish between the study we had planned — a study more fortunate researchers may some day complete in full — and the study we finally executed, which is described below.

The Actual Study

In general, at least six different kinds of data, or data sources, must ideally be examined to answer the questions we raised above: interviews with selected agency personnel and questionnaires completed by all personnel; observation of personnel at work; examination of agency records; collection of data on networks of communication within the agency; also collection of data on communications with the outside; assessments of information file quality; and interviews with samples of clients.

Since little was known about computerization in social welfare organizations, our first step was to survey the extent and nature of computer use by such organizations. A total of 253 social welfare organizations with full-time paid staff located within an 80-kilometre radius of Toronto were asked to complete a questionnaire about the size of the organization, type of service rendered, sources of income, level of use of computers, length of time computers had been used, type of hardware and software used, and planned future use of the computer system. Of these, spokesmen for 172 agencies responded and almost one-half, 82, were using computers. It may be important to note that the respondents were typically in upper management, as we later learned while carrying out case studies of eight selected organizations.

The survey found that, of the organizations using computers, more than half had been using them two years or less. Large organizations, with at least 45 full-time employees, used computers more than small (12 full-time employees or less) or medium (13 to 44 full-time employees) size organizations. Large organizations specifically designed software to meet their own requirements, while small and medium size organizations used packaged programs.

Five activities accounted for most of the computer use. Computers were used most often to keep track of accounts and expenditures. The next four computer uses, ranked in declining order of frequency, were for preparation of periodic report writing; word processing; planning or policy making; and analyzing client characteristics. When grouped by services provided, health-related services made the greatest use of computers, followed by income maintenance; rehabilitation and vocational services; child welfare; mental health and mental retardation, recreation and group work; correctional services; family and individual counselling and community support services. The benefit of computerization spokesmen mentioned most often was greater efficiency, i.e., more work can be accomplished in less time by fewer people. The two problems spokesmen most often associated with computerization were inappropriate software and limited resources. On the basis of the survey results, we decided to do a multiple case study. We would use questionnaires, documents, participant observation studies and interviews to collect data. A pilot study was conducted to test the research strategy and the planned data collection methods.

The pilot study was carried out in a large organization outside the geographical area from which we later selected organizations to study. This organization was selected because of its size, range of activities and experience in computer use. A total of 53 staff completed questionnaires and 21 people were interviewed.

The pilot study results convinced us that the first phase of data collection in the larger study should consist of a review of documents including planning reports, minutes of earlier meetings, budgets, correspondence with other agencies, annual agency reports, forms filled out by agency staff for the computer and the printouts generated by the computer. The second phase comprised unstructured interviews with certain staff, called "key informants," who were particularly knowledgeable about agency history, funding, organizational structure, reasons for computerizing, staff orientation towards computerization and staff attitudes regarding computerization. These "key informants" were usually still employed in the agency. However, former staff members were interviewed when appropriate.

A three-section questionnaire (see Appendix), consisting of 59 items, was administered to all staff after we finished reviewing documents and interviewing our key informants. The first section sought information on staff attitudes toward computerization, the respondents rating 18 statements on a four-point scale of possible responses ranging from strong agreement to strong disagreement. This section had been pre-tested with approximately 100 staff in non-participating organizations. The remaining two sections of the questionnaire sought information on attitudes and experience with respect to their computer system; and personal data, including age, sex, education, professional association, and prior computer training or use.

Semi-structured interviews were then conducted with a quarter of the staff selected at random from all levels within the organization. However, the major emphasis was on front line and support staff as primary or potential users of computer technology. The interviewer could pursue questions in some depth and discuss responsibility of the respondent for the introduction, implementation and use of the computer; perceived major costs or benefits of computerization to the organization and staff; impact, if any, of computerization on attitudes or values, particularly on professional staff; and what changes were perceived as necessary to improve the use of computers with respect to access, orientation, applications and service delivery.

Participant observation continued throughout the six to eight month data collection period. This included attending meetings, talking with staff, and observing the ways data were inputted and used.

In our pilot study, a sample of clients was interviewed. They proved uninformed or uninterested in the extent and nature of computer use in the organizations. As a consequence, we decided not to pursue the interviewing of clients in the larger study.

Our survey findings, the pilot study and the literature review convinced us to carry similar case studies in eight organizations. These were selected from among the 51 who reported they were presently using computers and met the criteria used for selection. These criteria were size, type of organization, and level of computer use. These critera were employed because we believed these variables would partially explain the response of the organizations to computerization. We initially selected 24 organizations that met the criteria and priorized them in terms of their "fit" on all criteria.

We are indebted to Hasenfeld for the concept of "people-changing" and "people-processing" organizations which we used to classify organizations according to anticipated outcome of service. People-changing organizations "attempt to alter directly the attributes or behaviour of their clients through the application of various modification and treatment technologies" (Hasenfeld and English, 1974, p. 5). People-processing organizations "attempt to change their clients not by altering basic personal attributes, but by conferring upon them a public status and relocating them in a new set of social circumstances" (ibid.).

We thought the difference in resources between large and small organizations would produce different types and levels of computer utilization. Specifically, we expected larger organizations would have a greater need for computers but also, being more bureaucratic, would have greater difficulty changing over to computer use than small organizations. We also thought staff in people-changing organizations would be more concerned about confidentiality, professional discretion, and control than staff in people-processing organizations.

Organizations were selected for "level of computer use" to allow us to compare organizations at different levels of implementation, confronting different types of technical and organizational difficulties and representing different "stages" in the process of computerization. Stated otherwise, the selection of agencies at different levels of computer utilization allowed us to compare the kinds of organizations reaching these different levels; and also to examine sequential cross-sections of organizational development. The study of different stages at one point in time is a commonly used alternative to studying change over a long period of time. Combined with longitudinal study, this comparison across organizations at different stages provided a partial corrective to errors of memory within "advanced" organizations.

Stratification of the sample according to type (people-changing and people-processing organizations) and size of organization enabled us to examine the effects of professional socialization and commitment to individualized decision-making (more common in small than large organizations, and more common in people-changing than in people-processing organizations), on the implementation and utilization of computer technology.

Diagram 2.1 illustrates the use of these criteria to select the eight organizations. Data were collected in the eight organizations by four field staff with experience in social research and academic backgrounds in sociology and social work. The field staff collected data during a six to eight month period in each organization. This amount of time was needed to minimize agency disruptions resulting from data collection; and to familiarize the researchers with the organization and the organization with the researchers.

Throughout the period of data collection, the principal investigators met regularly, at some points weekly, with the field staff, to construct data collecting instruments, review progress, assess the findings, and clear up problems. Interaction among the field staff, and between the field staff and one investigator (John Gandy) was facilitated by the location of the project office in the Faculty of Social Work. There was no shortage of communication about problems and findings.

That would seem to be a plus for the project, in that we were always reasonably certain our field staff were headed in roughly the same direction. Some might raise the objection that such frequent communication might bias the results by introducing a closure on findings: that expectations about results were created by such interaction and sharing of ideas. While in many instances this might be so, ours was never a project suffering from excessive or premature closure. There was much marvelling at any discovered pattern or similarity between organizations. What the field staff found was simply so distant from what the literature had led us to expect that we were constantly confused, constantly at a loss. As we will show below, the variation among organizations was quite considerable. It was, and is, difficult to generalize across the eight cases in the easy way commentators who have studied no organizations have done.

So, in retrospect, the frequent communication during data collection and after was a small bulwark against total chaos. The results of our research are not what we expected, nor what the literature predicted; and no one foresaw, much less created, that finding.

One of the field staff began data collection about six months before the others, and finished earlier too. As all data collection reached completion and

Diagram 2.1
The Organizations Selected for Study

| Stage of Computer Use | Type of Organization | | | |
	People-Processing		People-Changing	
Intermediate	Immigrant Aid	District Office/Correctional Services	Urban Youth Counselling Services	United Family and Child Services
	N = 25	N = 45	N = 25	N = 38
Advanced	Parkside Community Centre	County Dept. of Social Services	Suburban Treatment Centre for Children	Dominion Family and Child Service
	N = 15	N = 135	N = 30	N = 61

Notes

(a) "People-processing" organizations provide assistance or a service but make no attempt to change behaviour or attitudes. They include public assistance, homemaker services, meals-on-wheels, hostels, homes for the aged.
"People-changing" organizations attempt to change behaviour and/or attitudes using a range of strategies. They include children's aid societies, family service agencies, marital counselling services.
(b) Small agencies are those with fewer than 25 direct service personnel.
(c) By "intermediate" computer use, we mean use restricted to the processing of budgets and administrative records. By "advanced" computer use, we mean case management, research-oriented data analysis, and computer-assisted decision-making to any degree.
(d) "N" indicates the number of questionnaire respondents in that agency.
Each cell contains the pseudonym of an organization we actually studied.

report writing began, interaction and communication in the research group declined rapidly. In the last six months of the project, one of the field staff accepted another job while completing final reports and another staff member failed to complete the analysis of data for one organization. Thus the final products of our work, conceived by the principal investigators and implemented as part of a frequently interacting team, were brought forth largely in isolation.

By the project's end, the principal investigators possessed detailed field notes on eight organizations, completed interviews with over 100 people, completed questionnaires for 374 people, and eight case studies ranging from sketchy to magnificently rich. The questionnaire data were computerized and analyzed using SPSS. These data, as well as field notes, excerpts from organizational documents, materials from interviews, and field worker observations written down in organizational reports, constitute the basis for this monograph.

The findings of this research process are stated in the chapters below. Because the eight organizations we studied varied so much, we have adopted a mix of case study and generalization across organizations. An attempt is made at the end of each thematic chapter to draw some cross-agency conclusions. Overall conclusions about the causes and effects of computerization are set down in the final chapter of this monograph.

Summary

Our initial survey of human service organizations in and around Toronto produced a list of 82 agencies that were using computers. These agencies tended to cite greater efficiency as the chief benefit of computerization. The most commonly mentioned problems had to do with inappropriate software and insufficient resources. We decided to do a pilot study in order to determine the most appropriate data collection techniques.

The pilot study convinced us that our methodology should proceed through the following phases:

1. review of the agency's documents;
2. unstructured interviews with key informants;
3. administering of a questionnaire about the staff's attitudes towards and experiences with computerization plus personal data on each respondent; and
4. in-depth interviews with randomly selected employees.

In addition, our four field staff would conduct ongoing, participant observation for six to eight months at each agency selected for study.

The eight agencies were selected on the basis of size (more or fewer than 25 professional staff), level of computerization (advanced vs intermediate), and kind of service provided (people-processing vs people-changing). We expected to find that the staff in people-changing organizations would be more concerned about issues of confidentiality, professional discretion and control than would their counterparts in people-processing organizations; that large agencies would computerize earlier but with more difficulty; and advanced users would make at least some use of computers in a way that transformed the service clients received. The next chapter sets the background for our findings by briefly describing each of the eight organizations we studied.

Chapter 3

The Eight Organizations

This chapter describes the organizations, the services they provide and the staff who completed questionnaires. The first section covers the four "people-processing" organizations and the second section the "people-changing" organizations. In Chapter 4, we examine the experience of these organizations with the introduction and implementation of computerization.

We used pseudonyms for the eight organizations, to ensure the anonymity that was a condition of their participation. However, one organization was so specialized that complete anonymity would have been impossible. In this case, we have not identified the specific administrative unit involved.

People-Processing Organizations

County Department of Social Services

This is a large organization created in 1974. It delivers the social services formerly administered by two area municipalities. Its primary function is to deliver general welfare assistance to qualified area residents. In addition, the County Department of Social Services, hereinafter referred to as CDSS, provides counselling and support services (to qualified low-income applicants) in areas such as life skills, job training and employment, day-care, and placement of the elderly. In 1984 it employed 166 full-time staff. The Department has five divisions, supported by financial, systems and staff training resources. These divisions are Income Maintenance; Employment Placement; Support Services Division; Social Planning and Policy Development; and Services to the Elderly. The main users of computers are found in the Income Maintenance Division.

Social Service Workers determine the eligibility of applicants for general welfare assistance, and monitor changes in eligibility status once clients have qualified for assistance. They maintain client files that consist of basic client data; a client profile; medical data; job search forms; release of information forms; documentation from other agencies; income statements; change of information forms; notices of confirmation; and case summaries (which may range from one line, to a page and a half of notes on each contact, including contacts with employers, landlords, and/or other agencies).

Every few days, workers receive the names of new applicants, whom they must interview (at home) within 48 hours. Concurrently, they make regular (usually monthly) home visits to all clients on their active caseload, and also respond to "emergencies" or inquiries, as they arise. When the eligibility status of a client changes, the change must be recorded. Status changes are required on an estimated eight or nine out of every ten cases, each month.

Unit supervisors, area managers and the Divisional Director oversee worker-client activity, and monitor the performance of direct service staff. The area managers and director work primarily with aggregated data while unit supervisors have detailed summaries of worker activity to supplement their "hands-on" review of client files and worker performance.

The parental support and special income unit falls within the Income Maintenance Division of the Social Services Department. Workers in this unit monitor court decisions concerning support payments, to ensure parents are contributing to the support of their dependents. A special monthly report (the Parental Support Listing), which shows all recoveries through the courts, was designed to facilitate case management for this unit.

For duties pertaining to Special Income, including assistance for glasses, dental work, and basic appliances (fridges, stoves, etc.), this unit relies heavily upon information already on the mainframe for G.W.A. (General Welfare Assistance) clients. Otherwise, workers obtain information pertaining to F.B.A. (Family Benefits Assistance) recipients from the Province, and/or directly from applicants (especially those who qualify as low-income earners).

Sub-specializations within this unit are the Eligibility Review and Overpayment Recovery officers, the Family Benefits Liaison workers, and the staff assigned to specific community hostels. Usually they rely upon, or update and verify, data already available from social services. In the overpayment recovery function, however, a monthly report has been designed (the "overpayments listing") for all clients deactivated, but owing money.

The employment program is split into two units. The Employment Services Unit handles employment assessment and training (i.e., work activity) projects. Only qualified G.W.A. recipients are referred to these programs, and while in training, clients are monitored by case workers.

The Employment Placement unit, a separate division, works closely with Canada Employment Centres, provincial employment projects (i.e., Youth Corps) and community action groups (including those for older workers, ex-offenders and ex-psychiatric patients) to achieve as many job placements for G.W.A. clients as possible. A core clerical pool in the Finance and Systems Group is closely aligned to the major focus of Departmental activity: the Income Maintenance Division. The activities performed in Finance and Systems include inputting changes of client information, monitoring program statistics and expenditures, liaising with Regional Finance, and advising department heads on annual budgeting.

District Office/Correctional Services

This large government organization is responsible for administering decisions affecting the release of prisoners from penal institutions. The operation of the parole service at the district level is the focus of this case study.

Overall management of the District Office/Correctional Services, hereinafter referred to DOCS, is conducted from the head office, which handles planning, policy development and program implementation, monitoring and evaluation. A senior executive is responsible for managing the service. The organizational structure also includes a Senior Management Committee which makes and monitors policy decisions. Branches are part of the management structure with each Branch having responsibility for a component of the service.

The DOCS we studied covers a large geographic area and maintains four sub-offices, three sub-sub-offices, two interviewing locations, and two community correctional centres, for offenders on day parole. The staff complement is 69 full-time staff. Of these, Area Managers, Superintendents, the Coordinator of Community Resources, the Administrative Assistant and the Secretary to the District Director report directly to the District Director. Other personnel include parole officers, Office Services Supervisors, office managers, Case Documentation Clerks, and support staff. The staffing of a typical sub-office/centre consists of the Area Manager or Superintendent who, as the senior manager, is responsible the day-to-day operation of the unit; six or seven Parole Officers; an Office Services Supervisor; and two or three Case Documentation Clerks. These personnel report to their respective Area Manager or Superintendent, the parole officers and Office Services Supervisor directly, and the Case Documentation Clerks indirectly through the Office Services Supervisor.

The 'sub' offices and the centres are the service delivery units. Parole officers provide offenders released from institutions with supervision which may include assessment, counselling, assistance with employment and, at community correctional centres, residential services.

Management staff at the district office include the District Director, the Administrative Assistant and the Coordinator of Community Resources. Other managers include the Area Managers, who supervise the sub-offices and their associated bureaus, and the Superintendents in charge of the community correctional centres.

The District Director is the senior executive for the District. As such, he is responsible for the overall operation of the various offices/centres in the region. Policy directives for the district are agreed on by the District Director, the Area Managers and the Superintendents, and the Coordinator of Community Resources at a monthly district management meeting. While standing orders for the district emanate from the District Director, these orders must be consistent with the orders of Regional Headquarters which, in turn, are consistent with those issued by the Commissioner. As well, the District has to adhere to directives put out by the branch heads although the various branches have no direct authority over parole offices.

Parkside Community Centre

This small organization provides recreational, counselling, and group activities to seniors, teens, parents and children. The Centre's stated purpose is:

> To promote and enhance the well-being of people in the context of their community and within an adaptive service framework which fosters social interaction, personal growth, effective support systems, improved mental and physical health, community participation and mutual self-help.

Parkside Community Centre, hereinafter referred to as PCC, employs 12 full-time permanent staff, supplemented by seven full-time staff on contracts established under various grants and 45 part-time staff. In addition, 25 to 30 students are hired on short-term contracts, under government grants, during the summer. Although the Centre's funding comes primarily from the United Way and, secondarily, from the municipality, many programs are offered under provincial and federal government grants and some small charitable foundations.

Programs for seniors, teens, children and parents are conducted by the Centre. Recreational programs such as fitness, swimming and sports are offered to people of all ages, as are social and cultural programs such as arts and crafts, ceramics, computer training, dances and special events (i.e., parties, film nights). The Centre also conducts outreach and camping programs for children 6 to 17 years of age. People 14 to 24 years old may be eligible for the centre's Employment Training and Placement Services program. Adults with young children can enroll in the Centre's Child/Parent Centre. Special programs for seniors include transportation, informal drop-in centres, and individual counselling. Finally, the Centre frequently offers special intergenerational programs.

The Centre's total clientele was about 1300 to 1600 when we studied it. Of these, 850 were youths, aged 6 to 17 years, and 500 to 750 were senior citizens and adults.

The Board of Directors has undergone many changes over the past three years, changes that resulted from growth and change within the Centre. Prior to this growth, the Board was made up of a wide cross-section of people from different occupational backgrounds. In the last three years a deliberate attempt was made to recruit board members for the Centre's programs. For example, several members have expertise in computers while others have expertise associated with the Parent-Child Centre. Thus, increasingly, Board membership was shaped by the character of the Centre's programs.

The re-organized Board has taken a more active role in program advisory committees. However, it also makes decisions about salaries, the hiring of non-contractual employees, budgets, program and policy development, and grant applications.

Within the current structure, decisions are made at several levels. Day-to-day decisions involving service or minor program changes are made by middle management — Executive Assistant, Program Director — in consultation with front-line workers. Administrative decisions are made by the Executive Director. The Board of Directors decides on proposed new programs; new grants being sought; and proposed expenditures of more than $2,000.

The planned growth and change in the Centre's organizational structure has caused staffing problems. Programs for children and adults have expanded but the number of staff has not expanded accordingly. Because the United Way could not fund three full-time positions, heavier time demands have been made on existing staff.

Immigrant Aid

Immigrant Aid, hereinafter referred to as IA, was established in the 1970s to provide free services to help all new immigrants and refugees adapt to life in Canada. The services included an English as a second language (E.S.L.) school for those not yet eligible for E.S.L. classes provided by Employment Canada; a nursery school for children, aged two months to five years, whose parents are in the E.S.L. program; settlement services which provide initial information about housing, employment, schools, health care, recreational facilities and government and community services; and a service which helps clients to apply for programs such as Family Allowance and Health Insurance. About 60 percent of clients are refugees requiring special assistance. In recent years, refugees have come from Eastern Europe (especially Poland and Romania), the Middle East, and Central and South America; however the largest group are Chinese-speaking persons from Southeast Asia. In 1984, the staff handled approximately 34,000 cases including 6,000 new clients and about 7,000 telephone enquiries.

Besides the services already mentioned, the organization operates three storefront shopping plaza locations, opened in response to the growing trend by immigrants and refugees to settle on the urban periphery.

There are 17 full-time direct service staff in this organization and they report directly to one of three supervisors. In addition, there is an administrative assistant, a intake clerk and two clerk/typists. The administrative assistant reports directly to the manager as does one clerk/typist. The other clerk typist and the intake clerk report directly to the supervisor of settlement services.

People-Changing Organizations

Dominion Family and Child Service

This large multi-faceted organization has three service groups — Developmental Assessment and Treatment Services (DATS, under the clinical direction of a pediatrics department), Children's Services and Adolescent Services (both under the clinical direction of a psychiatry department), and 11 distinct program units.

As part of a large teaching institution, affiliated with a university, a community college and a regional hospital network, many "staff" are supplied through faculty appointments, and others as part of their professional training (i.e., residents, interns and students on placement). As such, the staff size is constantly in flux, ranging from 90 to 125, but averaging slightly over 100 members.

The service is administered as a matrix system, with professional staff reporting to department heads for administrative purposes, and to program heads for clinical direction. Consequently, contracts must be negotiated between department heads and program heads for allotments of staff time and professional service.

The Dominion Family and Child Service, hereinafter referred to as DFCS, is a secondary and tertiary-level service facility. That is, all referrals must come from primary service providers (including family physicians, social service organizations, schools, etc.) or other secondary level treatment facilities. As the only tertiary-level service provider in the area, it offers both consultation to human service providers and treatment for children with severe disorders.

To fully appreciate the organizational context in which computerization took place, it is necessary to refer to several events which were concurrent with or immediately preceded computerization. Perhaps the major event, in the 1970s, was the amalgamation of the Service with the University Medical Centre. The amalgamation resulted from a Provincial demand for rationalization of local health care facilities, and a Regional plan to combine the Dominion Family and Child Service with the University teaching programs, under one administration. After that, the Service took on a different personality. No longer was it a relatively small, close-knit and informal treatment facility, where staff could deal with one another face to face. It became part of a much larger entity, considered by some remote, complex and full of bureaucratic 'red tape.'

Funding and reporting relationships also changed in 1978 to 79. At that time, the provincial government reorganized its Ministries, and children's mental health programs came under the jurisdiction of the Ministry of Community and Social Services, and no longer under their traditional sponsor, the Ministry of Health.

New working relationships had to be established, and old assumptions set aside. External control increased sharply. More significantly, operating revenues failed to keep pace with the rate of inflation, and year after year the organization had to cope with (relatively) fewer resources. Not only were staff unable to keep up with the growing patient waiting lists, but staff numbers were often reduced as vacancies were not always filled. Along with the funding shift came demands for more detailed reporting of professional activity. If programs were to survive, they would have to 'prove' their worth in facts and figures. Staff at every level experienced pressure to 'produce.'

The third major event to influence the organizational environment into which computers were thrust occurred in the early 1980s. Staff experienced dramatic shifts in the style and emphasis of leadership and their professional activity, if not competence, was repeatedly subjected to review. Past performance was no longer significant, and high levels of productivity were no longer assumed.

United Family and Child Services

This large quasi-public organization has a mandate, from the provincial Child Welfare Act, to provide protective services to children and counselling to families. The United Family and Child Services, hereinafter referred to as UFCS, also identifies resources available and needed in its catchment area and assists in securing needed resources.

The UFCS has 59 employees, including nine supervisors/managers, 12 support staff and 38 direct service staff. Most, excluding support staff, have formal training in social work or child care work. The agency receives about 2,200 requests for service per year.

Like other quasi-public child welfare organizations, this one has a permanent funding base; 80 percent of its $3.5 million budget is provided by the provincial government and the rest by the local municipality. If it runs a deficit, the agency can apply to the provincial government for additional funds through an Exceptional Circumstances Review. In the past few years, the agency's funds have been restricted by maximum increases allowed by the province, but funding is still guaranteed.

UFCS is managed by a Board of Directors which determines agency policy. It consists of 15 elected members and four representatives appointed from the Regional Council. Elected members come from many backgrounds including school principalships, corporate tax law, pharmaceuticals, social work, construction, social planning and foster parenthood. The Board actively assists management without becoming involved in the day-to-day operation of the agency. Its work is completed through committees. Currently, there are seven Board committees: Personnel, Program and Planning, Property, By-Law, Nominating, Executive, and Finance.

The Executive Director is hired by the Board to oversee day-to-day functioning. Staff who assist the Director include accounting, court service, volunteer coordinator/staff trainer and Director of Services. The Director of Services coordinates all agency services. Under his supervision are: two Family Service teams (child protection and family counselling); one Intake and Abuse team (also providing emergency after-hours services); one Child Management team (caring for protection and children's services cases); one Residential unit (children's services); one Foster Care unit (children's services); one Adoption unit; one Community Organizer; and all clerical support staff. The Family Service, Intake and Abuse, Foster Care, Child Management and Residential teams all have supervisors who oversee the work of five or six direct service staff, and who report to the Director of Services. The Director of Services supervises the Adoption team and the community organizer.

There are three levels of decision-making for general policy matters: the Team Supervisors' Group, the Management Group and the Board of Directors. Team Supervisors meet every second week with the Director of Services. This group decides issues concerning team policy, and stress accountability. The Management Group consists of team supervisors, the Director of Services, the Comptroller and the Executive Director. It decides on program changes, service planning and personnel issues. Finally, the Board of Directors makes the decisions regarding new staffing, agency policy, budgeting, monthly expenditures, and new programs which will have a financial impact on the agency. Staff members are frequently involved in decision-making through membership on committees.

Urban Youth Counselling Service

This small mental health centre, for youths 12 to 19 years of age, is funded by the Ministry of Community and Social Services. Urban Youth Counselling Service, hereinafter referred to as UYCS, was established in 1975 as the result of an increasing concern of mental health professionals about the lack of services for severely disturbed adolescents.

One major concern of those professionals and lay persons who founded UYCS was the lack of continuity and follow-up when adolescents moved from program to program. To fill this gap UYCS was "built into a formal network of children's mental health services," to monitor the progress and treatment of those in the system.

The stated objectives of UYCS are to provide responsive and effective direct treatment services to youth in their homes and communities; to assist troubled youth and their families to become as self-reliant as possible; and to provide coordinated treatment planning and continuity of service to all referred youth.

Although funded by the provincial government, UYCS is a registered non-profit charitable organization with a private Board of Directors. This Board establishes the overall policy and general direction of the organization.

The full-time staff of 30 includes 22 who provide direct service, five management or supervisory personnel and three support staff. One support staff member is employed part-time. These staff deliver service through the following major programs and services: Intake/Service Coordination Team; Home Treatment Program; and Day Treatment Program.

The Intake/Service Coordination Team, consisting of a program director and five social workers, accepts referrals from various health and social service agencies. The team does a needs assessment, develops a treatment plan and arranges a placement in an appropriate setting either within the UYCS system or in other community services. The Community Support Program, a responsibility of this team, was established in 1978 to help adolescents accomplish short-term goals, and to provide crisis back-up and extra staffing where necessary.

The Home Treatment Program, staffed by a program director and seven social workers, provides professional at-home social work services to adolescents and their families. The services provided include family counselling, individual counselling of an adolescent or parent(s), liaison with other community agencies, and advocacy for adolescents involved with schools, courts and hospitals.

The Day Treatment Program, staffed by a program manager, nine youth workers, and three special educators provided by the local Board of Education, serves from 10 to 12 adolescents at each of three satellite locations. This program, which receives most of its referrals from several Boards of Education, is open Monday through Friday, 9:00 a.m. to 3:00 p.m., and provides a therapeutic milieu that tries to help adolescents return to school or enter the work force.

Suburban Treatment Centre For Children

This small organization serves physically disabled and multi-handicapped children and young adults. The Suburban Treatment Centre For Children, hereinafter referred to as STCC, seeks to recognize the special needs of people with physical disabilities and those of their parents, and to provide specialized services to meet those needs; to work cooperatively with community services, educational and recreational facilities to ensure that wherever possible, children can participate in community programs; and to act as an advocate for the Centre's children.

STCC serves handicapped children and young adults up to and including age 21. The services include four age sequential programs — Infant, Preschool, Children, Adolescent and Young Adult — in which multidisciplinary teams provide therapeutic services to clients. The Centre also has an assessment service; a consultation service, i.e. consulting with other community agencies; and other special services including medical clinics, life skills training, and social/recreational programs.

STCC is funded by the provincial government and by donations from service clubs, other charitable organizations, businesses and individuals. An annual fund raising appeal raises most of the private donations. Of total funding, 84 percent is provided by the provincial government and 16 percent by community donations.

The Centre is managed by a 20-member Board of Directors who set organizational policy. The Board also helps with management issues, but not on a day-to-day basis. An example of the responsibility undertaken by a Committee of the Board is the Program Advisory Committee's task of examining the kinds of programs to be offered, and their staffing requirements.

STCC has a three-tiered management structure, direct service staff, support workers, and 36 full-time staff. In addition, four teachers employed by the Surburban Board of Education operate school programs at STCC. The organization also hires casual staff to run recreational and leisure programs; and its operation is assisted by approximately 150 volunteers.

A senior manager, the Executive Director, oversees the overall operation of STCC, particularly the financial management of the organization. The Assistant Executive Director, the second tier, manages all aspects of the clinical service.

The third tier of management consists of coordinators. Two coordinators whose functions pertain to organizational concerns — volunteers and community relations — report to the Executive Director. Other coordinators manage the clinical service and report to the Assistant Executive Director.

Service coordinators identify client needs and plan service and delivery. Program coordinators lead multi-disciplinary teams and are concerned with identifying needs, developing programs and coordinating service activities. Discipline coordinators are more concerned with maintaining qualitative and quantitative standards of service within each speciality.

Direct service staff allocated to these programs report directly to their program and discipline coordinators.

Other employees include the office staff and an accountant who has recently been appointed the data processing manager. These personnel report directly to the Executive Director. Two services have particular relevance for understanding the extent and nature of computerization at STCC. One, the school program operated by the Board of Education, was established for handicapped children who cannot attend community based classes. The program has used computers as learning tools since its inception. The other is the Assistive Devices Resources Service (A.D.R.S.). A.D.R.S. assesses the therapeutic utility of assistive devices, i.e., computers, for children with communication disabilities, and serves as a technical resource for the Centre's personnel. As a designated Communication Clinic in the provincial government's Assistive Devices Program, the Service orders prescribed assistive devices for physically disabled children.

Summary

Table 3.1 compares the eight organizations we studied. It is interesting to note that all of the people-changing organizations are primarily provincially funded agencies geared to serving young people. The people-processing organizations, on the other hand, constitute a more diverse group.

A few other facts, not apparent from Table 3.1, also need to be noted. First, DOCS is probably the most rigidly hierarchical structure of the eight organizations we studied. Its policies are made at head office and the local management has less autonomy than managers at the other agencies have. Secondly, two of these organizations — PCC and DFCS — had morale problems even before (and during) computerization. In both cases, the staff was feeling over-worked, and at the DFCS the problem was compounded by the rapid and confusing changes in personnel at the upper management levels.

The staff in the 8 organizations who completed questionnaires were: predominantly female (73 percent); average age 32.5 years; average length of time employed five years; two out of three staff were employed in the organization before computerization; more than two out of three staff were providing direct service or supervising direct service staff; about one of five reported that they had professional social work qualification while just over one-third reported that they had a professional qualification other than social work; and almost two-thirds reported that their education included an undergraduate degree or graduate study.

We will examine in later chapters whether the environments of these organizations had any influence on the success of computerization. Most particularly, we shall examine the ways computers were introduced and implemented in each agency. As we shall see, the earliest experiences with computers frequently determine whether computerization will subsequently prove easy or difficult in the long haul.

Table 3.1
Characteristics of the Eight Organizations Studied

Organizations	Service Provided	Major Source of Funds	Staff Breakdown
People-Processing			
County Department of Social Services	General welfare assistance	Government	166 full-time
District Office/Correctional Services	Supervision of parolees	Government	69 full-time
Parkside Community Centre	Recreational and social programs for children and adults	United Way	19 full-time time; 45 part-time; 25-30 summer students
Immigrant Aid	Information/referral services and language classes	Government	24 full-time
People-Changing			
Dominion Family and Child Service	Clinic for children with severe disorders	Government	approx. 100
United Family and Child Services	Protective services for children and family counselling	Government	58 full-time
Urban Youth Counselling Service	Treatment centre for adolescents	Government	30 full-time
Suburban Treatment Centre for Children	Treatment centre for handicapped youths up to age 21	Government	36 full-time; casual help volunteers

Chapter 4

The Introduction of Computers

It is essential to manage the implementation process, and to recognize the effect the different organizational levels can have on productivity and the successful adoption of a new system if their needs and concerns are not addressed. There are three prerequisites for the successful introduction of new systems: an underlying infrastructure; design of the hardware and software to meet the requirements of the people in the organization; and an implementation strategy that considers the immense social and organizational changes these systems imply (Wallersteiner, 1982, p. 60).

The importance of how computers are introduced in organizations has been amply documented. This chapter describes how and why computers were introduced in each of the eight organizations which will be grouped, for this analysis, according to their reported use of computer technology prior to the arrival of our field staff. As was pointed out earlier, an organization that reported three to five uses of the computer was classified as an intermediate user of computer technology. Organizations reporting 6 or more uses were classified as advanced users. Remember, however, that "advanced" and "intermediate" have meaning only in relation to each other: in reality, the "advanced" users prove much less advanced than many have imagined in the social work literature.

Advanced Computer Use

County Department of Social Services

CDSS had been using computer technology for about 9 years before this research was undertaken. In the early 1970s, CDSS used the main-frame computer of the municipality. The first program computerized was income maintenance. However, this practice proved unsatisfactory: poor design resulted in a failure to generate relevant data, and/or inadequate report formats.

In 1974, the Executive Director appointed a small committee, composed of a staff member, a programmer from the municipality, and a representative from the Province, to study the problem. Financing half of the cost of devel-

oping a new system, the Province insisted that any new system maintain separate files for client, financial and other data.

The design phase lasted one year. The Committee met regularly to identify system requirements and construct the data base. The staff member on
the Committee (program manager — Income Maintenance) felt he knew
exactly what was required. Thus, the involvement of other staff was minimal,
and many (if not most) staff knew little of the on-going process. The next
eight months were taken up with programming the system. This included
developing forms, writing a manual, and making decisions about hardware
and other technical matters. The program manager designed draft copies of
forms to be used and distributed them (informally) to staff, for feedback.
Based upon the response, the forms were often reworked before they were
adopted for use.

The system was gradually put in place over a six-month period. A clerk
volunteered to input data and test the system, to ensure that it worked. By the
end of the fourth month, direct service staff had been trained in using forms,
and from then on, they were expected to do one new case, per day, on the
new system. In the sixth month, staff converted their remaining caseload to
the computer.

A few structural changes occurred in the Department as the system was
being introduced. At least two new staff positions were created, and the
Income Maintenance program was consolidated into one location. Computer
Terminal Operators were needed to input client data, and Control Clerks
were designated for each team of welfare workers, to manage (among other
things) the paper flow between the workers and the input operators. As the
new positions were introduced, others (in the clerical and reception areas of
decentralized offices) were discontinued. Existing staff had to reapply to the
Department for one of the new positions, or lose their jobs. Most did reapply,
as the Terminal Operator and Control Clerk positions were more senior, and
higher paying, than their previous jobs.

Training of staff at all levels has been limited from the beginning. Staff
were taught only what they had to know, in terms of form filling or operating
terminals. Often "hands-on" training was provided by senior workers, in the
absence of a training officer or more formal methods. However, many staff
did not consider more thorough training efforts in computer technology to be
necessary despite the limited use that staff made of the system.

Dominion Family and Child Service

The push to develop a computer system in this organization can be traced to
one person — an experienced clinician who became a Program Manager.
While reviewing case management procedures, he discovered little was
known about the number of staff, or patients. The manual recording system

was clearly inadequate, as it could not provide him with a current list of open cases. After examining randomly selected patient records, he concluded that anywhere from 30 to 50 percent were not being well managed. Either the charts were out of date, or cases that should have been closed were still open, or cases in some clinically bad state had not been followed up. Furthermore, he had heard several complaints that people responsible for planning couldn't get the data they needed.

In May of 1980, the Program Manager met with the Centre Administrator to compare the options of maintaining the manual system versus developing a new computerized one, in terms of the problems and the costs involved. This followed a roundtable discussion by senior staff, the consensus of which had been to try the new system that he would develop, for a year. The Administrator agreed, and funds were made available to develop the system using the main-frame computer of the teaching instruction with which it is affiliated.

The Administration saw several advantages to going ahead with the proposal. First, the need for an improved information system was widely acknowledged. Something would have to be done to generate the data needed by planners and funding bodies. Second, the impetus for the system came from within, and was led by a staff member highly regarded as a clinician, as well as a Program Manager; whatever he developed could not be interpreted as imposed by the administration or some outside source. Third, the system was sufficiently flexible to accommodate the needs of both the research unit and management. Finally, it called for no new staffing, just a reallocation of existing personnel. It may well have been the simplest, if not the least expensive, response, and this seemed like an opportune time to move in that direction.

The Program Manager prepared a paper describing the purpose, design, features and costs of the computer information system. Within six months, work on the system had been completed.

However, within eight months dissatisfaction was evident among the staff. Statistics which recorded only their "direct service" to patients averaged two to four hours, per clinician, per day: an embarrassment both individually and collectively. Especially embarrassed were senior staff, whose responsibilities included not only direct service but also teaching, supervision, consultation and community support, none of which were being counted as service. An information system that ignored these other activities seemed to question not only their productivity, but the very legitimacy of non-direct patient service. If such statistics were going to be made available to funders and external bodies, changes would have to be made.

Concerned staff discussed the problem, and produced a "Team Statement" on the use of computers, which recommended, along with some procedural changes, the redefinition of service categories that allowed for the recording of all staff activities. Program and Department heads reviewed and approved the proposals, and the system was changed to record 100 percent of staff working time.

There have been many revisions to the system since then, but the only major one was the switch from a "batch" to a more "interactive" system. This change occurred because of pressure from the Hospital. Its computer systems group successfully argued the DFCS system should conform to a software package (MEDUS/A) purchased for all hospital programs. The switch resulted in integrated records and helped rationalize (if not reduce) overall computer-use expenditures.

MEDUS/A is a more "powerful" system, enabling users to tap otherwise inaccessible data. Since it is also an interactive system, users can input or obtain data (given basic system knowledge and security codes) as they require it. Data need not always be printed in "hard copy" to be read, and therefore, data are far more accessible and current than they would be in a system dependent upon batch reports and systems experts.

Only two obstacles still stood in the way: DFCS support staff would have to input raw data, rather than send it to an external keypunch service; and many staff would now have to become familiar with the system — they would have to be trained to input and access data from a (mainframe) computer. But the Hospital insisted the DFCS change. It would not support the rising costs of independent computer use, but was willing to participate in the one-time costs of conversion at the Centre. A special effort was mounted and by April of 1983, all cases seen within the previous 12 months had been transferred to the new system. In May, the first four (of 11) computer terminals were installed, and the input operators began training. By mid July, department heads received their first monthly printouts showing ratios of the expected hours worked by each staff member.

Within a year of the switch from a batch to a more interactive system, ten terminals and one printer were operational; training had been given to 13 program secretaries; and a medical billing system had been introduced, criticized, and improved. But staff compliance with the system was less than desired. Senior staff (notably physicians who were not employed directly by the Hospital) often resisted or refused to participate.

In 1985, two years after computerization was introduced, training sessions were organized for key personnel, including team managers, senior support staff and interested program directors. The training of front line staff was given lower priority.

Suburban Treatment Centre for Children

In 1981, three years before our research began, this organization obtained a microcomputer from the local Board of Education for use in therapy. However, one middle manager recognized the computer's potential for upgrading the organization's information system. A first task was to convince senior management that various software packages could be useful to the organization. At the same time, this staff member developed a simple medical records program, based on the rolladex system, that produced case review reports. The next step was teaching the Director of Medical Records how to key in the medical records data. The Executive Director later assigned the data entry to this person. However, during the initial phase of implementation procedures were computerized without any formal decisions being made. The staff remember that computerization had no definite beginning point: "it evolved: it was all experimenting" — "it came about through bit by bit development."

In the spring of 1984, considerable progress had been made in operating the computer. Data from the medical records program was being used to track clients, prepare reports, analyze client characteristics and monitor therapy services. The accountant also had the payroll on the computer.

However, personnel involved in developing the computer operation, including the Executive Director and Assistant Director, had decided back in 1983 that the existing system was inadequate. The software packages for the Apple II were not flexible and sophisticated enough for them. Furthermore, the hardware was being shared with therapy services, so organizational procedures were not always being run when needed. The solution was to obtain better hardware which would be used solely for organizational purposes.

Limited options were available for obtaining funds to upgrade the computer operation. STCC receives most of its funding from the provincial government and the government was unwilling to provide either financial support or consultative assistance for the computer system.

Consequently, the Executive Director asked the Board of Directors for funding from the monies collected through community donations. The request was accompanied by a proposal outlining the rationale for upgrading the computer system. It argued the upgraded system would increase operating efficiency and maximize productivity with no appreciable increase in operating expenses.

The Board approved, in principle, funding for computerization; but it stipulated that the Executive Director use an outside consultant to help identify which functions were potential candidates for computerization and to select the appropriate hardware.

A Board member arranged for the Executive Director to meet with a senior consultant from a management consulting firm. Following the meeting, they submitted a proposal which contained a workplan for the required study, and indicated that the firm would prepare a Request for Proposal for issuance to prospective suppliers. The proposal, acceptable to the Executive Director, was approved by the Board of Directors.

The consultants indicated the following applications were appropriate for computerization: General Ledger — The requirement was for a straightforward system that followed generally accepted accounting principles; Payroll/Personnel — A system was needed to replace the program designed by the management consultant firm and being run on the Apple II. Although TPS had proved generally satisfactory, STCC wanted a system that provided more flexibility in reporting areas; Fixed Assets — STCC required a system to process Straight Line Depreciation with a 5/10/15 year life and provide sufficient flexibility for future changes as required by the Ministry of Health; Membership/Donation Control — The requirement was for a system with identification, tracking, labelling and report preparation facilities. As well, the system had to interface with word-processing for newsletter preparation, and with general ledger to record donations received; Word Processing — A system capable of generating personalized form letters and customized letters was needed. The program would have to interface with the medical records database; and Medical Records System — The requirement was for a database management program for a still developing/evolving medical records system. The program needed an expandable storage feature; file manipulation capabilities; and had to produce — or be adapted to produce — both standard and customized reports. The program also had to offer mathematical, statistical and graphics options.

Vendor responses to the Request for Proposal indicated the IBM PC/XT could run the above applications. Approval for buying the necessary hardware was given by the Board and the equipment was installed in the summer of 1984.

Parkside Community Centre
In 1982, the Board of Directors and management staff of this organization began discussing computerization. They had found that, due to increased accountability demands, they needed quicker, easier access to information. The only "pressure" they felt from an outside source came from the United Way following a funding meeting in 1982. Although all information requested had been presented at the meeting by the President of the Board, some information had been difficult to collect. Following the presentation, the United Way representative asked if the agency could afford to purchase a computer to assist in funding applications. The President of the Board responded by asking whether they could afford not to, given the statistical requirement for funding application. The administrative staff thought com-

puterization would enable them to meet demands for increased accountability, increased management and increased manpower requirements.

Although discussions about computerization started in 1982, the Centre lacked sufficient funding for all new programs that year. In 1983, the Board and administrative staff acquired funding from the provincial government. Hence, they began making serious inquiries about buying and using a computer.

The Executive Director and Executive Assistant found shopping for a computer difficult because they did not know what computers could do. They approached the Board for assistance. The Board asked them to identify their needs but, when they were unable to do so, a Board member who was employed by a management consultant firm arranged to have a colleague assist in decision-making. He met with the staff and, using information from their meeting, recommended types of hardware and software. He also developed a "Vendor's Questionnaire" to be distributed by the centre.

The proposal identified the Centre's needs, the objectives of computerization and equipment needed. The principal needs were said to be: General Ledger, including sub-fund accounting; management reporting; member registry file and ad hoc reviews of member profiles; time management and service delivery statistics; word-processing with mail merge; spreadsheet analysis capabilities; research capability to study effectiveness of clinical programs; and such additional needs as room and program scheduling, inventory control, donor and donation recording, and member alumni lists.

Four objectives were identified: namely, to provide better management information in the form of member profiles, service rendered, and costs of different clinical programs; to assist the agency in meeting the reporting requirements of the various funding applications; to reduce the clerical effort required to complete funding applications; and to support the research needs of the agency by assisting in the evaluations of program effectiveness.

Management recommended the organization purchase a tailor-made package from a computer company but the Board did not agree. Board members thought any system used by the Centre had to be flexible, given the Centre's growth and development. In addition, the package cost more than a new software package would. The Centre, therefore, purchased an IBM PC and software identified by the consultant. It was anticipated that staff could also use the system, thus avoiding the expense of hiring a full-time programmer. The Board assumed staff would have time to write their own programs. Ultimately, they purchased a microcomputer (IBM PC/XT) which was installed in February 1984.

With money from the federal government, the centre hired two people to establish a computerized information system.

Both the Board and management staff determined what information would be entered into the computer. They decided service information (membership files, donor files, time management files) should be entered first since this seemed the most necessary to secure funding and ensure day to day services.

One of the programmers' job requirements was to design and conduct a training course for all full-time staff. They also wrote a users' manual which was distributed to each staff member. Originally, the course was designed to take place over ten three-hour sessions and to combine theoretical knowledge and hands-on experience. However, many of the staff members found they could not afford the time away from their jobs to attend the course and the frequency of meetings was reduced to once a week. The content of the course changed from a combination of theory and "hands-on knowledge" to demonstration.

The programmers were also to have trained the Executive Assistant and Director to use the computer, but neither manager found time to learn the system. As a result, the Centre's computer system was inoperable for the first three months of 1985. The Director kept applying for grant funding to hire a new programmer on a contract basis. The Centre received temporary funding from the federal government, again for eight months, to hire (on a contract) a programmer who had a degree in computer science and experience with microcomputers and with working in a human service organization.

The new programmer found numerous difficulties with the programs already established. Program documentation had not been completed, and the new programmer had to spend the first three months determining how each program had been designed, in order to create documentation for them. He then evaluated each program and changed computer forms to suit any changes to the programs. He also began creating new programs to enable management to complete funding package statistics. The difficulties in implementation appear to have resulted from a lack of money to adequately fund the venture; planned growth and change in the agency's structure over the past three years; a lack of time on the part of managers and staff to learn how to use the system; and the (excessive) amount of authority given to the computer staff hired to establish the system.

Intermediate Computer Use

United Family and Child Services

In the early 1980s this organization experienced a sharp increase in the demand for its services. Because of an increase in the number of children in residential facilities outside the agency's jurisdiction and a 78 percent increase in staff over a four-year period, an operating deficit developed.

Computer technology was first introduced in UCFS by the comptroller for use in preparing financial reports and payroll. The programming and processing of data were done outside UFCS.

However, the Management Group composed of senior staff began exploring how computer technology might also meet their needs for information and case management. A new comptroller, recently hired to replace the comptroller who had introduced computerization in the finance office, viewed computerization favourably and saw that computer use would help both him and the agency get more work done.

The Management Committee felt the computer might also be used to assist the organization in keeping track of children in care, to reduce the number of children in residential facilities outside UFCS's jurisdiction; to enable the agency to quickly and effectively meet the information requirements of the government; and, to track expenses for residential care and overall budgets to avoid overspending.

The Management Group decided the agency could not afford an in-house, mainframe computer system similar to those found in large Child Welfare agencies. They, therefore, began examining programs available through computer companies and eventually purchased the Accounting and Children's Services packages, feeling these packages would meet the three computerization needs identified above. The Board saw these packages as inexpensive, compatible with the provincial government's recording and reporting system for Service Planning, and having the potential to become increasingly cost-effective. In addition, the agency could purchase more computer packages and equipment later if they proved necessary. The province approved the capital expenditures required and encouraged UFCS in its efforts to computerize.

UFCS made the Comptroller a liaison between themselves and the computer firm. This decision was based on two considerations. First, the Comptroller's job would be assisted through computer use, since the Comptroller maintains accounting and other statistics and completes the annual Service Plan. Secondly, the Comptroller was already interested in computerizing the agency and was considered by some management staff to be a key backer of the computer system.

After the Board decided to purchase the system a representative of the vendor came to the organization to introduce the staff to the system and train them in its use. The system was introduced as a management system rather than one designed to assist front-line workers. The information collected was not directly related to casework and was therefore acceptable to staff. The potential benefits of the system to management, staff and organization were discussed with the staff by a senior officer of the computer company. He understood the difficulties faced by front-line workers when agencies computerize, because of his work with other agencies; thus, he realized the importance of staff acceptance of the two computer programs.

Once staff were trained, the organization began submitting batched forms for the programs. A staff users' group, consisting of representatives from social work, supervisory, child care, secretarial and management staff, was set up to identify problems. This group submitted recommendations to the company and as a result of their input, forms were changed.

In 1983, the organization purchased a microcomputer (IBM PC) with a hard disk attachment. The computer company had recently developed equivalent software packages for microcomputers. Initially, the agency used only the financial package in its computer. Recently, they began processing Children's Services information on the computer also. But they continued to submit these forms to the computer company in order to receive the same printouts they were accustomed to receiving. They have found they are losing reports with their microcomputer because it does not have the capacity of the larger system.

The organization purchased a second computer terminal in 1984, hooked it into their microcomputer, and housed it in the Executive Secretary's office. She was to use it for word-processing. Eventually the terminal will be accessible to social workers so they can 'call up' information on cases.

District Office/Correctional Services

In 1978 to 84, DOCS developed several program modules which provided an information package on incarcerated criminal offenders, a Mail Manager program which links all Correctional Services Management and operational units, and a word-processing package. This package was on a main-frame computer located in the head office. In 1983 systems-oriented personnel at head office decided to extend computerization to parole districts. Several District Directors who recognized the potential of the technology supported their decision. Terminals were supplied to the District during the fall of 1983. Soon afterwards the modules, the Mail Manager program and the word-processing package, came on line. These programs were introduced for use in the parole system without any modification to their basic design.

Training for the initial stage of computerization, when the programs became operational, was conducted by a senior staff member who was responsible for teaching personnel how to use the hardware and software packages. The instruction was targeted at the Area Managers/Superintendents and the Office Services Supervisors as they, and especially the latter, would be on site to teach, manage and encourage the Case Documentation Clerks to use the system. Approximately five hours were allotted for each training session, after which it was assumed the staff could operate the system with the help of supporting documents and manuals. Following this, the systems people spent several days studying the District's operational procedures. Consultations with staff of the sub-offices and the community correctional centres elicited their concerns and requirements for the Parole Supervision System. This process identified some ways computerization could facilitate the operation of the District.

The Parole Supervision System (PSS) was designed to help parole offices. The database contains information on the type of release, the relevant dates, the name of the supervisor, and a wide range of additional material which can be updated and amended as required.

Training for the Parole Supervision System was held about a year after the training for the initial stage of computerization. This time, however, the trainers came from Operational Information Services at head office. Although attendance at these one-day sessions was limited to Office Services Supervisors, on occasion a Case Documentation Clerk was deputized to take the training. Supervisors were then expected to train the support workers who would bring the backlog of PSS data on-line. The directive issued by head office suggested this should be accomplished quickly, in two to three weeks.

The training of the Office Services Supervisors, their training of the Case Documentation Clerks, and the implementation of the system all within a compressed time frame, created stress in some offices. In interviews, several people commented that this was a poor way to introduce a system. As one person said: "You should train first; then you bring in the program."

Due to a rushed and inadequate training program, workers have had to learn to use the system through trial and error experimentation. But work demands and the time lag in logging on the mainframe made this type of learning difficult. Other staff members, especially parole officers, received no training, but some of them tried to learn informally through hands-on use.

For the most part, staff regarded the training as haphazard because different procedures and trainers were used to introduce the existing programs and the computerized Parole Supervision System. Others knew how to operate only one or two modules. Because of this, many staff members said they would like to be given an overview of the entire computer operation. According to one worker, this instruction would make her work more meaningful and interesting as she would then understand how the various modules fit together.

Immigrant Aid

In 1973, demands for service from this organization increased sharply. The manual system used until then for collecting data on clients became overloaded and unmanageable. In June 1979, the Ministry decided to help IA comply with its mandate to provide information on immigrants settling in its catchment area. This information was to be made available to all government offices and departments with responsibilities in this area.

At that time, the staff manually recorded Telephone and Public Inquiry Reports and Daily Case Reports. In the former case, inquiries of various types were simply tallied up by area of major concern. In the latter case, information fell into three categories: (1) Client Information, consisting of the client's name, who referred her/him (if applicable) and other personal information, (2) Initial Services section, which listed the most commonly provided services and (3) Referrals, consisting of the name, address, and type of agency to which the client was referred (if applicable). Additionally, each counsellor kept a summary of information requested on the telephone by clients, members of the public, and employees of agencies. Each client had a Case History Card, containing personal information and notes made by counsellors. The Ministry made the following recommendations regarding computerization following an inquiry into the informational needs of Immigrant Aid: "that the decision be made to implement a computerized information system for . . . statistics," and "that the decision to computerize be made as soon as possible."

However, change was not to be immediate, since: "Pending . . . changes (e.g., the development of a common intake form for (a) the general client population (b) the language school and (c) the nursery) and the resulting need to consider fully their implications suggest the desirability of postponing any discussions of possible changes to data collection and processing procedures." At this time, a new senior staff appointee, dissatisfied with the data collection system, convinced the administration that more systematic data collection could and should provide information on the clients of Immigrant Aid: namely, services given, frequency of use of the services provided by counsellors, and planning and program development that would be useful to other Ministries.

A computer systems expert was hired to design a system for use on the Ministry's mainframe computer. Many meetings took place during which a set of forms was developed. The initial meetings involved the systems designer, Management Systems personnel and the supervisors of the services. The forms were then pre-tested on two counsellors, some modifications were made and a few forms were printed. The system had a trial run in August 1980, was modified slightly and the forms were revised again, twice. The staff were trained by the systems designer in two one-hour sessions with groups of three people. In these sessions, the systems designer noted most of the staff "were terrified of computers" and job evaluation seemed uppermost in their minds but, after a few training sessions, the staff seemed to be less resistant to the computer technology. The comments of staff would suggest that the two hour training provided was not adequate: "I just picked up the use of the computer by asking whoever was around." "It was an hour and a half of 'teach yourself'. . . . After a while, it was fun. Now it's just part of the job." "I don't remember getting any instruction on it . . . I was just taken over to the computer and shown how to do it." "Overall, the introduction to the computer, and training period, were inadequate. . . . The manual was 'the pits.' "

The data processing was done on a three-step "Batch System." Data forms were sent once a month to a Provincial mainframe computer. The raw data were then sent to an outside company for keypunching and verifying, then were entered on a computer tape. This tape was sent back to the Provincial systems people and the data were run from the tape. This process took so long that data were frequently out-of-date by the time they were received in report form by Immigrant Aid. In some instances it took weeks to obtain an "ad hoc" information report.

By 1983, senior staff realized their computer system was outdated and in May 1983, they proposed revamping it. The following excerpts from their proposal indicate what they felt was needed to deal with the problem in the system.

> We have tried to cover all aspects of the problems involved and believe that the purchase of a microcomputer as soon as possible will prove to be much more cost effective than the present system which is archaic and expensive. Clearly time is of the essence since otherwise we are in danger of wasting our funds on the old ineffective system.

The proposal was passed along to the appropriate department. It was put on hold pending a review of computer systems within the Ministry and had not been accepted by the time this study ended.

Urban Youth Counselling Services

In this organization the move to introduce computer technology was initiated by the Executive Director and the Program Manager of the Intake/Service Coordination Team. In 1983, in a proposal to the Board of Directors, the Program Manager recommended that UYCS purchase a microcomputer and the appropriate software. The report identified the following "immediate" (within one year) uses for the system: word processing, accounting, fiscal planning and budgeting, and home treatment direct service statistics. The report also identified the following future uses (as soon as possible after one year): day treatment attendance records; night duty helper schedule; monthly reports and graphs; and a management information system. The Board was very receptive; but before making a final decision, it asked the Executive Director to prepare a report on the costs of different microcomputers and their respective capabilities.

Early in 1984, the Executive Director recommended to the Board that the organization purchase a microcomputer. He hoped to develop a computerized system that would process client-related data and financial and budgeting data.

As early as December 1982, the Ministry had distributed a memorandum encouraging its funded organizations to consider buying office automation equipment including word-processors, micro-processors, and personal computers. While this memorandum may have supported the two senior staff in their request to the Board of UYCS, the Executive Director stated there had been "little or no pressure on the organization to computerize."

The Program Director, regarded as the computer expert in the organization, assumed the major responsibility for planning and initiating computerization in UYCS. He undertook this task with the support of the Executive Director, who shared his enthusiasm about the potential of computers. The move also had the full support of the Board.

In the spring of 1985, when data were collected for this research, UYCS was using the mainframe computer at a local University once a year to process data from the intake and assessment forms. In addition, once a month data were sent to the Children's Mental Health Services Information System for processing. This processing of data is a requirement for support of the children's mental health centres. The microcomputer was used by UYCS for word processing, book-keeping and accounting, and as a decision support system using a program that the senior Program Manager adapted for the use of the Community Support Team. In addition, microcomputers were used for educational purposes by the teachers in the three centres of the Day Treatment Program.

When UYCS purchased its microcomputer there was no computer programmer/analyst on staff, a situation that still existed when data collection for this study ended. UYCS used some packaged and some specially designed programs to prepare periodic reports on services provided, to analyze client characteristics, to assist management in policy/program planning and evaluation, and for some accounting procedures.

When computerization was introduced, a few workshops, conducted by the Program Manager, were held to acquaint staff with very basic aspects of computerization. Support staff were assisted in learning to use the computer as a word-processor and to enter and update information. Training disks and manuals were made available and support staff were expected to use these to learn how to enter and retrieve data. However, no pressure was put on the professional staff to use computers and a "free and easy" approach was taken with regard to their access to the computer.

Table 4.1
Selected Data Relevant to the Implementation
of Computerization

Organizations	Length of Time since Computer Introduction	Type of Computer	Software	Structured Training Program for Staff	Planning Involvement
People-Processing					
County Department of Social Services	9 years	main-frame and micro	Developed within organization	Yes, limited in content	Senior staff*
District Office/ Correctional Services	1 year	main-frame	Developed outside organization	Yes, for senior staff	None
Parkside Community Centre	1 year	micro	Programmer on contract	No, planned but not implemented	Senior staff
Immigrant Aid	4 years	main-frame	Developed outside organization	Yes, a total of 2 hours	Senior staff
People-Changing					
Dominion Family and Child Service	5 years	main-frame	Developed within organization	Yes, 2 years after	All staff
United Family and Child Services	4 years	main-frame	Developed outside organization	Yes, by vendor	All staff
Urban Youth Counselling Service	1 year	main-frame	Developed outside organization	Yes	Senior staff
Suburban Treatment Centre for Children	3 years	micro	Developed outside organization	No	Senior staff

*Senior staff includes executive directors and managers.

Summary

Table 4.1 summarizes selected information on the implementation of computerization in the 8 organizations.

In CDSS, STCC, UYSS and UFCS supervisors or managers were the moving force in the introduction of computerization and they convinced the executive director or the Board of Directors to find the necessary funding. For IA and the DFCS, computerization appeared to have come about through a combination of factors. Both organizations had key upper managers who were computer enthusiasts, but both also had pressure from the outside. IA was being encouraged to computerize by the provincial government, while

DFCS felt the need to computerize to become more accountable to its funding sources. The Board of Directors of PCC felt pressure from the United Way to improve the accountability of the organization. DOCS, on the other hand, had computerization imposed on it by its head office.

Typically, these systems were all designed as management tools and very little input was sought from, or training given to, staff at the direct service or support levels. The organizations that had the most problems during implementation appear to have been PCC, DOCS, and DFCS. At the first two organizations, inadequate training seems to have been the main problem. At the DFCS, computerization caused bad staff relations when a computerized staff monitoring system produced data that implied the staff (especially the senior staff) were unproductive.

The organizations in which the impetus to computerize came solely from within had fewer problems during the implementation stage. It is interesting that the two agencies where staff felt particularly overworked prior to computerization — the DFCS and PCC — both faced problems during computer implementation. Most of the organizations made no provision for input of support or direct service staff in planning implementation.

We have now ''met'' the eight organizations and learned about the conditions under which they came to adopt computers. We shall now consider how computers were actually being used at the time our field staff studied these organizations.

Chapter 5

Staff Use of Computers

One comment frequently expressed in the literature is that the success of computerization in an organization is directly related to the participation of users in planning and maintaining the system. In this chapter we examine the extent, nature and implications of the involvement of staff in the planning and use of computer technology.

Advanced Users

County Department of Social Services

At the time of our data collection, almost 10 years had passed since computer technology was introduced into this organization. But, despite the rapid changes to computer technology in that time, the system was substantially the same as when it was introduced, with small refinements of the original design. One constant has been the Systems Programmer, employed by the Municipality, who designed the original system. Since 1979, a "systems monitor" has acted as the liaison with the Municipal Systems Department. It is a trouble-shooting role, used when staff identify problems with the system, or want to obtain information not normally accessible. While not an expert on highly technical aspects of computers, the systems monitor can resolve many problems internally, and effectively communicate Departmental concerns to the experts. The system was designed, primarily, to support the income maintenance function. But apart from the social service workers, and their supervisors, managers and directors, there are several other users directly or indirectly related to income maintenance. These include clerical and accounting staff, who support Departmental activity generally, and the special divisions or units that assist welfare recipients with respect to life skills, job training and/or finding employment.

In support of the income maintenance function, the computer routinely generates the following reports:

Daily
- Client Change Listings;
- Payment Change Listings;
- Cheque Issuance Register.

Bi-Monthly
- Cheque Run (for specified cases, where necessary);

Monthly
- Advance Cheque Listing (for accuracy and audit checks by workers);
- Cheque Run (all cheques produced by client and district);
- Client Profiles (updated for case files, maintained by worker);
- Last Home Visit Listing (which lists all outstanding cases by date priority);
- Form 4 Data (the managerial report of activity by team and worker);
- Form 5 Data (the statistics and expenditures required for Provincial subsidy).

At the time our research was conducted, the Department had no computer-assisted learning capability, although it was committed to implementing such a program in the near future. The Training Officer sees computer-assisted learning as a tremendous benefit, as it will enable her to concentrate on teaching professional values, and discretion, for which computers are not well suited. Acquiring a microcomputer for training (and other) purposes was planned within the year.

Almost three-quarters (73 percent) of staff who completed questionnaires indicate they use computer generated output. However, there is considerable variation by position, ranging from 50 percent of support staff, to 70 percent of supervisors, to 82 percent of direct service staff, to 100 percent of the managers.

Among respondents who stated that they use computer generated output "for any purpose" the overall ranking of use is shown in Table 5.1. More than 9 out of 10 of these respondents use the computer to monitor client service data and more than half the respondents use it to determine eligibility for financial assistance or service. When the relative weighting of computer applications is analyzed by staff position, distinctive patterns emerge. The most obvious pattern is that the range and extent of computer applications increases with rank in the Departmental hierarchy. Support staff name only three applications used by a quarter or more of their number; direct service staff name five; supervisors, ten; and managers, nine applications used by 25 percent or more of their group. Of the three applications regularly used by support staff, only one is used by a sizeable percentage (45 percent use computers "to monitor client service"). By comparison, computers are applied to eight distinct tasks by 50 percent or more of the managers polled.

All levels of staff include "monitoring client service" among the top

Table 5.1
Ranking of Overall Computer Use by Type of Application

Rank	Type of Application	Percent of Users (N = 95)
1	Monitor client service data	93
2	Budget and manage resources	64
3	Determine amount of financial assistance	59
4	Determine eligibility for agency service	58
5	Refer clients to other departments or agencies	46
6	Revise existing services/programs	30
7	Conduct research	27
8	Revise existing services/programs	25
9	Monitor staff performance	21
10	Formulate policy	16

two computer uses, but when viewed in relation to other computer applications, "monitoring client service" takes on different meanings for each group. Support staff, for example, primarily process clients and direct client data to the appropriate files. Direct service workers use the system to manage their caseloads, by establishing who is eligible for service, at what level of entitlement; when to review each case; and when to refer, if necessary. Supervisors "monitor client service" to ensure the maintenance of service standards and case flow. When discrepancies appear, supervisors may intervene to correct a worker, advise a unit, revise service patterns or relocate staff resources. For managers, monitoring client service data is part of overall program management. Client service and staff performance data (in aggregate) are indicators of current program status. Along with more specific, issue-oriented data (some of which may be generated from the existing data base), these indicators provide the basis for program planning and the development of new services.

More than half (54 percent) of the respondents indicate they make more use of the computer system now than they did when they started using it. Among those who reported that they make more use of the system now, most (78 percent) attribute the change to "job requirement," but other reasons given include "experience in using computers" (49 percent), the fact that the "system is easier to use" (35 percent), "faster response time" (33 percent), a "wider range of applications" (31 percent), and "formal training" (15 percent).

Notably, those making significantly more use of the system than before include managers (80 percent) and support staff (64 percent). By comparison, only 44 percent of direct service staff and 40 percent of supervisors make more use of computers than before. This suggests administrative applications have expanded at a faster rate than clerical or direct service applications. Not everyone who uses the computer, however, completes forms. About two-thirds (64 percent) do so as part of their jobs, but this group is predominantly (88 percent) direct service and support staff (who represent 53 percent and 16 percent of the total, respectively). Among those who complete input sheets, 71 percent do so on a daily basis, although others report weekly (8 percent), monthly (4 percent), quarterly (2 percent), or other (2 percent) patterns of data input.

Client profiles and case management reports are the most commonly completed forms, followed by time-management (i.e., activity logs) and accounting forms.

Almost three-quarters (73 percent) of the survey sample enter or retrieve data from the computer. Of those, nearly twice as many retrieve (90 percent) as enter (49 percent) data. Among those who enter data (predominantly support staff) three-quarters do so daily, while others report weekly (10 percent) or monthly (31 percent) data entry. Among those who retrieve data (predominantly direct service workers, but representing every staff category) 85 percent do so daily, while others report weekly (14 percent) or monthly (2 percent) data retrieval.

Approximately one-fifth (22 percent) of those who enter or retrieve data have been doing so for a year or less; one-third (34 percent), for less than 3 years; and about half (48 percent), for less than five years. About half of the respondents in their first year of data entry are new employees and the other half have shifted over from older procedures. This suggests a higher rate of mobility into data entry than into some other jobs that involve computer use.

Dominion Family and Child Service

Two types of "files" are kept in the computerized information system of this organization: one for patient data (a clinical record), and another for staff data (an activity record). When patients are admitted to a CFC program, they are issued a "patient master-file" identification number (unless referred within the Hospital, in which case a number already exists) and their data is entered onto MEDUS/A. Clinical data are then routinely collected on an "out-patient service sheet" (OPSS), considered the backbone of the system. Information derived from the OPSS is entered (or "filed") in the "patient service record" (PSR). Data relevant to staff activity are then automatically gleaned from the PSR and transferred to the "resource record."

Forms completed by staff to maintain the system include "Patient Diagnosis," "Comments," "Transfer," and "Discharge" forms, as well as the OPSS daily activity/encounter form. In addition, staff must submit "Staff Activity Plan" forms, on an occasional basis, which state the formal expectations of their professional activity by department and program.

In terms of data feedback, the following are generated on a monthly basis:

1. Clinicians receive

    a) Clinician Caseload Reports (of active, closed, and follow-up cases, listed by patient name);

    b) Individual Clinician Statistics (aggregates of professional activity over the period, as compared to expected performance);

2. Program Managers receive

    a) Program Summary Reports* (of patient status and service);

    b) Clinicians within Program Statistics (showing the time spent, by clinician, in program activity);

3. Department Heads receive

    a) Department Summary Reports* (of the hours worked by professional staff as compared to contracted expectations);

    b) Department Non-Patient Summary Reports* (of time/activity by clinician);

    c) Department Education Reports* (itemized lists of staff and their respective educational inputs);

4. The Centre Administrator receives

    a) Milieu Program Statistics (of patient attendance in Centre programs, for reporting to the Ministry of Community and Social Services);

    b) Physical and Occupational Therapy Reports (from the C.P. Centre and the pre-school programs for government reporting).

    Note: Program Management and Advisory Committee (PAMAC) Members receive all asterisked (*) reports.

In addition, a number of special reports are generated through MEDUS/A. They include two administrative reports, on resource management (a staff 'contract' summary) and records management (a record of encounters for specified patient groups); two program planning and analysis reports (patient populations analyzed by birthdates, type and location of service); two in the area of program management (a summary of CFC active, closed, and follow-up cases, and a team caseload summary); one for epidemiological research (a referral/diagnosis report); and one required by the courts (a patient encounter report).

Most reports are called up by the Assistant to the Centre Administrator who formats monthly reports in advance, so they can be printed as soon as the data are in (and/or deadlines have passed). More specialized reports are generated by, or with the assistance of, a system consultant.

A handful of other staff also take a special interest in computer use, and sit on a committee called the "Data Cluster Group." They monitor ongoing computer use, address problems, and recommend system improvements. Several are receiving training from the systems consultant, so that they can begin designing their own computer applications. Some see this as the first step towards more meaningful use of data, for program planning and analysis. As staff become familiar with applying data in their respective departments, programs, and teams, they will likely begin developing new information packages to facilitate case management.

Only 28 percent of respondents on staff when computers were introduced report they were consulted about the change. Among those who were not consulted, 41 percent think they should have been. This view is voiced more strongly as one moves up the organizational hierarchy. For example, while none of the support staff who were on staff when computers were introduced were consulted about the implementation, only 22 percent think they should have been. By comparison, a majority (55 percent) of the managers and directors were consulted initially; but all of those who were not consulted think they should have been.

A third of the respondents were consulted about the kinds of computer programs now being used. Half of those who were not consulted think they should have been, including 15 percent of support staff, half of the direct service staff, and all of the supervisors, managers and directors who were missed.

Nearly two-fifths (39 percent) of the survey participants indicate they were consulted about the types of computer reports generated. Of the majority (61 percent) who said they had not, however, three-fifths (59 percent) think that they should have been consulted. This view is shared by 18 percent of support staff, 75 percent of direct service staff and all of the (admittedly few) supervisors, managers and directors left out of the process.

Staff who fill input forms were asked if the "forced-choice classification" of data presents problems; the vast majority (76 percent of the total) characterize their problems with forced-choice as "slight." Four-fifths of the study population fills out forms for computer input, including all managers and supervisors, and 86 percent of direct service staff; but only 62 percent of support staff and half of the directors. Among those who fill out these forms, most (55 percent) describe it as a daily activity, while the remainder describe it as a weekly (39 percent) or monthly (3 percent) occurrence. Time and case management forms are compiled by the vast majority (88 percent) of respondents, while one in five (19 percent) enters client profile data and 4 percent report entering accounting data.

Staff who fill out computer forms as part of their job have noticed a definite increase in the amount of "paperwork" they are required to complete. Overall, 84 percent report an increase in paperwork, and nearly two-fifths describe the increase as substantial. Only 9 percent of those who do computer-related paperwork say that it has decreased, while 3 percent believe it has remained the same.

Less than half (43 percent) of the respondents enter or retrieve data (directly) from the computer. Those who do are principally support staff (92 percent) and managers or directors (55 percent) as compared to a reported 17 percent of supervisors and 18 percent of direct service staff. Data entry, which is performed almost exclusively by support staff, is a daily (30 percent), weekly (39 percent) and monthly (24 percent) activity. Data retrieval, performed by a wider range of staff, tends to be on a monthly (42 percent) or weekly (30 percent) basis, although some report it as a daily (21 percent) activity. Three out of four users (76 percent) say it is "much easier" to retrieve data than before. No one finds computerized record keeping (data entry or retrieval) to be more difficult than before, although a few (9 percent, comprised mainly of direct service staff) think data entry has "remained the same." This finding is interesting since most respondents (60 percent) have been using the computerized recording system for less than a year, and only 5 percent report having used it for more than two years. The system, it would seem, is readily adopted by those with direct, "hands-on" experience.

Table 5.2
Ranking of Overall Computer Use by Type of Application

Rank	Type of Application	Percent of Users (N=62)
1	Monitor client service data	82
2	Develop new services/programs	37
3	Revise existing services/programs	36
4	Budget and manage resources	34
4	Conduct research	34
6	Monitor staff performance	30
7	Formulate policy	16
8	Other, including: Refer clients to other departments or agencies; Determine eligibility for agency service; Determine amount of financial assistance.	4

About two-thirds (62 percent) of respondents indicate they use computer generated output; but it is clear that few applications are used extensively. Among respondents who use computer generated output "usually" or "sometimes," the overall ranking of uses is as shown in Table 5.2.

Only one application, "to monitor client service data," is reported by more than half (82 percent) of those who use computer generated output. The next five most common applications, chiefly supervisory and/or management responsibilities, include the development (37 percent) and revision (36 percent) of services/programs; budgeting and resource management (34 percent); research (34 percent); and the monitoring of staff performance (30 percent). Finally, policy formulation (cited by 16 percent of computer output users) also falls within the supervisory and/or management sphere.

The data indicate that the extent of computer use, and not only its application, may vary by position. Only 31 percent of support staff and 61 percent of direct service staff use computer output, compared to 83 percent of supervisors and 91 percent of managers/directors. Furthermore, when the relative weighting of computer applications is analyzed by staff position, distinctive patterns emerge. The most obvious is that the range and extent of computer use increases with rank in the organizational hierarchy.

Table 5.3
Ranking of Major* Computer Applications by Position

Support Staff (N=7)	Direct Services (N=28)	Supervisors (N=8)	Managers/Directors (N=16)
Monitor client service (23%)	Monitor client service (54%)	Monitor client service (83%)	Monitor client service; monitor staff performance (91%)
		Budget and manage resources (67%)	Budget and manage resources (73%)
		Revise services/programs; develop new services/programs (50%)	Revise service/programs (64%)
		Monitor staff; conduct research; formulate new policies (33%)	Develop new programs; conduct research (55%)
			Formulate policy (45%)

*Applications identified by less than 20% of any group are excluded.

Support staff and direct service staff identify only one computer application used by one fifth of their members or more. Supervisors, managers and directors, on the other hand, list seven qualifying applications. Furthermore, while none of the applications listed are performed by one-half or more of the support staff, and only one is performed half of the direct service staff, supervisors list four and managers/directors list six distinct applications performed by a half or more of their members.

Every occupational group includes "monitoring client service" as its primary use but, as was also the case within CDSS, each group performs this function differently.

Just over half (54 percent) of the respondents indicate that they make more use of the computer system now than they did when they first started using it at. Among those using system more now, most (53 percent) attribute it to a "job requirement" but some cite "experience in using computers" (44 percent); the existence of a "wider range of applications" (34 percent); "faster response time" (25 percent); the system being "easier to use" (19 percent); and "formal training" (14 percent).

These results are also similar to answers given by the staff at the County Department of Social Services. And, again as at CDSS, we find considerably increased use of the system over time by supervisors (83 percent), managers and directors (82 percent). Yet only a third (32 percent) of direct service staff, and half (54 percent) of the support staff use computers more than they did before.

The reasons for more extensive computer use reveal a distinctive pattern. Managers and directors give equal weighting (45 percent) to experience, improved ease, and a wider range of applications as reasons for their increased use of the computer system; all other staff list "job requirement" and "experience" as primary reasons. In fact, increased computer use as a job requirement (i.e., imposed rather than self-initiated or a matter of choice) is reported by more than two-thirds of all (qualifying) support staff (71 percent) and direct service staff (67 percent).

Table 5.4
Reasons for More Use of Computers by Position
(Percent)

Reasons	Support (N=11)	Direct Service (N=15)	Supervisors (N=8)	Managers and Directors (N=15)
Job Requirement	71	67	40	27
Experience	71	44	40	45
Wider Applications	43	33	20	45
Faster Response	43	—	40	27
Easier to Use	—	—	20	45
Formal Training	—	—	—	36

Parkside Community Centre

Because it reported six uses of computers in our initial survey, we classified this organization as an advanced user; but few who completed questionnaires actually report using the system. Specifically, eight staff members indicate they complete forms and seven use computer output. Only five state they enter or retrieve data. Forms are completed by people in all positions except support staff; but only supervisors and managers use computer output. These findings are consistent with the fact that the computer system was initiated to assist managers in completing administrative duties.

Of the eight respondents who report completing forms, all use time management forms, while two use client profile and client update forms. No regular trends for completion of forms (i.e., daily, weekly, monthly, etc.) can be found. Table 5.5 indicates the respondents' reaction to forced-choice classification of data. The interviews reveal staff do not complete time management forms consistently; gradually they have stopped using them altogether because of difficulty with time management categories. Most find their work does not match any of the codes available.

Table 5.5
Difficulties with Forced-Choice
Classification of Data

Degree of Difficulty	No.
Total	8
Serious problem	3
Slight problem	3
No problem	1
No response	1

As noted, supervisory and management staff are the sole users of computer output. Table 5.6 shows, in order of frequency, the uses they make of the output.

Table 5.6
Ranking of Overall Computer Use by Type of Application

Rank	Type of Application	No.
1	Monitor client service data	6
2	Conduct research	3
3	Monitor staff performance	2
4	Formulate policy	2
5	Determine amount of financial assistance	2
6	Revise existing services and programs	2
7	Budget and manage resources	2
8	Develop new services	2
9	Refer clients to other services	1

It should be noted that the number of people reporting some of these activities is quite small. The responses indicate, as one would expect given the reasons for computerizing and the stage of implementation, that the system is used predominantly for administrative purposes.

Suburban Treatment Centre For Children

In this organization the projected new or expanded uses of the computer include word-processing, accounting, volunteer control, and community relations functions, and medical records. The least progress has been made in word-processing, and the computer is seldom used for correspondence or other documents.

Several factors have contributed to this situation. First, it appears the executive director did not make a firm decision, during the planning phase, to computerize this work. Consequently, the support staff were not pressured to use the program. Secondly, the workers were not convinced that the word-processing program was a useful tool. Their resistance may stem from the fact they did not participate in the decision to purchase the microcomputer and institute a word-processing program. Their involvement was limited to selecting the Wordstar program and, later, attending a workshop on word processing. During an interview, one person commented that the clerical staff may feel computerization ''was being laid on them from the top.''

Difficulties the accountant experienced with the program also caused a false start in getting the accounting functions on-line. After solving this problem, it took considerable time to reconstruct the parallel manual accounting system. During this period payroll, previously handled on the organization's microcomputer, was farmed out for processing. An accountant with extensive computer training was employed to generate the kinds of reports (i.e., spread sheets and budgetary forecasts) that are useful to management in decision-making.

The coordinators of volunteers and of community relations have made extensive use of computer technology. The coordinator of volunteers, who has word-processing training, uses the program to store the information on the volunteer application form. As this information is then broken down and stored by categories (for example, the interests/skills attributes of the volunteers), it is easy to search the file when a volunteer with these attributes is required.

Similarly, the coordinator of community relations has used the computer to keep track of donor records and donor mailings; to print and illustrate newsletters and media handouts; and for campaign purposes.

The data base for the Medical Records System (MEDREC) is comprehensive and must be updated daily. Consequently, significantly more data are entered with MEDREC than with the former system. This change led to resistance from support workers who were expected to take on the additional work. One support staff has been reassigned to do all the data inputting; but there is no back-up support for this person.

Table 5.7 illustrates the amount of staff involvement in decisions regarding computerization. These findings reinforce the impression gained during interviews that many staff members had no, or limited, involvement in the decision-making process, or else they did not avail themselves of opportunities to participate in these decisions.

Table 5.7
Staff Involvement in Decisions Regarding Computerization

Involvement in Decision-Making	Yes (Percent)	No (Percent)
Consulted re: the introduction of the computer (N=20)*	40	60
Consulted re: kinds of computer programs being used (N=30)	37	63
Consulted re: kinds of computer reports being generated (N=30)	47	53

*The other 10 respondents had not been hired when these decisions were being made.

Some staff members, particularly therapists, report they were not consulted about buying the computer, implementing MEDREC, or computerizing other organizational procedures. However, the Assistant Director says she consulted the therapists, especially the program coordinators, on the kind of information that had to be collected and the best format for computer generated reports. When designing the Client File, comments on the Client Profile Sheet were sought from the coordinators and therapists, but this request brought only two responses.

MEDREC was introduced during the field work for this research and before it was fully operational, the Assistant Director and the program coordinators were using MEDREC reports to allocate staff to various programs. Discipline coordinators use the reports to assist with performance reviews, and the therapists are using them to administer their caseload.

Other features of the system include a procedure which merges a word-processing function — labelling — with information on the MEDREC system. This is particularly useful and saves time when preparing mailings to parents.

Some staff members think MEDREC's usefulness would increase if the data were more up-to-date and the reports were generated on a regular basis. Others comment that it takes too long to implement the system, to have the support staff input data, and/or to have the therapists fill out the daily activity sheets. A few wonder if the payoff will be great enough to justify this time expenditure. But most staff think the system will help to keep track of client recall times — "an expensive but real use." It is anticipated that MEDREC will be a useful tool for the clinical services.

Intermediate Users

Urban Youth Counselling Service

As in three of the four organizations previously discussed, computerization at the UYCS appears to have been instituted with little staff input into the decision-making process. (At the fourth organization, the County Department of Social Services, the key computerization decisions were probably made long before this study was conducted, so the present staff may not remember or know who was consulted initially.)

In this organization, only four of the 18 respondents report they were consulted when the decision was made to computerize (see Table 5.8 below). Of the 14 respondents who said they were not consulted, only three feel they should have been. Indeed, only one of 18 direct service staff was consulted at this stage of computerization; by contrast, two of three supervisory and managerial staff were consulted.

There was slightly more consultation about the kinds of programs being used, as six of 25 staff members report being consulted at this stage. Only a minority (four) of the 19 staff who were not consulted feel they should have been.

Table 5.8
Staff Involvement in Decisions Regarding Computerization
by Position in Organization*

	Position of Staff					
			Direct		Managerial and Executive	
	Support		Service			
Involvement in Decision Making	Yes	No	Yes	No	Yes	No
Consulted about the introduction of the computer	1	3	1	12	2	1
Consulted about kinds of computer programs being used	2	2	2	16	2	1
Consulted about kinds of computer reports being generated	1	3	6	12	3	0

*5 no responses

Staff are consulted most often about the types of computer reports being produced; ten of the 25 respondents say they have been consulted on this matter. As one might expect, all supervisors and managers have been consulted recently. The most marked change is in the proportion of direct service staff consulted, six of 18 recently, compared with one or two out of 18 at the earlier stages. Only one out of three support staff have been consulted about computer reports; yet only a minority (four) of all the staff who are not consulted think that they should have been.

One staff member observes that, basically, two people make all the decisions related to computer use. However, it seems that the staff feel comfortable with this arrangement.

Fewer than half (nine) of the respondents complete forms for the computerized system as part of their jobs. Of these nine, seven are direct service and two are support staff. One staff member (in direct service) completes forms daily, four workers complete them weekly, and three respondents, monthly. Of the four staff who report both weekly and monthly completion of forms, one is support staff and three are in direct service.

Eight respondents reported on the type of forms they complete (see Table 5.9). Of these only two are support staff, contradicting research that shows support staff usually carry a major responsibility for this function. At the same time, only one-third of the direct service staff complete forms. This finding is consistent with an administrative staff member's comment that there are "no threatening forms to feed into the computer." One professional staff member simply decided not to use the computer in any way.

Table 5.9
Type of Form Completed, by Position

| | | Type of Form | | | |
Position	Accounting	Time Management	Case Management	Client Profile	Other
Support	1	—	—	—	1
Direct Service	—	3	4	4	1

One-third of the respondents report they enter and/or retrieve data from the computer. But only three of the nine staff reporting they complete forms also report they enter and/or retrieve data. Those reporting they enter and/or retrieve data include one manager, three support and four direct service staff.

Thus, a total of 14 respondents (8 who say so, plus 6 who earlier said they complete forms) input or retrieve data. When cross-tabulated by position we find two of the four support, ten of the 18 direct service, and one of the three management/supervisory staff enter or retrieve data. Given the permissive attitude regarding staff participation in computerization, the involvement of professional staff is higher than expected.

Of nine respondents who report they use computer generated output, one is support staff, one is supervisory/managerial, and seven are direct service staff. Table 5.10 presents the frequency of use of computer generated output for selected organizational activities.

As with every other organization we have discussed thus far, computer generated output is most often used in this organization for administrative purposes such as monitoring client service data, budgeting, and managing

Table 5.10
Ranking of Overall Computer Use by Type of Application

Rank	Type of Application	No.
1	Monitor client service data	9
2	Budget and manage resources	7
3	Determine amount of financial assistance	7
4	Revise existing services/programs	5
5	Refer clients to other departments or agencies	3
6	Conduct research	1
6	Formulate policy	1
6	Determine eligibility for agency service	1

resources. But the UYCS is unique among agencies discussed so far in that no one reports using the computer to monitor staff performance. Most of the various uses reported involve a small minority of staff. Fewer than half the respondents use computer generated output at all. It is surprising, in view of the importance attached to referrals of youths to appropriate organizations in the network, that so few staff use the computer when referring clients to other agencies.

United Family and Child Services

In this organization staff at all levels receive computer printouts routinely. Computer forms are batched and submitted to outside consultants who enter the information into their mainframe computer to produce reports. Some reports must be specifically requested, but routine reports are also made. Support staff receive caseload listings for their team members, by team and by worker. Front-line protection workers receive caseload lists, "record due" lists, and child information lists. Team supervisors get caseload listings by worker, and summaries of admissions and discharges of children assigned to workers in their teams. Both the Comptroller and Director of Services receive all routine reports. Finally, the Executive Director and Board of Directors receive reports upon request. All statistical case reports deal only with children in a residential care setting (foster care, group home, OPI, etc.).

Computerized reports seem most useful to upper management, especially the Comptroller, for Service Planning purposes. Below this level, reports are used less frequently. Only a few team supervisors indicate using reports and front-line workers tend to use reports only if their supervisors do.

Agency personnel maintain manual files to record cases and completed computer forms are also kept in the manual file. Paradoxically, the manual files have become more accurate since computerization, when information began to be collected systematically for the first time.

Although information is available on printouts, some staff continue to use two manual systems for reminders. All staff maintain up-to-date 'black book' notes for court purposes and some staff supplement their notes with printouts. In addition, the 'tickler' system is used. Secretaries manually record important dates several days in advance, to allow preparation time.

Most respondents use the system by completing forms and by making use of computer output but, as expected, few actually input or retrieve information.

Most respondents, 79 percent (30), fill out computer forms. All direct service workers complete forms; but respondents in other positions are divided on the use of forms. One would expect this, as the system is a management tool utilizing information provided by those at lower levels of the hierarchy.

Of those who complete forms, 43 percent (13) do so weekly. However, support staff and supervisors who complete forms at all do so daily use as Table 5.11 indicates.

Table 5.11
Frequency of Completion of Forms

Position	Frequency		
	Daily	Weekly	Less than Weekly
Support Staff	4	2	0
Supervisors	2	0	0
Direct Service Staff	2	10	2

Variation in the completion of forms by position of the respondent may be due to the fact that both support staff and supervisor must complete their own forms after receiving completed forms from direct service staff. Supervisors also correct forms and support staff record statistics about cases and occasionally complete forms for direct service workers. Both supervisors and support staff receive completed forms from about eight people, and no regular days are established on which forms must be submitted in bulk. Direct service staff fall behind in their form filling, and for this reason, supervisory and support staff must regularly help service workers submit their forms.

Forms of three major types are used: accounting forms, case management forms, and client profile forms. A few respondents report completing computer forms for other purposes, including time management and client information up-date. Which types of forms are completed apparently depends upon one's position. As Table 5.12 shows, accounting forms are generally completed by support staff and middle managers. Both support staff and direct service staff report that they complete case management forms. Finally, client profiles are usually completed by direct service staff and supervisors. Support staff are evenly divided in their use of these forms. Clerical staff indicate that as noted earlier, some team secretaries have begun completing client profile forms for their team workers who cannot complete them on time.

Table 5.12
Type of Form Completed, by Position

| Position | Type of Form | | |
	Accounting	Case Management	Client Profile
Support Staff (N=10)*	Yes	Yes	Yes-No
Direct Staff (N=19)	No	Yes	Yes
Supervisor (N=8)	No	No	Yes
Upper Management (N=8)	Yes	No	No

*2 support staff reported Yes and 2 reported No.

A minority of respondents (21 percent) report entering and/or retrieving data. Since support staff have access to the in-house computer, we expected those claiming to enter and retrieve data to be predominantly support staff. However, respondents from all positions within the agency report entering and retrieving data. Most report retrieving it monthly. (Given the responses, respondents must have been including indirect entry or retrieval; case data are retrieved indirectly through the consultants, rather than by using the in-house system.)

Table 5.13
Ranking of Overall Computer Use by Type of Application

Rank	Type of Application	No.
1	Monitor client service data	17
2	Revise existing services/programs	6
3	Budget and manage resources	5
4	Conduct research	5
5	Develop new services/programs	5
6	Formulate policy	4
7	Determine amount of financial assistance	4
8	Monitor staff performance	3

Of the 33 responses concerning use of output, 67 percent (22) indicate they do use output. Position held in the agency does not affect one's use of output. This is as expected, since people in different positions receive different reports relevant to their own position. Uses of data to assist in agency-related activities are ranked in Table 5.13. Note that no respondent uses output to refer clients to other departments or agencies, or to determine eligibility for agency service.

The way computer output is used depends upon one's position in the agency (see Table 5.14). Respondents in all positions except support staff use output to monitor client data. Managers use output for more activities than respondents in other positions, because the system was established as a tool for management. Managers do not use computer output to monitor staff performance, however, as this computerized management task is performed by supervisors. As in all the other organizations we studied, in UFCS monitoring client data is the most widely used computer function. As mentioned UFCS, like the others, also uses the computer to monitor staff performance.

Table 5.14
Computer Use by Type of Application and Position

Type of Application	Position			
	Support	Direct Service	Supervisor	Managers
Monitor client data	No	Yes	Yes	Yes
Revise services	No	No	No	Yes
Manage resources	No	No	No	Yes
Develop new services	No	No	No	Yes
Conduct research	No	No	No	Yes
Make policy	No	No	No	Yes
Monitor staff	No	No	Yes	No

Interviews indicate that most clerical (support) staff do not use the computer reports they receive. Those who do use the reports do not use them for any activity listed in the questionnaire. Secretaries receive listings of their team's caseload and recording due dates. They use the information to remind direct service staff of overdue recordings. Direct Service workers use output to ''monitor client data'' by verifying client information, and for quick, easy access to client data (i.e., they carry output in briefcases when out of the office). Finally, supervisors use output to monitor client data and staff performance by compiling statistics on team caseloads, tracking 'difficult' cases, and ensuring team members maintain up-to-date files.

District Office/Correctional Services

When this research ended, the computerized Parole Supervision System had just become operational. Thus, the staff's system use was still developing and the system was still being debugged.

Two technical problems were encountered. First, the district offices and computerized institutions all logged on to the same mainframe computer. This overload caused long delays — a two to three hour wait is not exceptional — and much frustration, especially for the Case Documentation Clerks who are the main users.

Numerous hardware breakdowns also cause frustration. Workers initially try solving problems by telephoning staff members who have expertise with computers. Whenever this fails, the equipment has to be shipped to head office for repairs. While the office is without the equipment, staff record incoming messages and/or reports and relay the information. Many direct service staff think the computer systems are inadequate for their needs and find the data to be incomplete and out-of-date. Support workers mention that a computerized version of the warrant procedure, which would have been a real work saver, was not implemented.

Staff were not involved in the decision to introduce computer technology, but some staff provided input when the computerized Parole Information System was developed. However, Table 5.15 indicates only a minority of staff were involved at any stage of the introduction and implementation of the system.

Table 5.15
Staff Involvement in Decisions Regarding Computerization
(Percent)

Involvement in Decision-Making	Yes	No
Consulted re: the introduction of the computer (N=40)*	27	73
Consulted re: kinds of computer programs being used (N=45)	29	71
Consulted re: kinds of computer reports being generated (N=45)	22	78

*The other 5 respondents were not employed in the Central Ontario District when these decisions were being made.

Unlike staff at the UYCS, the majority of the staff of this organization feel they should have been consulted. In fact, fully 69 percent of the respondents feel they should have been consulted about the types of reports being generated.

Although computerization is relatively new in this organization, staff report substantial use of computer generated records and statistics. Of the 45 respondents, 30 (67 percent) think computer generated output assists their work. As Table 5.16 shows, the staff of the District Office of Correctional Service Canada, like employees at all the other organizations we studied, use the computer most often to monitor client service data.

The Mail Manager program is also used extensively. It is seen as less expensive and more efficient than the mail or telex and is credited with decreasing the time required for communications between the District Office and the Regional and head offices.

Table 5.16
Ranking of Overall Computer Use by Type of Application

Rank	Type of Application	Percent (N=30)
1	To monitor client service data	60
2	To budget and manage resources	27
3	To revise existing services/programs	27
4	To refer clients to other departments/offices	20
5	To conduct research	20
6	To monitor staff performance	16
6	Electronic Mail	16
8	Develop new services/programs	12
9	Formulate policy	6
10	Determine eligibility for service	6

Immigrant Aid

In this organization there was limited involvement of staff in decisions surrounding the introduction and implementation of computers (Table 5.17). Here, as at DOCS, the majority of staff who were not consulted feel they should have been. The proportion of staff consulted has remained constant at approximately 40 percent at each level of decision-making.

Table 5.17
Staff Involvement in Decisions Regarding Computerization*

Involvement in Decision Making	Yes	No	N/R
Consulted re: the introduction of the computer	4	6	4
Consulted re: kinds of computer programs being used	6	14	5
Consulted re: kinds of computer reports being generated	10	11	4

*Eleven respondents were not employed by the agency when the decisions were made about introducing computers.

More than half of the staff complete forms as a part of their job. These forms are completed daily and include time management, case management and client profile forms. The forms most often completed are client profiles. Although half of the staff complete forms, only 8 percent (2) say they enter data and none retrieve data. This apparent anomaly results from the fact that the completed data forms are sent once a month to the provincial mainframe computer. Raw data are then sent to an outside company for keypunching, verifying, and entry on to a computer tape. The tape is sent back to systems people at the Province, and data are rarely run from the tape. This process takes so long that reports are rarely available when needed and the information is often out-of-date when finally received.

Ten of the 24 respondents (40 percent) report they use computer generated output. Table 5.18 presents the range of uses reported. As at all the other agencies we studied, the most common use of the computer is to monitor client service data. As referring clients to appropriate community resources is a major function of this organization, it is surprising that only 3 staff report using the computer to assist them in this activity.

Table 5.18
Ranking of Overall Computer Use by Type of Application

Rank	Activity	No.
1	Monitor Client Service Data	8
2	Conduct Research	7
3	Budget and Manage Resources	5
3	Revise Existing Services and Programmes	5
5	Develop New Services/Programmes	4
5	Formulate Policy	4
7	Refer Clients to Other Departs. or Agencies	3
8	Monitor Staff Performance	2
8	Determine Eligibility for Service	2
10	Determine Amount of Financial Assistance	1

Summary

Certain patterns of computer use seem common to all the organizations we studied. The number one use of computers is "monitoring client data" while the second most common use is for budgeting and accounting. Invariably computer use increases with rank in the organization, reflecting of the fact that these systems were designed primarily as management tools. Computer use also increases over time and invariably leads to increased paperwork. Although the staff were not often consulted about computerization, the majority of workers at most of the organizations do not think they should have been consulted. The exceptions to this rule are DOCS and IA where the majority of staff say they should have been consulted. At the DFCS, higher status employees also resent the lack of consultation. All three organizations have had staff-management problems following computerization.

The heaviest user of computers (in terms of staff involvement) is probably the CDSS. The second heaviest user is probably DOCS, where 66 percent of the staff use computer output in their work. The lightest users of computers (mainly just management) are the UFCS, the UYCS and PCC. The other three agencies fall somewhere in the middle in terms of staff computer use.

It should be noted here that "staff involvement in computer use" was not the measure we employed to classify organizations as "advanced" or "intermediate" computer users. This classification referred only to the number of different ways an organization reported using its computer, not the number of employees who used it in those ways.

Given the widely varying patterns of implementation, how do staff view the computer? Do they see it as enhancing efficiency? As increasing control over their work? Generally, how do these perceptions vary from one organization to another, and from one position to another? These are questions we intend to answer in the next chapter.

Chapter 6

Staff Attitudes to Computers and Computerization

Central to understanding the computerization process is an examination of staff attitudes towards the computer and computerization. We began with 54 attitude items derived from the literature, other studies, and hunches. These 54 items were pretested on the pilot study population (described in Chapter 2) and a variety of convenience samples, including social work staff and students at the University of Toronto.

The 54 items were examined for their intercorrelation. The items least correlated with other items were removed, leaving 36 of the original items. These 36 were then factor analyzed, and the 18 items loaded most highly on three main factors were retained for use in the larger study. These 18 items appear in part A of the questionnaire.

Both the literature review and results of the pre-test led us to expect three factors would emerge in people's attitudes towards computers: an "efficiency factor," a "control factor," and an "integration factor." The first would supposedly address issues of efficiency, effectiveness (or quality of service), and organizational rationality. The second would address issues like control, regimentation and compulsion over the workers and clients. The third would address issues of organizational integration, coordination, interaction, cooperation, communication and information sharing. However, when we factor analyzed the 18 items included in the final version of the questionnaire, only two main factors, not three, emerged. The "integration factor" disappeared and its items were now loaded on one of the remaining two main factors. A number of other relatively trivial factors were identifiable; but for all practical purposes, they could be ignored. Diagram 6.1 below displays the important contribution made by factors 1 and 2 to the *eigenvalues,* which are interpretable as the variance accounted for by the factors. Clearly, after factors 1 and 2 were identified, no other factor contributed a large additional amount to our understanding. On this basis we decided to ignore all but factors 1 and 2.

Factors 1 and 2 were rotated to clarify their meaning. Rotation redistrib-

utes the loadings of the items on factors, making the relative importance of
factors more nearly equal. Often, rotation also assigns items to one and only
one factor, thus clarifying each factor's meaning. We tried both varimax and
procrustean rotation, to see which best separated the factors and clarified
their meaning. Varimax rotation sets the factors at right angles to one
another, eliminating their correlation with each other. Procrustean rotation,
instead, seeks the best fit between the items and factors, whether the factors
remain intercorrelated or not.

Diagram 6.1
Initial Factor Method: Iterated Principal Factor Analysis
Plot of Eigenvalues

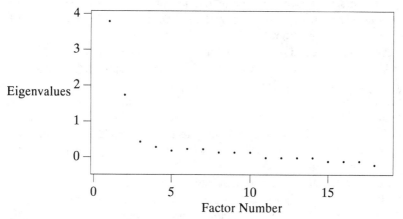

We found virtually no difference in results, regardless of type of rotation. Naturally, the total eigenvalue (5.644) (Table 6.1) was the same, regardless of rotation. The two factors together accounted for a little more than 30
percent of the variance in the 18 items. Both methods of rotation assigned
slightly higher eigenvalues to factor 1 than factor 2 after rotation, although
the two were more nearly equal after than before rotation. And, for both
methods, the squared multiple correlation of items-to-factors was approximately 80 percent, a very respectable result. Either method, then, would give
us construct validity: a high item-to-scale correlation, and (especially with
the varimax rotation) a high degree of separation between factors.

In all the analyses that follow, the varimax rotation is used. That the
two identified factors indeed measured efficiency (factor 1) and control (factor 2), respectively, is clear if we look at the most heavily loaded items for
each factor in Table 6.2. Most heavily loaded on Factor 1 were: "Computerization will result in more coordination of services in an organization" (A18
in the questionnaire); "A well organized computer system improves the

Table 6.1
Eigenvalues and Squared Multiple Correlations, by Factor
and Type of Rotation

| | Type of Rotation | | | |
| | Varimax | | Procrustean | |
	Factor 1	Factor 2	Factor 1	Factor 2
Eigenvalue*	2.945	2.704	3.328**	3.113**
Squared multiple correlation***	.802	.787	.825	.812

*Variance in items accounted for by factor
**Ignoring other factor
***Based on item-to-factor correlations
Total eigenvalue = 5.644   % variance explained = 5.644/18 = 31.4   N = 374

overall efficiency of an organization'' (A8); and ''Computerization results in improved delivery of service to clients'' (A3). Most heavily loaded on Factor 2 were: ''Computerization dehumanizes the clients by treating them as numbers'' (A15); ''Computerization reduces the amount of social interaction on the job'' (A14); and ''Computerization poses a threat to the autonomy of staff working with clients in a human service organization'' (A10).

From these factors, factor scores were created: each respondent (N=374) was now characterized by a score on perceived efficiency of the computer and perceived control by the computer. These factor scores, normally distributed with a mean of 0, could be used in conventional parametric analyses to determine what kinds of people were most likely to see the computer as efficient or inefficient, controlling or not controlling. We began by calculating one-way analyses of variance for the more obvious explanatory variables. The results, shown in Table 6.3 below, reveal that in only a few cases did an explanatory variable account for more than 1 percent of the variance in a factor score. Among these, the most important influence on attitudes towards computers was the extent of social work education: this variable accounted for 6.25 percent of the variance in the efficiency factor, and 5.23 percent of the variance in the control factor. The first effect was statistically significant at p=.086, while the second just missed being significant at p=.14; significance levels were low because the relationship was calculated on a subsample of just over 100 cases that reported some social work education.

Though the amounts of variance accounted for and levels of statistical significance were poor, the results at least tended in directions one might have predicted. Table 6.4 below displays the mean factor scores for variables with significant R-squares in Table 6.3. A high positive score on factor 1 reflects a belief that computers are efficient; a high negative score on factor 2 reflects a belief that computers control people.

Table 6.2
Rotated Factor Loadings of Attitude Items, by Factor*

	Factor 1	Factor 2
Computerization will result in more coordination of services in an organization.	.689	—
A well-organized computer system improves the overall efficiency of an organization.	.665	—
Computerization results in improved delivery of service to clients.	.598	—
Computerization will result in more cooperation between organizations providing similar services.	.544	—
Computers are the best means of distributing information in an organization.	.523	—
Computerization fosters the sharing of information in an organization.	.504	—
Computerization results in more rational decision-making within an organization.	.477	—
Computerization helps to clarify the tasks and the responsibilities of staff.	.444	—
Computerization will not improve the quality of service provided by an organization.	-.415	—
Computerization upsets good relations between managers and workers.	(-.278)	.400
People place more value on conclusions arrived at by computer analysis than by human evaluations.	—	.379
Computer technology threatens the privacy of clients.	—	.438
Computerization in human service organizations reduces the amount of discretion exercised by staff working with clients.	—	.510
Computerization decreases the flow of informal communication within an organization.	—	.511
Computer use forces client data into artificial categories.	—	.531
Computerization poses a threat to the autonomy of staff working with clients in a human service organization.	—	.588
Computerization reduces the amount of social interaction on the job.	—	.619
Computerization dehumanizes the clients by treating them as numbers.	—	.702

*Using Varimax Rotation

The data show quite unequivocally that managers think computers are efficient and not controlling, while direct service providers think the opposite. This sets the stage for a conflict between these two groups. Second, people who own and use home computers do not think computers are controlling, not surprisingly since they know more than others about how to con-

Table 6.3
Variance Accounted (R^2) in Factor Scores,
by Selected Explanatory Variables

Explanatory Variable	No.	In Question #	Value of R^2 Factor 1 "Efficiency"	Factor 2 "Control"
Age	325	C2	.0179	.0086
Education (yrs.)	329	C3	.0078	.0031
Level of soc. wk. educ.	104	C5	.0625*	.0523
Prof. qualifications	200	C4	.0143*	.0002
Prof. associations	316	C6	.0039	.0000
Gender	327	C1	.0001	.0023
Position in organization	318	B1	.0199*	.0203*
Computer use outside	329	C7	.0000	.0007
Computer training	328	C9	.0011	.0021
Years in agency	319	B2	.0089	.0271
Own/use home computer	326	C8	.0040	.0081
Employed in org. before computerization	322	B4	.0075	.0064

*Statistically significant F value, $.05 < p < .10$

trol a computer. Owner/users are also likely to think that a computer is efficient; but their difference from non-owners in this respect is not statistically significant. Finally, people with social work qualifications do not tend to think the computer is efficient, and do think it is controlling. Among those with social work qualifications, the people feeling most controlled are those with the lowest social work qualifications (i.e., community college diplomas). However, these differences in views about control are not statistically significant. What is statistically significant is that social workers with a BSW degree are the most skeptical of all social workers about the efficiency of the computer.

Is the apparent effect of social work education really due to position held in the organization, since people with higher degrees are also more likely to hold high positions? To better answer this question, we calculated two-way analyses of variance. We find suggestive but not statistically significant interactions between professional qualification — i.e., whether trained as a social worker or not — and position in the organization. In general, respondents with social work qualifications, and people lower down the organizational ladder, are disinclined to believe in the efficiency of computers. When the two qualities are combined, the result is an extreme denial of efficiency. People with social work training who occupy direct service positions are very much more negative about computer efficiency than support staff with no social work qualifications; and conversely, managers with no

Table 6.4
Mean Factor Scores for Specified Subcategories

Subcategory	No.	Mean Score* Factor 1 "Efficiency"	Factor 2 "Control"
Social Work Education Level			
Comm. College Diploma	33	-.002	-.170
BSW	36	-.347	-.165
MSW, DSW, Ph.D.	28	-.129	.220
Other	8	.511	.474
Professional Social Work Qualifications			
Any (Diploma/BSW/MSW)	97	-.167	-.055
None	104	.057	-.027
Position in Organization			
Support Staff	66	.098	-.034
Service Providers	176	-.102	-.052
Manager, Dept. Head	39	.107	.165
Branch/Agency Director	38	.243	.309
Home Computer Owner/User			
Yes	48	.147	.214
No	279	-.013	-.011

*A strongly positive score on factor 1 means high perceived efficiency; a strongly negative score on factor 2 means high perceived control.

social work qualifications are very much more convinced of the efficiency of computers than managers with social work training are.

That is, managers without social work training are more positive about computers than one would predict by simply adding together the effects of position and type of qualification; and likewise, support staff with social work qualifications are much more negative than one would have predicted by simply adding together the separate effects. Likewise, social-work-trained support staff are strongly convinced that computers control people, while social-work-trained managers are not so convinced. In this last respect, the social-work-trained managers are even more convinced that computers do not control than are the managers without social work qualifications.

The interaction between professional qualifications (in social work) and position is nearly significant, at $p=.1656$. Likewise, the interaction of age and position is nearly significant at $p=.1013$: position in the organization has a very strong effect on perceptions of control by computers at older but not younger ages. Among respondents aged 45 and over, fear of computer control increases markedly as you go down the organizational hierarchy. There is no such variation among workers aged 20 to 29; in this younger group, the support staff is least concerned of all groups about control by computers.

Gender also interacts with other variables to influence scores on Factor

2 — attitudes towards computer control. Specifically, gender interacts with position at a near significant level (p=.1154), and with professional (social work) qualifications at a highly significant (p=.0028) level. The first interaction, between gender and professional qualifications, reveals that the two groups most strongly convinced that the computer is controlling are females with social work qualifications and, even more so, males without social work qualifications (presumably, occupying support or supervisory, though not managerial, positions).

It is difficult to explain these interaction effects except with reference to the notion of "status inconsistency." A qualified social worker holding a support position in a social work organization is in a position inconsistent with his/her education. This inconsistency may cause the respondent to affirm conventional social worker's views (that computers are not efficient and are controlling) all the more emphatically. Likewise, a person without social work qualification who is managing a social service organization may feel all the more obliged to affirm non- (or anti-) social work sentiments regarding the computer where efficiency is concerned: presumably, the manager who doesn't know much about social work does know something about efficiency!

The social-work-trained manager is in the most inconsistent position where control is concerned; for in fact, the computer is chiefly a management tool in social service organizations, and therefore it is an instrument of control. The control function of the computer will be less tolerable to a social-work-trained manager, who will therefore strive the most strenuously to deny this unpleasant fact.

Not only does position in the organization interact significantly with type of education and qualification: as we noted earlier, it also interacts with gender. The attitudes of men in different positions vary more widely than attitudes of women in different positions. In particular, men who are not managers are much more likely than women to feel the computer is controlling. The numbers involved are small and one is cautious about drawing strong conclusions from so few cases. But one hypothesis worth considering is that non-managerial men will be more sensitive about control by computers than managerial men (who *have* control over the computer) or non-managerial women (who are socialized in a culture where submissiveness is considered a desirable or at least normal female trait). If this hypothesis is valid, we would expect to find the concern about control diminishing among men who are promoted into management or in cultures where gender differences in overall dominance/submissiveness are less pronounced.

Gender-based variation in beliefs is less marked on the topic of efficiency, but still noticeable: for example, male direct service staff express more doubts about computer efficiency than female direct service staff, while

Table 6.5
Mean Scores on Factor 2 (Control by Computers)
by Explanatory Variables

	No.	Mean Score on Factor 2 Soc. wk. qualif.	No.	Other qualif.
A. Professional (S.W.)				
Qualification, * *by Position:*				
Support	6	-.832	6	-.092
Direct Service Staff	65	.046	59	-.168
Supervision of D.S.S.	13	-.175	14	.258
Manager	9	.326	21	.251
B. Professional (S.W.)				
Qualification, * *by Gender:*				
Female	68	-.140	77	.126
Male	28	.148	26	-.473
C. *Position, by Gender:*		*Female*		*Male*
Support	57	-.008	8	-.308
Direct Service Staff	121	.003	48	-.191
Supervision of D.S.S.	28	.291	11	-.156
Manager	19	.222	18	.414

*Including only those with any professional qualification.

male supervisors appear much more strongly convinced of computer efficiency than female supervisors.

Again, small numbers of responses make drawing strong conclusions dangerous. However we are once more drawn to cultural explanations of this gender difference. In our culture, men are socialized to value efficiency more than women, for whom "how the job is done" — for example, the consensus and good feeling a process generates — is at least as important as its outcome. This must remain more speculation until tested through a cross-cultural comparison of male and female responses to computerization.

In general, then, the respondents most positively disposed towards computers are managers (male and female), especially managers without social work qualifications. They are most likely to view the computer as efficient, and least likely to view it as controlling. By contrast, respondents holding the least favourable attitudes are male support and male direct service staff with social work training. These respondents are less likely than managers to see the computer as efficient and more likely to see it as controlling. These perceptions are not surprising, in light of the ways the computer is actually being used, as we show in other chapters.

The most important finding of this analysis of factor scores is, however, the most obvious: the strongest influence on attitudes towards computers is not position, type of education or gender, but organization. Attitudes toward computers differ quite a lot from one organization to another.

To determine whether the observed organization differences in scores on factors 1 and 2 were statistically significant, we examined them using an analysis of variance. A one-way analysis of variance showed the effect of agency on factor 1 (the efficiency factor) to be significant at p=.0088 and the effect of agency on factor 2 (the control factor) to be not significant (p=.1748).

We then determined whether organizations displayed significantly different patterns of relations between the factor scores and some of the variables we had earlier found to be correlated with these factor scores: notably, position, education in social work, professional qualifications and age.

The first interaction considered was between organization and position. Before introducing the interaction term, both effects on Factor 1 were statistically significant (at p=.0026 and p=.0131, respectively); after the interaction term was introduced, the entire model was still significant, but none of the three terms was significant in its own right.

The situation was similarly puzzling where some other interactions were concerned, although puzzling in different ways. The two-way analysis of variance for organization and social work education produced a statistically significant model (p=.0348) and statistically significant main effects on Factor 1 for organization and social work education (p=.0730 and p=.0381, respectively). Introduction of an interaction effect, however, reduced the significance of the overall model to p=.1058, and rendered the main effects and the interaction effect statistically insignificant.

In this case, the interpretation was somewhat simpler. Introducing an interaction term had lost us 12 degrees of freedom which, in the context of an already small subsample (only 105 had any kind of education in social work), had reduced the possibility of a significant finding for the model as a whole.

We followed a similar procedure in studying the interaction between organization and professional qualifications in respect to Factor 1. Here, the overall model without an interaction term was significant at p=.0851; of the individual terms, only professional qualifications were significant at p=.0228. The significance of the organization effect had fallen to p=.1384. Accordingly an interaction term was not introduced. We concluded that some of the observed variation was due to a variation between organizations in the kinds of professional qualifications present.

Finally, we examined the relationship between organization and age. The overall model was significant at p=.0044 and effects of agency and age on Factor 1 were each statistically significant at p=.0064 and p=.0642, respectively. When the interaction term was introduced, the significance of the overall model fell slightly to p=.0157. The significance of the organization effect fell slightly to p=.0314, and neither the age effect nor the age/agency interaction was now statistically significant.

What did this exercise indicate? Where factor 1, the efficiency factor, was concerned the significance of organization variations declined in two instances with the introduction of test factors. From its initial value of p=.0088, the significance of the organization effect was reduced to p=.0730 by the introduction of education in social work and to p=.1384 by the introduction of professional qualifications. This was partly due to the loss of degrees of freedom and reduced sample size. However the original sum of squares associated with organization fell from 14.8335 (alone) to 10.3453 when education in social work was introduced and 9.4538 when professional qualifications were introduced. This means that a substantial part of the observed variation between organizations in the perception of computer efficiency is due to the fact that different organizations contain different mixes of professional qualifications and educational backgrounds in social work.

The fact that these test variables did not eliminate the organization effect entirely suggests that other factors may have been at work in making organizations more or less likely to view the computer as efficient. One possible explanation is the real difference in the effectiveness of the computer installation itself, which we cannot measure with data we collected. Another is the perceived difference: organization subcultures must vary significantly in their view of computer efficiency, even holding the composition of the organization constant.

On the other side, the introduction of the test factors "position" and "age" did not lessen the effect of organization but increased it slightly: from sums of squares of 14.8335 (for organization alone) to 17.4327 and 15.5428 with the addition of position and age, respectively. This means, at the very least, that organization differences did not merely reflect different hierarchical structures (or the positions of people responding in each organization) or age compositions. Instead, introducing "position" and "age" sharpened the organization effect.

We have seen that the interaction effects were not significant in their own right. Yet they noticeably reduced the "organization" sum of squares where position and age were introduced. Position and age were more likely in some agencies than in others to influence the perception of computer efficiency. Therefore we must interpret the positive or negative effects of position and age on perceptions of computer efficiency within particular organization contexts. In some agencies, being in a particular position, or being younger or older, will have one effect on perceptions; in another organization, a very different effect.

Where perceptions of control are concerned, the matter is somewhat different. The independent effect of organization on factor 2, perception of control, is not statistically significant. This fact is unchanged by the introduction of the test factors "position" and "age." On the other hand, introducing the test factors "education in social work" and "professional qualifications" has the effect of making the organization effect statistically significant, at $p=.0548$ and $p=.0565$, respectively. This implies the presence of interaction effects: which organization you work in influences your perception of control by computers if you have some kinds of training or qualifications and not others.

However, inclusion of social work education and professional qualifications also reduced the size of the group on which the organization effect was being calculated, from 332 cases (one way ANOVA) to 105 cases (where social work education was also considered) and 202 cases (where professional qualifications were also considered). The change in importance of the organization effect could have resulted in part from subsampling, as well as from specification by test variables. To check this, we calculated a one-way analysis of variance for organization and each factor, using the sub-samples $N=105$ and $N=202$ noted above. The result reversed what we had found earlier. For people with a social work education or social work (versus no social work) qualifications, organization now had a statistically significant effect on Factor 2 (the control factor) and no significant effect on Factor 1 (the efficiency factor).

Whether we view these findings as illustrating the effect of subsampling or another verification of the interaction between organization and other key variables (such as social work qualification) hardly matters. What does matter is the following: (1) organization has important main and interactive effects with other explanatory variables; (2) perceived control varies most markedly from one organization to another among those most sensitive to control, namely, social-work-trained personnel; and obversely, (3) perceived efficiency varies most markedly from one organization to another among those most sensitive to efficiency, namely, non-social-work trained personnel — mainly, support staff and managers.

That we were unable to find statistically significant interaction effects, despite our many efforts to do so, reflects a problem of small sample size overall and, even more, considerable size variation among organizations. An ideal analysis of variance, with equal numbers of cases in each cell of a two or three way table, might well have given the statistical confirmation we sought in vain.

To conclude this portion, we have seen that "organization" has a complex relationship with the two attitude factors, perceived computer efficiency and perceived computer control. In some instances, the effect is partly a result of compositional differences between organizations: organizations containing a larger proportion of certain types of people (e.g., social work-

ers) inclined one way or another towards computers will make that organization as a whole look more or less inclined in that direction. The perception of
computer efficiency is more affected by "position" and "age" in some
organizations than in others. Likewise, perception of computer control is
more affected by social work education and professional qualifications in
some organizations than in others.

It is time, therefore, to examine the attitudinal data organization by
organization, to see how this operates. We begin with an examination of the
average factor scores for each organization, then consider responses to individual items.

Organization by Organization Comparisons of Mean Scores

For easier understanding, we have displayed the mean factor scores for the
eight organizations in Diagram 6.2. Here, in parentheses after the name of an
organization, the first number is the mean loading on the efficiency factor,
and the second is the mean loading on the control factor. Recall that a positive loading on factor 1 (efficiency) means a perception that computers are
efficient. A negative loading on factor 2 (control) means a perception that
computers are controlling.

Note first that six out of eight organizations are on the diagonal that
links low efficiency with low control, and high efficiency with high control.
This suggests a hypothesis to be examined further: computer efficiency and
control often go together, and where both are lacking, computer use simply
isn't very extensive or "advanced." Conversely, extensive use will produce
strong perceptions of both efficiency and control. (That this finding is not a
mere artifact of measurement is guaranteed by the varimax rotation which,
over all cases, sets the two factors at right angles, or independent of each
other.) However note that two of eight organizations (i.e., Correctional Services and PCC) are exceptions to this "rule." We should expect to find
unusual circumstances in these organizations to explain the deviation, circumstances that may include exceptionally good (or bad) leadership, planning, and luck.

Extent of Computer Use: Advanced versus Intermediate

However the data reveal no simple correspondence between degree of computer use and perceptions of efficiency and control. The four "intermediate"
computer using organizations — DOCS, UFCS, IA and UYCS — are located in
three different cells; and so are the four "advanced" users. This suggests that
no relationship exists between these variables; that "advanced" organizations
are not as different from "intermediate" ones as we originally believed; or that
perceptions of efficiency and control are largely independent of real efficiency
and control, which may indeed vary with the extensiveness of computer use.

People-Processing versus People-Changing Organizations

Second, note that all but one of the people-processing organizations are all in the bottom half of the diagram, and people-changing organizations are all in the top half. This says that perceptions of control are strongest in the people-processing organizations, and weakest in the people-changing organizations.

Third, note that all four people-changing organizations fall on the left side of the chart, indicating a perception of relatively low computer efficiency. By contrast, people-processing organizations are evenly split in their perceptions of computer efficiency between very positive and very negative assessments. Computerization is obviously something that affects people-processing organizations more variously than it does people-changing organizations.

Diagram 6.2
Average Perceptions of Computer Efficiency and Control,
by Organization

| | | Perceived Efficiency is | |
		Low*	High*
Perceived Control is	Low**	UYCS (-.179, .337) STCC (-.053, .139) DFCS (-.225, .013) UFCS (.0004, .286)	
	High**	DOCS (-.201, -.138)	IA (.337, -.112)
		PCC (-.289, -.226)	CDSS (.225, -.066)

*"Low" scores are below the overall mean (N=333) on this factor, and "high" scores above the mean. The mean score is 0.0130.
**"Low" scores are above the overall mean (N=333) on this factor, and "high" scores below it. The mean score is -0.0088.

Large versus Small Organizations

As well, note that the four largest organizations — UFCS, DFCC, DOCS and CDSS — are in three different cells. This fact suggests that size *per se* is an unimportant factor in predicting perceptions of efficiency and control. Several interpretations are possible. One is that organizational size, at least within the size range of organizations we have examined, doesn't influence (perceived) computer efficiency and control at all. Another is that size does influence actual efficiency and control, but perceptions of computer efficiency and control are largely independent of the organizational reality. This possible disjuncture between perception (attitude or sentiment) and reality is something we will consider further in chapters to come.

Participation in Implementation

Finally, we consider the effect on attitudes of a variable that looms large in the literature as influencing people's acceptance of computers: namely, their participation in the implementation process.

Strictly speaking, this refers chiefly to the involvement of staff in the planning of what is to be computerized, and how. Secondarily, it refers to the availability of structured training for staff personnel in how to use the new technology. However, in the eight cases we studied, we found little variation in either involvement or training. This makes measuring the impact of participation on attitudes and perceptions very difficult.

In one organization (District Office/Correctional Services), no staff were involved in planning. At the other extreme, in another organization (Dominion Family and Child Service), all the staff who would be affected by it were involved in planning for computerization. Between these extremes, involvement in planning was limited to senior staff in the remaining six organizations.

The organizations varied more in the training they provided for use of the computer and information system. In one organization (STCC) no training was provided or planned for; in another (PCC), training was planned but never implemented. In the remaining organizations training was variably available: in one (DOCS) training was limited to senior staff. In two organizations (UFCS and UYCS), a limited amount of training was provided by the vendor of computer software. Finally, in-house training was provided in three other organizations: in one (IA), it consisted of two one-hour sessions, in a second (DFCS), it came two years after computers had been introduced and in a third (CDSS) the content was very limited.

Given this history, it is difficult to claim that staff in one organization received significantly more training than staff in another organization. It is even more difficult to draw conclusions about the relationship between training given and type of organization: large versus small, people-changing versus people-processing, advanced versus intermediate user. The variation among organizations is simply not wide enough.

This forces us to draw in a third variable less centrally related to agency participation: that is the location where software for the information system was developed. It could be argued that in-house development of software would require at least some staff participation, as compared with an "off-the-shelf" purchase of standard software.

Even here the variation is not great. Still, software was developed within the organization in three of the organizations studied (i.e., CDSS, PCC and DFCS).

Rather than try to scale these three "participation variables" and array the eight organizations along a scale from most to least participation — an effort that would have doubtful accuracy and validity — let us try instead to contrast the most extreme cases.

On the one extreme are two "low participation" organizations. STCC got pre-packaged software from outside the organization, provided no staff training in its use, and limited involvement in planning to senior staff. The DOCS also purchased pre-packaged software, limited training in its use to senior staff, and involved no staff in the planning for computerization.

At the other extreme are three "high participation" organizations. DFCS developed software wthin the organization, (eventually) provided staff training for all, and involved all staff in the planning process. PCC developed its own software, planned (but did not finally provide) staff training in its use, and at least allowed senior staff involvement in planning for computerization. Finally, IA bought pre-packaged software, provided some (two hours) staff training in its use, and involved senior staff in planning for computerization.

Referring back to Diagram 6.2, we find no correlation whatever between the type or extent of staff participation and perceptions of computer efficiency and control: the five organizations are more or less evenly distributed across the three cells in Diagram 6.2. If, as we believe, the acceptance of computerization is reflected in perceptions of computer efficiency and control, then acceptance is not influenced by the type or extent of staff participation.

The failure of this finding to confirm one of the most strongly held beliefs in the computerization literature suggests one or more of several possibilities. The first is that computer acceptance and perceptions of control and efficiency are not, in fact, connected. However, the data we examine later seem to rule out this possibility. A second is that there is simply too little variation in "staff participation" among the agencies we studied to allow for a good test of this hypothesis. This conclusion is probably warranted. However, we will return to this issue briefly in a few pages.

Comparisons of Variance by Organization

One further characteristic differentiating the eight organizations is the amount of agreement (consensus) or disagreement (dissensus) expressed about the effects of computerization on efficiency and control. This characteristic is measured by comparing each agency's standard deviation of factor scores (for a given factor) with the corresponding standard deviation for the entire population. The results of this comparison are tabulated in Diagram 6.3 below.

Here we find a pattern similar to the one in Diagram 6.2. Namely, of 6 organizations on the main diagonal in Diagram 6.2, 4 remain on the main diagonal in Diagram 6.3.

Diagram 6.3
Standard Deviations of Perceptions of Computer
Efficiency and Control, by Organization

| | | Deviations of Perceived Efficiency | |
		Low*	High*
Deviation of Perceived Control	Low**	UYCS (.643, .675) UFCS (.787, .858) STCC (.870, .833)	DFCS (1.091, .832) PCC (.927, .869)
	High**	DOCS (.877, .938) CDSS (.790, .911)	IA (1.038, 1.056)

*The standard deviation for Factor 1 (N=333) is .8939. "Low" deviations are below this mean for the entire sample, "high" deviations are above it.
**The standard deviation for Factor 2 (N=333) is .8890. "Low" deviations are below this mean for the entire sample, "high" deviations are above it.

Specifically, UYCS, UFCS, and STCC — all people-changing organizations expressing the (average) view that computerization increases neither efficiency nor control — display a high degree of intra-organization consensus on both issues. IA — a people-processing organization expressing the (average) view that computerization increases both efficiency and control — displays a high degree of intra-organization dissensus (perhaps, conflict) on both issues.

Of the remaining four organizations, DOCS and CDSS display consensus on efficiency, not control; and DFCC and PCC display the opposite pattern. If dissensus indeed implies conflict, we should look for signs of conflict over control in DOCS and CDSS, and conflict over efficiency (perhaps manifested in conflicts over productivity or paperwork) in DFCC and PCC.

Returning briefly to the question we raised a few pages ago about the effects of "staff participation" on perceptions of computer efficiency and control, we find an intriguing result.

Referring to the data in Diagram 6.3, the three organizations with relatively high staff participation display relatively high degrees of dissensus — i.e., high standard deviations — about computer efficiency; the reverse is true for organizations with low staff participation. (There is no such patterning on the issue of consensus about computer control.) This finding may be purely accidental and worth no further notice if our earlier conclusion is valid: namely, that the variation in staff participation among organizations is simply too slight to justify drawing conclusions.

On the other hand, if the finding is not purely accidental, it implies that staff participation, far from increasing consensus, does the opposite. Perhaps the more people actually know about computerization — the more first-hand experience they have with it through participation in planning and implementation — the less likely they will be to accept stereotyped perceptions of computer efficiency and the more likely they will be to form independent and varying judgements based on personal experience. Unfortunately we cannot go much beyond this speculation at the present. More will be said about "participation" later.

We now proceed to examine the organizations one by one, to better understand the configuration of attitudes we have summarized in the factor scores.

People-Changing Organizations

Urban Youth Counselling Service

As Diagram 6.2 showed, the staff of this organization do not think computer technology threatens their control over the discretion and autonomy in working with clients, nor that it has a negative impact on clients (Table 6.6).

The staff indicate a belief in the potential of computer technology for increasing the efficiency of the organization, and support the opinion that computer technology will increase the overall efficiency of an organization; but staff are divided on the perceived impact on rational decision-making (A1), on the sharing of information (A11) and on clarifiying of the tasks and responsibilities of staff (A13). In general, staff of UYCS do not believe computerization increases efficiency to any marked degree (see Diagram 6.2).

Further, an examination of the factor scores shows a relatively high degree of consensus that computerization neither increases efficiency nor control. (Such consensus is indicated by standard deviations which are below the standard deviations for the entire sample, N=333.)

Staff were also asked about their attitudes towards computers when they first started using them. Four of the 23 were "somewhat negative," and 3 out of 4 staff were "positive" at the time of implementation. Today, all staff responding are either "positive" or "very positive." Thus, acceptance of computers has grown even stronger.

United Family and Child Services

Staff responses to the 18 statements concerning computerization and computer technology are generally favourable with respect to the organizational impact of computers on control and efficiency. But as in UYCS and the other people-changing organizations, computers are viewed here as having little positive effect on either efficiency or control, comparatively speaking (see Diagram 6.2 above). Like UYCS again, there is relatively strong consensus on these issues, judging from the standard deviation of factor scores.

As indicated in Table 6.9, more than four out of five respondents indicate they currently have positive attitudes toward computers and there does

Table 6.6

Attitudes of UYCS Staff Toward Computer Technology and
Computerization in Organizations: Grouped According
to Factors of Control and Efficiency

Attitudes	Agree* (Percent)	Disagree (Percent)
	(N=25)	
Control Factor		
A2. Computerization in human service organizations reduces the amount of discretion exercised by staff working with clients.	20	72+**
A5. People place more value on conclusions arrived at by computer analysis than by human evaluations.	32+	60
A7. Computer use forces client data into artificial categories.	48	44+
A10. Computerization poses a threat to the autonomy of staff working with clients in a human service organization.	12	84+
A15. Computerization dehumanizes the clients by treating them as numbers.	16	76+
A17. Computer technology threatens the privacy of clients.	32	60+
A4. Computerization upsets good relations between managers and workers.	4	84+
A9. Computerization decreases the flow of informal communication within an organization.	8	84+
A14. Computerization reduces the amount of social interaction on the job.	15	76+
Efficiency Factor		
A1. Computerization results in more rational decision-making within an organization.	44+	48
A3. Computerization results in improved delivery of service to clients.	64+	28
A8. A well organized computer system improves the overall efficiency of an organization.	88+	4
A11. Computers are the best means of distributing information in an organization.	40+	52
A12. Computerization will not improve the quality of service provided by an organization.	20	76+
A13. Computerization helps to clarify the tasks and responsibilities of staff.	44+	48
A6. Computerization fosters the sharing of information in an organization.	68+	28
A16. Computerization will result in more cooperation between organizations providing similar services.	68+	24

Table 6.6 (continued)

Attitudes	Agree* (Percent)	Disagree (Percent)
	(N=25)	
A18. Computerization will result in more coordination of services in an organization.	64+	28

*"Agree" category is made up of "strongly agree" and "agree" responses on question-naire. "Disagree" category is made up of "disagree" and "strongly disagree" responses. "Don't know" and no responses are not included in totals.

**For each statement the opinion that is considered positive to the introduction of computer technology is indicated by a +.

Table 6.7
Attitudes of UYCS Staff Toward Computer Use

Time	Very Positive	Somewhat Positive	Somewhat Negative (Percent)	Very Negative	Not Reported
When first started using computers	32	44	16	–	8
After implementation	40	52	–	–	8

not appear to be any significant shift in attitude from the time respondents first used computers to the present. This may reflect satisfaction that computerization has not increased control, since it does not reflect a conviction that computerization has increased efficiency, comparatively speaking.

Thus, all in all, the UFCS staff view computers and computerization in much the same way as the staff of the Urban Youth Counselling Service do.

Suburban Treatment Centre For Children

The attitudes of staff at STCC are also positive towards computerization and computer use. Like the staff of UFCS and UYCS, they perceive relatively little organizational effect of computerization on either efficiency or control (see Diagram 6.2). As in the other two organizations, there is a fair degree of consensus in these views.

In two areas, staff feel computers will not have a positive impact: in respect to the privacy of the clients, and, as with the previous two organizations, the distribution of information within the organization. Two thirds regard computers as a threat to the privacy of clients (Q.A17) and 60 percent do not think computers are the best means of distributing information in an organization (Q.A11).

The attitudes of staff before and after computerization indicate computerization was implemented in a "friendly" environment. During the initial

Table 6.8
Attitudes of UFCS Staff Toward Computer Technology and
Computerization in Organizations: Grouped According
to Factors of Control and Efficiency

Attitudes		Agree* (Percent) (N=38)	Disagree (Percent)
Control Factor			
A2.	Computerization in human service organizations reduces the amount of discretion exercised by staff working with clients.	32	66+**
A5.	People place more value on conclusions arrived at by computer analysis than by human evaluations.	55+	45
A7.	Computer use forces client data into artificial categories.	50	47+
A10.	Computerization poses a threat to the autonomy of staff working with clients in a human service organization.	16	84+
A15.	Computerization dehumanizes the clients by treating them as numbers.	26	77+
A17.	Computer technology threatens the privacy of clients.	26	74+
A4.	Computerization upsets good relations between managers and workers.	13	84+
A9.	Computerization decreases the flow of informal communication within an organization.	32	66+
A14.	Computerization reduces the amount of social interaction on the job.	16	82+
Efficiency Factor			
A1.	Computerization results in more rational decision-making within an organization.	69+	29
A3.	Computerization results in improved delivery of service to clients.	53+	45
A8.	A well organized computer system improves the overall efficiency of an organization.	95+	03
A11.	Computers are the best means of distributing information in an organization.	47+	53
A12.	Computerization will not improve the quality of service provided by an organization.	39	61+
A13.	Computerization helps to clarify the tasks and responsibilities of staff.	55+	42
A6.	Computerization fosters the sharing of information in an organization.	71+	26

Table 6.8   (continued)

Attitudes	Agree* (Percent)	Disagree (Percent)
	(N=38)	
A16. Computerization will result in more cooperation between organizations providing similar services.	71+	26
A18. Computerization will result in more coordination of services in an organization.	79+	18

*"Agree" category is made up of "strongly agree" and "agree" responses on question-naire. "Disagree" category is made up of "disagree" and "strongly disagree" responses. "Don't know" and no responses are not included in totals.
**For each statement the opinion that is considered positive to the introduction of computer technology is indicated by a +.

Table 6.9
Attitudes of UFCS Staff Toward Computer Use
(N=38)

Time	Very Positive	Somewhat Positive	Somewhat Negative	Very Negative	Not Reported
			(Percents)		
When first started using computers	25	50	19	6	—
After implementation	32	50	18	0	—

period of use, 53 percent of the respondents had a 'positive' attitude towards computer use. When these responses are combined with the 'very positive' responses, 77 per cent of the respondents were favourably disposed to computerization at the outset. Moreover the percentage of respondents with a 'positive' attitude towards computer use has, as in the previous two organizations, increased with time.

Dominion Family and Child Service

As in the other people-changing organizations, attitudes of the DFCS staff toward computerization and computer use are generally positive. Again, an examination of Diagram 6.2 reminds us that this positive attitude correlates with a general perception that computerization has increased neither efficiency nor control. Here we find slightly less agreement on the efficiency of computers than in other people-changing organizations but just as much consensus on the control issue.

Like the staffs of the previous three organizations, respondents here do not think computers are the best way of distributing intra-agency information (Q.A11). Slightly more than half the staff have reservations about the contri-

Table 6.10
Attitudes of STCC Staff Toward Computer Technology and
Computerization in Organizations: Grouped According
to Factors of Control and Efficiency

Attitudes		Agree* (Percent) (N=30)	Disagree (Percent)
Control Factor			
A2.	Computerization in human service organizations reduces the amount of discretion exercised by staff working with clients.	26	73+**
A5.	People place more value on conclusions arrived at by computer analysis than by human evaluations.	60+	40
A7.	Computer use forces client data into artificial categories.	40	60+
A10.	Computerization poses a threat to the autonomy of staff working with clients in a human service organization.	13	83+
A15.	Computerization dehumanizes the clients by treating them as numbers.	27	70+
A17.	Computer technology threatens the privacy of clients.	26	74+
A4.	Computerization upsets good relations between managers and workers.	13	87+
A9.	Computerization decreases the flow of informal communication within an organization.		
A14.	Computerization reduces the amount of social interaction on the job.	23	77+
Efficiency Factor			
A1.	Computerization results in more rational decision-making within an organization.	57+	40
A3.	Computerization results in improved delivery of service to clients.	67+	27
A8.	A well organized computer system improves the overall efficiency of an organization.	90+	10
A11.	Computers are the best means of distributing information in an organization.	40+	60
A12.	Computerization will not improve the quality of service provided by an organization.	33	67+
A13.	Computerization helps to clarify the tasks and responsibilities of staff.	50+	47
A6.	Computerization fosters the sharing of information in an organization.	63+	33

Table 6.10 (continued)

Attitudes	Agree* (Percent)	Disagree (Percent)
	(N=30)	
A16. Computerization will result in more cooperation between organizations providing similar services.	80+	17
A18. Computerization will result in more coordination of services in an organization.	77+	20

*"Agree" category is made up of "strongly agree" and "agree" responses on questionnaire. "Disagree" category is made up of "disagree" and "strongly disagree" responses. "Don't know" and no responses are not included in totals.

**For each statement the opinion that is considered positive to the introduction of computer technology is indicated by a +.

Table 6.11
Attitudes of STCC Staff Toward Computer Use
(N=20)

Time (n=30)	Very Positive	Somewhat Positive	Somewhat Negative (Percents)	Very Negative	Not Reported
When first started* using computers	23	54	20	3	—
After implementation	23	70	7	—	—

*Only 29 responded to this question as 1 respondent indicated he/she did not know the answer.

bution of computerization to clarifying their tasks and responsibilities. Staff are least positive about the control that they feel will, or may, result from computerization. Their concerns are indicated by the proportion who feel that there are dangers in people overvaluing computer generated data (48 percent), forcing client data into inappropriate categories to accommodate the computer (50 percent) (Q.A7) and using the computer to violate the privacy of clients (64 percent) (Q.A17). These concerns all also shared by staff at other agencies discussed so far; but they are concerns even more commonly voiced in people-processing organizations, as we shall see.

When computers were introduced into DFCC, 61 percent of the staff were receptive to the technology, a lower initial acceptance level than at the other people-changing organizations we studied. This increased to 76 percent after implementation, but again, this level of acceptance is slightly lower than at the other agencies. Almost 1 out of every 4 staff at the DFCC reports negative attitudes towards computers several years after computerization.

Table 6.12
Attitudes of DFCS Staff Toward Computer Technology and
Computerization in Organizations: Grouped According
to Factors of Control and Efficiency

Attitudes	Agree* (Percent)	Disagree (Percent)
	(N=61)	
Control Factor		
A2. Computerization in human service organizations reduces the amount of discretion exercised by staff working with clients.	26	70+**
A5. People place more value on conclusions arrived at by computer analysis than by human evaluations.	46+	48
A7. Computer use forces client data into artificial categories.	50	43+
A10. Computerization poses a threat to the autonomy of staff working with clients in a human service organization.	33	62+
A15. Computerization dehumanizes the clients by treating them as numbers.	16	82+
A17. Computer technology threatens the privacy of clients.	64	33+
A4. Computerization upsets good relations between managers and workers.	25	74+
A9. Computerization decreases the flow of informal communication within an organization.	13	82+
A14. Computerization reduces the amount of social interaction on the job.	–	–
Efficiency Factor		
A1. Computerization results in more rational decision-making within an organization.	65+	31
A3. Computerization results in improved delivery of service to clients.	58+	38
A8. A well organized computer system improves the overall efficiency of an organization.	84+	15
A11. Computers are the best means of distributing information in an organization.	26+	70
A12. Computerization will not improve the quality of service provided by an organization.	38	61+
A13. Computerization helps to clarify the tasks and responsibilities of staff.	45+	51
A6. Computerization fosters the sharing of information in an organization.	64+	33
A16. Computerization will result in more cooperation between organizations providing similar services.	67+	26

Table 6.12 (continued)

Attitudes	Agree* (Percent)	Disagree (Percent)
	(N=61)	
A18. Computerization will result in more coordination of services in an organization.	70+	23

*"Agree" category is made up of "strongly agree" and "agree" responses on questionnaire. "Disagree" category is made up of "disagree" and "strongly disagree" responses. "Don't know" and no responses are not included in totals.
**For each statement the opinion that is considered positive to the introduction of computer technology is indicated by a +.

Table 6.13
Attitudes of DFCS Staff Toward Computer Use
(N=61)

Time	Very Positive	Somewhat Positive	Somewhat Negative (Percents)	Very Negative	Not Reported
When first started using computers	13	48	30	5	5
After implementation	20	56	16	7	—

People-Processing Organizations

District Office/Correctional Services

The staff of the DOCS displays, by far, the most negative attitudes towards computerization among the eight organizations we studied. Diagram 6.2 showed respondents here expressing the view that computerization does not increase efficiency but does increase control. There is strong consensus on the latter (increased control). Eight of our questions elicit responses indicating negative attitudes and these eight questions address both control and efficiency. It is also interesting to note that the degree of consensus on negative attitudes is higher among the correctional service staff than it is in any other group.

For example, 83 percent of respondents in this organization agree that computerization upsets good relations between managers and workers (Q.A4) and 72 percent agree that computerization decreases the flow of informal communication within an organization (Q.A9). At no other agency are negative responses to any question given by such clear majorities. Similarly, while staff at other agencies disagree with the notion that computerization helps to clarify the staff's responsibilities (Q.A13), no other group disagrees as strongly (78%) as the correctional service workers.

Table 6.14
Attitudes of DOCS Staff Toward Computer Technology and
Computerization in Organizations: Grouped According
to Factors of Control and Efficiency

Attitudes	Agree* (Percent)	Disagree (Percent)
	(N=45)	
Control Factor		
A2. Computerization in human service organizations reduces the amount of discretion exercised by staff working with clients.	56	40+**
A5. People place more value on conclusions arrived at by computer analysis than by human evaluations.	60+	38
A7. Computer use forces client data into artificial categories.	47	49+
A10. Computerization poses a threat to the autonomy of staff working with clients in a human service organization.	73	24+
A15. Computerization dehumanizes the clients by treating them as numbers.	60	38+
A17. Computer technology threatens the privacy of clients.	42	56+
A4. Computerization upsets good relations between managers and workers.	83	16+
A9. Computerization decreases the flow of informal communication within an organization.	72	27+
A14. Computerization reduces the amount of social interaction on the job.	58	42+
Efficiency Factor		
A1. Computerization results in more rational decision-making within an organization.	40+	58
A3. Computerization results in improved delivery of service to clients.	49+	49
A8. A well organized computer system improves the overall efficiency of an organization.	93+	7
A11. Computers are the best means of distributing information in an organization.	53+	47
A12. Computerization will not improve the quality of service provided by an organization.	31	69+
A13. Computerization helps to clarify the tasks and responsibilities of staff.	22+	78
A6. Computerization fosters the sharing of information in an organization.	67+	33

Table 6.14   (continued)

Attitudes	Agree* (Percent)	Disagree (Percent)
	(N=45)	
A16. Computerization will result in more cooperation between organizations providing similar services.	60+	38
A18. Computerization will result in more coordination of services in an organization.	78+	20

*"Agree" category is made up of "strongly agree" and "agree" responses on question-naire. "Disagree" category is made up of "disagree" and "strongly disagree" responses. "Don't know" and no responses are not included in totals.
**For each statement the opinion that is considered positive to the introduction of computer technology is indicated by a +.

Table 6.15
Attitudes of DOCS Staff Toward Computer Use
(N=45)

Time	Very Positive	Somewhat Positive	Somewhat Negative (Percents)	Very Negative	Not Reported
When first started using computers	24	47	20	7	—
After implementation	20	53	20	4	—

*Although 45 respondents answered the questions some indicated "don't know" or "no response."

As Table 6.14 shows, the majority of DOCS staff also feel that computerization reduces social interaction on the job (Q.A14) and dehumanizes the clients by treating them as numbers (Q.A15). In no other agency does as high a proportion of workers express these opinions. Other areas of concern expressed by a majority of staff have to do with the computer's effect on staff discretion and staff autonomy.

One should not, however, conclude that the staff of DOCS are anti-computer, *per se*. Ten of 18 questions elicit positive responses and 93% of the respondents agree that a well organized computer system improves efficiency (Q.A8). Thus it seems the staff are not opposed to computers in principle, despite their own organization's problems with implementation, lack of training, and technical breakdowns.

In light of these negative views, it is surprising that such a large majority of staff indicate that their attitude was positive to computer use when it began (71 percent) and is still positive now (73 percent) (Table 6.15). This suggests a discontent with management, not management technology.

Parkside Community Centre

Diagram 6.2 showed that respondents at this organization tend to see the computer as increasing control without increasing efficiency. Accordingly, staff in this organization are least favourable about the computer's effect on staff discretion and the control of clients. About half (47 percent) regard computerization as potentially dehumanizing to clients and 60 percent see it as a threat to the privacy of clients. More than half the respondents feel computerization forces client data into artificial categories and threatens the autonomy of staff.

Table 6.16

Attitudes of PCC Staff Toward Computer Technology and
Computerization in Organizations: Grouped According
to Factors of Control and Efficiency

Attitudes		Agree* (Percent)	Disagree (Percent)
		(N=15)	
Control Factor			
A2.	Computerization in human service organizations reduces the amount of discretion exercised by staff working with clients.	27	73+**
A5.	People place more value on conclusions arrived at by computer analysis than by human evaluations.	66+	33
A7.	Computer use forces client data into artificial categories.	53	40+
A10.	Computerization poses a threat to the autonomy of staff working with clients in a human service organization.	53	47+
A15.	Computerization dehumanizes the clients by treating them as numbers.	47	47+
A17.	Computer technology threatens the privacy of clients.	60	40+
A4.	Computerization upsets good relations between managers and workers.	20	80+
A9.	Computerization decreases the flow of informal communication within an organization.	27	73+
A14.	Computerization reduces the amount of social interaction on the job.	40	60+
Efficiency Factor			
A1.	Computerization results in more rational decision-making within an organization.	53+	47

Table 6.16 (continued)

Attitudes		Agree* (Percent)	Disagree (Percent)
		(N=15)	
A3.	Computerization results in improved delivery of service to clients.	73+	27
A8.	A well organized computer system improves the overall efficiency of an organization.	87+	13
A11.	Computers are the best means of distributing information in an organization.	33+	60
A12.	Computerization will not improve the quality of service provided by an organization.	33	67+
A13.	Computerization helps to clarify the tasks and responsibilities of staff.	33+	67
A6.	Computerization fosters the sharing of information in an organization.	60+	40
A16.	Computerization will result in more cooperation between organizations providing similar services.	73+	27
A18.	Computerization will result in more coordination of services in an organization.	60+	33
A15.	Computerization dehumanizes the clients by treating them as numbers.	47	47+
A17.	Computer technology threatens the privacy of clients.	60	40+
A4.	Computerization upsets good relations between managers and workers.	20	80+
A9.	Computerization decreases the flow of informal communication within an organization.	27	73+

*"Agree" category is made up of "strongly agree" and "agree" responses on questionnaire. "Disagree" category is made up of "disagree" and "strongly disagree" responses. "Don't know" and no responses are not included in totals.
**For each statement the opinion that is considered positive to the introduction of computer technology is indicated by a +.

Staff responses to statements concerned with efficiency are positive with one exception, two-thirds disagreeing that "Computerization helps to clarify the tasks and responsibilities of staff." Sixty percent or more of staff respond positively to all statements dealing with the integration and coordination of services. Yet, in comparison with two other people-processing organizations, IA and CDSS, these perceptions of increased efficiency due to computerization are unenthusiastic.

Attitudes toward computers have changed little since staff first started using the computer about two years earlier. Ten staff say they were very positive about computer use when it began, as compared with nine today. In view of the difficulties this organization experienced in implementing com-

Table 6.17
Attitudes of PCC Staff Toward Computer Use
(N=45)

Time	Very Positive	Somewhat Positive	Somewhat Negative (Percents)	Very Negative	Not Reported
When first started using computers	27	33	27	13	—
After implementation	20	47	27	6	—

puterization, it is surprising that the proportion of staff expressing negative attitudes has not increased more. As with DOCS, respondents here may be endorsing computers as management tools while, by implication, criticizing the way management has used them.

Table 6.18
Attitudes of IA Staff Toward Computer Use
(N=25)

Time	Very Positive	Somewhat Positive	Somewhat Negative (Percents)	Very Negative	Not Reported
When first started using computers	44	35	17	4	—
After implementation	25	62	13	—	—

Immigrant Aid

The staff apparently had a somewhat disillusioning experience with computerization. Whereas 44 percent of the staff were originally "very positive" towards computer use (the highest score of any agency we studied), this total has since dropped to only 26 percent (see Table 6.18). This decline in enthusiasm for computers is by far the largest we found in any of the eight agencies. Perhaps it is due to unrealistically high initial expectations coupled with the implementation problems IA has experienced.

However, while their enthusiasm has dampened, staff remain generally positive about computers in principle. This is demonstrated by the fact that 96 percent of the respondents still agree that "a well organized computer system improves the overall efficiency of an organization" and only 12 percent of the respondents hold an even slightly negative view of potential computer use. A slight majority of the staff feel their discretion in working with clients is curtailed by computerization. Diagram 6.2 indicates that respondents in IA express comparatively strong beliefs that computerization

Table 6.19

Respondents' Attitudes of IA Staff Toward Computer
Technology and Computerization in Organizations:
Grouped According to Factors of Control and Efficiency

Attitudes	Agree* (Percent) (N=25)	Disagree (Percent)
Control Factor		
A2. Computerization in human service organizations reduces the amount of discretion exercised by staff working with clients.	56	44+**
A5. People place more value on conclusions arrived at by computer analysis than by human evaluations.	44+	44
A7. Computer use forces client data into artificial categories.	32	64+
A10. Computerization poses a threat to the autonomy of staff working with clients in a human service organization.	36	64+
A15. Computerization dehumanizes the clients by treating them as numbers.	24	76+
A17. Computer technology threatens the privacy of clients.	32	68+
A4. Computerization upsets good relations between managers and workers.	32	68+
A9. Computerization decreases the flow of informal communication within an organization.	28	82+
A14. Computerization reduces the amount of social interaction on the job.	40	60+
Efficiency Factor		
A1. Computerization results in more rational decision-making within an organization.	72+	24
A3. Computerization results in improved delivery of service to clients.	84+	16
A8. A well organized computer system improves the overall efficiency of an organization.	96+	4
A11. Computers are the best means of distributing information in an organization.	64+	36
A12. Computerization will not improve the quality of service provided by an organization.	32	68+
A13. Computerization helps to clarify the tasks and responsibilities of staff.	56+	44
A6. Computerization fosters the sharing of information in an organization.	80+	16

Table 6.19   (continued)

Attitudes	Agree* (Percent) (N=25)	Disagree (Percent)
A16. Computerization will result in more cooperation between organizations providing similar services.	92+	8
A18. Computerization will result in more coordination of services in an organization.	84+	12

*"Agree" category is made up of "strongly agree" and "agree" responses on question-naire. "Disagree" category is made up of "disagree" and "strongly disagree" responses. "Don't know" and no responses are not included in totals.
**For each statement the opinion that is considered positive to the introduction of computer technology is indicated by a +.

increases both efficiency and control. But there is stronger disagreement (a higher standard deviation) about both views in this agency than in any other we studied.

All in all, the IA staff seem to feel that computerization is potentially very valuable even though their own experience has been disappointing at times. In this respect, the IA staff have reacted to computerization in much the same way as the staff of DOCS.

Table 6.20
Attitudes of CDSS Staff Toward Computer Technology
and Computerization in Organizations: Grouped According to
Factors of Control and Efficiency

Attitudes	Agree* (Percent) (N=135)	Disagree (Percent)
Control Factor		
A2. Computerization in human service organizations reduces the amount of discretion exercised by staff working with clients.	43	54+**
A5. People place more value on conclusions arrived at by computer analysis than by human evaluations.	51+	46
A7. Computer use forces client data into artificial categories.	49	48+
A10. Computerization poses a threat to the autonomy of staff working with clients in a human service organization.	30	66+
A15. Computerization dehumanizes the clients by treating them as numbers.	32	67+

Table 6.20   (continued)

Attitudes		Agree* (Percent)	Disagree (Percent)
		(N=135)	
A17.	Computer technology threatens the privacy of clients.	57	42+
A4.	Computerization upsets good relations between managers and workers.	18	79+
A9.	Computerization decreases the flow of informal communication within an organization.	28	70+
A14.	Computerization reduces the amount of social interaction on the job.	34	64+
Efficiency Factor			
A1.	Computerization results in more rational decision-making within an organization.	55+	40
A3.	Computerization results in improved delivery of service to clients.	80+	19
A8.	A well organized computer system improves the overall efficiency of an organization.	90+	19
A11.	Computers are the best means of distributing information in an organization.	60+	37
A12.	Computerization will not improve the quality of service provided by an organization.	22	77+
A13.	Computerization helps to clarify the tasks and responsibilities of staff.	48+	47
A6.	Computerization fosters the sharing of information in an organization.	85+	15
A16.	Computerization will result in more cooperation between organizations providing similar services.	77+	21
A18.	Computerization will result in more coordination of services in an organization.	89+	11

*"Agree" category is made up of "strongly agree" and "agree" responses on questionnaire. "Disagree" category is made up of "disagree" and "strongly disagree" responses. "Don't know" and no responses are not included in totals.
**For each statement the opinion that is considered positive to the introduction of computer technology is indicated by a +.

County Department of Social Services

The staff of this organization feel very positive about computer technology's effects on efficiency (Table 6.20), but their attitudes are mixed on the organizational effects of computer use on control. They are about equally divided between positive and negative responses to statements dealing with effects of computer technology on staff discretion in working with clients; the categorizing of client data for computer processing; and threats to privacy of clients when data are computerized.

Diagram 6.2 shows that, like respondents in Immigrant Aid, CDSS respondents view computers as increasing both efficiency and control. While there is relatively high disagreement on the second issue (i.e., control), we find less disagreement that computers have increased efficiency. Nine out of ten staff hold the view that computerization will improve the overall efficiency of an organization and eight out of ten, that computerization will improve the delivery of service to clients.

Thus, in this agency where computer technology has been in place for several years, the attitudes of staff probably reflect a positive experience of computer efficiency. Table 6.21 shows that a high percentage of staff were initially very positive towards computer use and the proportion has since grown larger. The feeling some have that control has increased may offset otherwise positive feelings created by this gain in efficiency.

Table 6.21
Attitudes of CDSS Staff Toward Computer Use
(N=135)

Time	Very Positive	Somewhat Positive	Somewhat Negative (Percents)	Very Negative	Not Reported
When first started using computers	27	44	12	1	16
After implementation	32	50	8	–	10

Summary

The good news is that in every agency, computerization was never as bad as some people feared it was going to be. In every case, the percentage of people feeling positive increased after implementation. Table 6.22 shows the percentages of staff holding somewhat or very positive attitudes towards computerization, both at the time of, and since implementation.

Data in this table show that computerization has been accepted more widely in people-changing than in people-processing organizations. Recall, the former tend to view computers as not efficient but controlling; hence, their growth in acceptance may reflect a sense of relief that little is changed by computers, and feared scenarios do not actualize. In the two people-processing organizations where staff's worst fears have been justified — DOCS and PCC — and computers are viewed as inefficient but controlling, acceptance has grown only slightly since implementation.

Computerization was not as beneficial as the staff of some agencies had initially hoped. Table 6.23 shows the changes in percentage of staff members

Table 6.22
Positive Attitudes of Staff Toward Computer Use

Organization	First Using Computers	Now	Gain
		(Percents)	
People-Changing			
Urban Youth Counselling Service (N=25)	76	92	16
United Family and Child Services (N=25)	75	82	7
Suburban Treatment Centre for Children (N=30)	76	90	14
Dominion Family and Child Service (N=61)	61	76	15
People-Processing			
District Office/Correctional Services (N=45)	71	73	2
Parkside Community Centre (N=15)	60	67	7
Immigrant Aid (N=25)	78	88	10
County Department of Social Services (N=135)	71	82	11

Table 6.23
Rank by Increase in Percent of Staff Who View Computerization
Very Positively Today

1.	UYCS	+8	5.	STCC	0
2.	UFCS	+7	6.	DOCS	-4
3.	DFCS	+7	7.	PCC	-7
4.	CDSS	+5	8.	IA	-20

who felt very positively about computers, initially and now.

Computerization was obviously a disillusioning experience for a large portion of the staff at DOCS, PCC and IA, all people-processing organizations. Some of the reasons for this disillusionment should be evident from Table 6.24 which lists the questions, by agency, that elicited more negative responses than positive ones. The numbers in parentheses indicate the percentages of respondents who answered in a negative direction.

Probably the most striking feature of Table 6.24 is that DOCS staff have by far the most complaints, mainly about control; and four of their eight concerns are unique to their agency. What's more, the intensity of their negative feelings is unmatched by respondents elsewhere. For example, the staff is in overwhelming agreement (83 percent) that computerization upsets good relations between managers and workers.

Questionnaire results reveal that the most common concerns have to do with the loss of discretion in working with clients, the artificiality of data categories, the threat to client privacy, and the inefficiency of computers in distributing and clarifying tasks.

Table 6.24
Percentage of Negative Responses to Statements
in Attitude Scale**
by Factor and Organization

	Control Factor*	Efficiency Factor	Total Negative Items
UYCS	A5(60) A7(48)	A11(52) A1(48) A13(48)	5
UFCS	A7(50)	A11(53)	2
STCC	A17(65)	A11(60)	2
DFCC	A7(50) A17(64)	A11(70)	3
DOCS	A2(56) A10(73) A15(60) A4(83) A9(72) A14(58)	A1(58) A13(78)	8
PCC	A7(55) A10(53) A17(60)	A11(60) A13(67)	5
IS	A2(56)		1
CDSS	A2(54) A7(49) A17(57)		3

*Statements

A1: computerization does not result in more rational decisions
A2: computerization reduces discretion
A4: computerization upsets good relations
A5: people place more value on conclusions arrived at by computer analysis than by human evaluation
A7: computer use forces client data into aritificial categories
A9: computerization replaces informal communication
A10: computerization threatens staff autonomy
A11: computers are inefficient at distributing information
A13: computerization does not help clarify tasks
A14: computerization replaces social interaction
A15: computerization dehumanizes clients
A17: computers threaten a client's privacy
**Numbers in parenthesis are the percent of negative responses to specific questions.

In the next chapter we examine empirical evidence that any or all of these concerns are justified by organizational changes occurring since computerization.

Chapter 7

The Impact on Advanced Computer Users

This chapter will examine staff assessments of the impact of computerization on job control, productivity, client service, and the organization overall.

The data presented on this topic are quite detailed. For this reason, we have separated the presentation into two chapters. This first will consider only how computerization has affected the so-called ''advanced'' users of computers — those agencies making six or more uses of computers. We would expect to find the impact of computerization most marked in these organizations, since extent of computerization — the independent variable — is greatest here. The chapter following this one examines impacts of computerization on the so-called ''intermediate'' users, where computerization is somewhat less extensive.

Dominion Family and Child Service

Impact on Staff

In the last chapter, we saw that the factor scores for DFCS were relatively highly dispersed in respect to efficiency, and relatively undispersed in respect to control, indicating consensus on the latter issue. The average opinion was that computerization increased neither efficiency nor control in this people-changing organization. We now examine how these opinions are related to the actual effects of computerization on the agency.

Almost two-thirds of the DFCS staff who completed questionnaires were employed before computerization took place. Thus, it was not unexpected that 69 percent report they had to learn new skills after the introduction of computer technology. Of the 69 percent, the vast majority (81 percent) do not think acquiring these skills has affected their job security. Further, more than three-fourths (79 percent) of staff report their job descriptions have not changed to reflect their acquired knowledge and skill in computer technology.

Two-thirds of the DFCS staff reported that computerization results in increased paperwork; 30 percent report a substantial increase and 38 percent a moderate increase.

Table 7.1
Impact of Computerization on Staff Discretion
and Control of Job: DFCS
(N = 61)

Impact	Discretion (Percent)	Control (Percent)
A lot more	3	—
More	10	33
None	79	44
Less	8	18
A lot less	—	3
No response	—	2

Another surprising finding is presented in Table 7.1. The majority (79 percent) feel there has been no change in the amount of discretion they exercise. Of those perceiving a change, more (13 percent) think their discretionary power has increased, than those (8 percent) who think it has declined. Only 3 percent consider their exercise of discretion has changed "a lot" however (all of those finding it greater than before). With respect to the amount of control exercised, 44 percent report "no change" as a result of computerization; 21 percent a loss and 33 percent a gain. Again, only 3 percent feel they have "a lot less control" over their work since computerization.

There are important differences by position in staff assessments of the impact of computerization on both discretion and job control. The majority in each group (ranging from 64 percent in one group to 100 percent in another) report "no change" in job discretion. But among those reporting a change, support staff are evenly divided; direct services staff report marginal gains in discretion; and managers/directors, significant gains.

Computerization has had more impact on job control. Opinion on the impact is mixed in every category, but support staff and supervisors tend to report significantly more control; while direct service staff report a marginal decline in their exercise of job control due to computer use.

In terms of enhanced discretion and control, the clear winners are the managers and directors. Supervisors and support staff both report gains in job control. Direct service staff, on the other hand, benefit least (if at all) as a result of computerization: while they report (marginally) more "discretion," they also report (marginally) less "control" then before.

Half of the respondents indicate that their productivity has "remained the same," but a third report increases, while one in seven reports a decline due to computerization. Again, however, perception varies by position.

Almost half (45 percent) of the managers and directors report personal productivity gains while only 18 percent report losses; all of the supervisors who indicate any change (17 percent) report productivity gains; nearly a third (31 percent) of the support staff report gains, while 8 percent indicate losses; and 29 percent of direct service staff report enhanced productivity, while 18 percent report losses owing to computerization. Benefits outweigh losses in every category, but managers and directors have apparently gained most in personal productivity, and direct service staff have gained the least.

Table 7.2
Staff Appraisals of the Costs and Benefits of Computerization
by Position: DFCS
(N = 61)

Position	Total (Percents)	More Benefits*	Equal Ben./Costs	More Costs*	NR**
Support Staff	100	15	10	37	38
Direct Service Staff	100	21	8	48	23
Supervisors	100	28	11	22	39
Accounting and Fiscal Managers	100	30	5	5	60
Department Heads and Managers	100	35	5	8	52

*These categories combine "many more" and "some more" responses.
**Of the 61 respondents some say they are not qualified to answer, or else indicate "don't know" or "no response." These responses are combined in the NR column.

Staff see computerization as most beneficial to department heads and managers, accounting and fiscal managers, and supervisors (Table 7.2). Almost half (48 percent) of the staff see computerization as having more costs than benefits for direct service staff and more than a third (37 percent) make the same assessment for support staff. Although from 23 to 60 percent of staff were unable or unwilling to assess the costs/benefits for specific positions, the data would indicate that the benefits to supervisors and direct service staff are more limited than to administrators and managerial staff. The observation of a staff member responsible for providing direct service is indicative of the response of this group:

> I realize that the computer and stats sheets are there primarily in my particular situation for administrative purposes and budgeting, and I know that they're necessary for those things. But as far as my being able to use it in my clinical work . . . no [computer technology does not play a large role]. Nor do I see how it could.

In summary, staff position is a key variable influencing assessments of the impact of computerization. Those in more senior positions, particularly managers and directors, are seen by their colleagues as gaining the most from the new technology. Support staff, direct service staff, are seen as receiving limited benefits from the system.

While many staff are enthusiastic about the potential of the computer system, no one believes they have come anywhere close to achieving it. Compliance with the present system, operational for more than a year, has been slow and uneven, and some computerized data are still considered unreliable. Teams, programs, and departments vary widely in their computer utilization. Few staff understand the system well enough to know its capabilities, or the mechanics of entering and extracting desired information. Reports are generated in a difficult-to-use format which, consequently, is largely ignored. Given the time and energy required to supply the computer with input data, few staff members believe they have received a fair return on their investment of time and effort. This explains the average perception, seen in Diagram 6.2, that computerization does not increase efficiency. Recall, however, that DFCS is marked by strong disagreement on this issue: position determines perception here.

Impact on Clients

Clients were not approached directly for their opinions about computer use in DFCS. Judging by information from staff interviews, there is some question as to whether clients even know that a computer records patient data. Consequently, the information in this section is based upon the staff survey and interviews.

As reported earlier, most respondents think computerization has positive effects on patient recordkeeping, and neutral or marginally positive effects on patient service. Despite apparent improvements to the recording system, however, few clinicians use computer-generated reports to manage their cases better or provide improved service. Most rely upon their own files and records, as they find computerized reports unhelpful and/or confusing.

Staff were asked to assess the costs and benefits of computerization for clients; a surprising 50 percent were unwilling or unable to make this assessment. Of the 30 staff at all levels who were willing and able to assess the costs and benefits for clients, 27 percent reported more costs than benefits for clients, 56 percent equal costs and benefits, and 17 percent more benefits than costs. The assessments of the 17 direct service staff were: 35 percent more costs; 53 percent equal costs and benefits; and 12 percent more benefits than costs. The assessments of staff with a range of responsibilities for the delivery of service and the direct service staff are very similar — more than half of the staff see no costs or benefits for clients resulting from computerization and a large minority (27 and 35 percent) of staff in both groups reported that there are more costs than benefits for clients. On this point one direct service staff commented:

> I don't think it does anything for patients . . . I just don't think it's relevant or
> useful to case management . . . There are methods in place for monitoring
> those kinds of things in a much more effective way without having to have a
> really complex apparatus, with language and terms that you need a language
> course to interpret . . . If one takes better case management as a goal for clini-
> cians, one doesn't need this kind of system to do that.

The DFCS staff do not appear to believe that computer technology discourages dealing with clients as individuals. Two out of three (66 percent)
report "no justification" for such a fear. Of the remainder, no one cites
"considerable justification," although a third (33 percent) sees "some
justification" for concern here. No supervisor, and only 9 percent of the
managers and directors worry that computer technology discourages dealing
with clients as individuals, but close to half of the support and direct service
staff (46 percent in each case) express such concerns.

Some express unease about the possibility of unauthorized access to
confidential information stored in computers. More than four-fifths (82 percent) of those concerned about this issue indicate at least "a little" concern,
while more than a quarter (26 percent) express "a lot" of concern. Only 16
percent are wholly unconcerned about the issue.

Although confidentiality is a concern at every level, attitudes vary by
staff position. Almost all (91 percent) managers and directors polled express
concern, followed by supervisors (83 percent), direct service staff (82 percent), and support staff (77 percent). The greater sensitivity among managers
and directors may derive from their responsibility for the consequences if
serious breaches of confidentiality arise.

More than three-fifths (63 percent) elaborated their concerns about
confidentiality. Three areas of the system seem most worrisome: the storage
of "diagnostic or outcome" data; the storage of "personal" or "confidential" information; and "access" to (rather than the content of) computerized
information.

The storage of diagnostic or outcome data (identified as a concern by 43
percent of the respondents) is worrisome because medical terminology could
be used to "label," "stigmatize," or "exploit" the patient (specifically
mentioned by 5 percent of respondents). Those concerned about "personal"
(7 percent) or "confidential" data (3 percent), cite financial, legal, medical,
and social (a family marital or history) information, in addition to identifying
data such as names, addresses, phone, OHIP or social insurance numbers.
About 7 percent of respondents worry that the access to data might not be
controlled tightly enough.

The same themes prevail in a related question about the kinds of data that should not be stored in the computer after a case is closed. One out of four responses mentions diagnostic, outcome, or other data that might stigmatize patients; 9 percent refer to "personal" or "confidential" data and 7 percent to (any) identifying data; 3 percent refer to access considerations; and a few (2 percent) suggest data on closed cases should only be stored for a limited time.

Somewhat surprisingly, given their confidentiality concerns, nearly three out of five respondents (57 percent) admit they are "unfamiliar with present policies regarding access to client information." Ignorance and concern about the centre's confidentiality policies seem to go together, and both tended to decrease with rank. The vast majority of those expressing an opinion believe present policies "satisfactorily protect" client confidentiality.

Impact on the Organization

When staff weigh the costs and benefits of computerization for the organization, more estimate the technology to be a net cost. Two-fifths (40 percent) of the 52 staff who answered perceive more costs than benefits, and nearly half of these indicate "many more costs than benefits." On the other hand, a third of the respondents see more benefits than costs. (The remainder, one quarter, see costs and benefits as equal.) Staff also rated the impact of computerization upon eight organizational activities (Table 7.3).

Table 7.3
Impacts of Computerization on Eight Areas of
Organizational Activities: DFCS
(N = 61)

Rank	Activity	Total (Percents)	Positive	Negative	None	DNA* N/R
			Impact of Computerization			
1	Internal statistical reporting	100	69	13	5	13
2	Client records	100	67	5	20	8
3	Case management	100	48	7	34	11
4	Program management	100	45	8	25	22
5	External reporting	100	28	3	32	37
6	Financial management	100	28	5	28	39
7	Supervision	100	22	8	46	24
8	Policy making	100	18	7	38	37

*DNA – does not apply (respondents who were not able to rate the area of responsibility because they had no knowledge of it).

The data in Table 7.3 show that as the number of respondents indicating positive impacts diminishes, the number of respondents indicating "no impact'' or "does not apply'' or giving no response, increases. This may be because the study population is comprised largely of direct service staff who know more about internal statistical reporting, client records, and case management than they do about policy making, financial management and/or external reporting. (At the same time, some respondents may select the "no impact'' category rather than disqualify themselves, even when they have little knowledge about the activity involved.)

Further examination affirms that position may influence respondent perceptions. For example, direct service staff are the least positive about the impact of the computer system on seven of the nine activities (being somewhat more positive than support staff about its impact on "program management'' and "service to clients''). A bare majority are positive about "internal statistical reporting'' and "client records,'' while more direct service staff are negative than positive about the impacts of the computer on "supervision'' and "policy making.''

Support staff rate computerization more positively than direct service staff (with the few exceptions noted) but this difference is most evident in the 85 percent positive responses given to the effect of "internal statistical reporting'' and "client records.''

Most supervisors are positive about the effect on six of the nine activities listed. However, only a third of the supervisors rate computerization's impact on "supervision,'' "external reporting,'' or "service to clients'' as positive (the majority in each case see no change).

Managers and directors are the most positive about the impact of computers. Only with respect to "policy making'' are supervisors more positive than managers/directors. This may reflect differences in the definition of "policy making'' and/or more critical appraisals of the usefulness of computer reports at senior levels of decision-making.

When staff are asked about the potential consequences of reverting to a manual record-keeping system, they tend to consider it a change for the worse — at least with respect to internal statistical reporting (70 percent), client records (54 percent), program management (44 percent) and financial management (41 percent) (Table 7.4).

While fewer than 8 percent of the respondents consider a manual system better than the present one for any of the activities listed, the largest group sees "no change" for external reporting (39 percent), case management (43 percent), policy making (46 percent), service to clients (57 percent) and supervision (64 percent). In other words, large numbers of staff see reversion to a manual system of record-keeping as no particular loss in terms of "supervision," "service to clients," "policy making," and "external reporting." A large majority think computerization positively affects internal statistical reporting and client records. On the other hand, the computer's

Table 7.4
Staff Assessment of the Impact of Reversion to a
Manual Information System on Eight Areas of
Organizational Activities: DFCS
(N = 61)

Rank	Activity	Total (Percents)	Impact of Reversion to Manual System			
			Better*	Worse*	No Change	N/R
1	Internal statistical reporting	100	5	69	13	11
2	Client records	100	3	53	31	11
3	Program management	100	7	44	36	13
4	Financial management	100	7	40	33	20
5	Case management	100	3	42	44	11
6	External reporting	100	2	38	39	21
7	Policy making	100	5	28	46	21
8	Supervision	100	5	17	63	15

*"Better" combines "somewhat better" and "much better," while "worse" combines "somewhat worse" and "much worse."

impact upon two areas of prime importance to direct service staff, namely service to clients and supervision, is seen as negligible by the majority.

Table 7.5
Rating of Computerized Records According to
Five Quality Indicators: DFCS
(N = 61)

Rank	Quality Indicator	Total (Percents)	Rating			
			Good*	Fair	Poor*	N/R
1	Relevance	100	41	28	28	3
2	Clarity	100	40	26	33	2
3	Comprehensiveness	100	37	26	33	3
4	Timeliness	100	36	31	28	5
5	Accuracy	100	23	41	34	2

*"Good" combines "excellent" and "good," while "poor" combines "poor" and "very poor."

Computerization is judged to have a generally positive effect on record-keeping but this opinion is by no means unanimous. Positive responses outnumber negative ones in all categories except accuracy (Table 7.6). And again, a sizable minority feel computerized records are not particularly good or bad. As Table 7.6 shows, manual records receive a marginally higher score for "relevance" but are judged inferior to computerized ones in every other aspect.

Table 7.6
The Rating of Manual Records** (prior to Computerization)
According to Five Quality Indicators: DFCS
(N = 40)

Rank	Quality Indicator	Total (Percents)	Rating			
			Good*	Fair	Poor*	N/R
1	Relevance	100	43	27	23	7
2	Clarity	100	24	36	32	7
3	Comprehensiveness	100	24	36	33	7
4	Accuracy	100	20	30	43	7
5	Timeliness	100	17	25	46	12

*"Good" combines "excellent" and "good," while "poor" combines "poor" and "very poor."
**By staff employed at the Centre prior to computerization — 66% of the total sample.

Suburban Treatment Centre for Children

In the last chapter, we found that the average factor scores for STCC were relatively undispersed, indicating a strong consensus of opinion. The prevailing opinion was that computerization neither increased efficiency nor control to any great degree. We now examine how that perception is tied to actual effects of computerization on the agency.

Impact on Staff

Two-thirds of the STCC staff were employed before computerization and therefore had to adjust to working with this new technology. However, only 57 percent report they had to learn new skills as a result. Of this number, more than four out of five report that learning new skills did not affect their job security. A minority (18 percent) feel learning new skills even increased their job security.

Two-thirds of the staff completing computer forms report that paperwork has increased since computerization, 9 percent reporting a moderate and 57 percent a substantial increase. The amount of paperwork remained the same for 30 percent of this group while one person reports a moderate decrease.

Almost three out of four (73 percent) respondents think computerization has no impact on their productivity. The remainder report a moderate (20 percent) or substantial (7 percent) increase. No one thinks computerization has lowered productivity.

The perceived effects of computerization on discretion and control exercised by respondents are presented in Table 7.7. Almost all (27 out of 28) respondents think computerization has either had no impact (67 percent) or, indeed, has increased the discretion they can exercise (23 percent). Similarly, all respondents think computerization has had no effect on (57 percent) or

Table 7.7
Impact of Computerization on Staff Discretion
and Job Control: STCC
(N = 30)

Impact	Discretion (Percent)	Control (Percent)
A lot more	3	7
More	20	30
None	67	57
Less	3	—
A lot less	—	—
No response	7	7

has increased their control over their job (37 percent).

Sixteen of the respondents (53 percent) believe computerization brings about more benefits than costs, six (20 percent) saying the benefits and costs are equal and six (20 percent) that there are more costs than benefits; and two respondents (7 percent) did not answer the question.

Table 7.8
Respondents' Assessments of Benefits/Costs of
Computerization for Staff, by Position: STCC
(N = 30)**

Position of Staff	Perceived Benefits/Costs (Percents)			
	More Benefits*	Equal Benefits	More Costs*	NR**
Direct Service Staff	53	17	10	20
Supervisor	53	3	3	41
Support Staff	17	17	17	49
Accounting and Fiscal Managers	37	3	7	53
Executive Director, Dept. Heads and Managers	50	7	7	36

*The "more benefits" category includes both "many more benefits" and "some more benefit" responses. Similarly the "more costs" category contains both "some more costs" and "many more costs" responses.

**Of 30 respondents answered the question some say they are not qualified to answer, or else indicate "don't know" or "no response." These responses are combined in the NR column.

One half or more of the staff regard computerization as having more benefits than costs for direct service staff, supervisors and department heads and managers (Table 7.8). Computerization is seen as having more costs for support staff than for other staff. As expected some staff were unwilling or unable to assess the costs and benefits for specific positions, the proportion ranging from 20 percent for the position of direct service to 53 percent for accounting and fiscal managers.

Impact on Clients

The STCC staff think the impact of computerization on service to clients has been mostly positive. Two-thirds believe the impact has been either strongly positive (7 percent) or positive (57 percent) while 27 percent see no impact. No one thinks the impact on service is negative. Half the respondents see computerization bringing clients more benefits than costs. One in five respondents assesses the costs and benefits as equal and only seven percent conclude that costs outnumber benefits.

The STCC staff's concerns about lack of confidentiality for clients is presented in Table 7.9. One half of the respondents are unconcerned about this issue. Almost one-fourth (23 percent) are "a little" concerned, while the remainder report "some" or "a lot" of concern.

Table 7.9
Concern about Lack of Confidentiality of
Client Data Stored in the Computer: STCC
(N = 30)

Level of Concern	Percent
A lot	13
Some	13
A little	23
None	51

Further to the confidentiality issue, a majority of staff (60 percent) feel psychosocial data on a client should not be retained after a case is closed.

Given that a concern for clients' privacy is one of only two concerns cited by the STCC staff on the attitudinal questionnaire, we are somewhat surprised to find that 60 percent of the respondents don't even know the agency's present policies regarding access to client information. One-third say the policies are satisfactory, while a mere seven percent find them unsatisfactory.

The staff sense a "confidentiality issue"; but they don't consider it to be of overriding importance. Similar perceptions are reflected in the interviews. One therapist mentions that staff concerns over the confidentiality of computerized data are no greater than their concerns for the confidentiality of hard copy records. Others note that data presently stored in the computer are no more endangered than client information stored in the manual system. The interviewee remarks, "There is nothing on the computer that is not accessible by looking at the medical records."

One staff person feels that the computer operation is well controlled and anyone but a designated user would have difficulty accessing the data. As one person succinctly notes, "protection in the present system is the lack of anyone's ability to use it."

The STCC staff also reject the idea that computers make it more difficult for the staff to deal with clients as individuals. The great majority, 87 percent, see no justification (great or slight) for this fear; and no one sees great justification for this concern.

Again, staff views on this issue are borne out during interviews. For example, when asked whether the values associated with the helping professions are at odds with values associated with computer technology, one staff member suggests that the values operating in a human service organization are more affected by leadership milieu than by a technical tool like the computer.

Impact on the Organization

No STCC respondents assess the computer as having had a negative impact on any of the seven organizational activities. The most positive impact is reported for: internal statistical reporting, client records, and case management. Approximately 9 out of 10 staff see a positive impact in these areas. The staff is least positive about the impact on policy making, external reporting, and financial management. (Note, however, that 34 to 40 percent of the staff did not rate these three activities at all.)

Table 7.11 presents the respondent's ratings of records and statistics on selected characteristics that generally define an effective and efficient information system. The responses show the staff believe computerization has improved the statistics and records in STCC. Unlike DFCS staff, who see manual records as slightly more relevant, STCC staff believe relevance is the area that shows greatest improvement after computerization.

The respondents also rate the hypothetical effects of reverting to a manual record-keeping system. These results, plotted on a better/worse scale, are presented in Table 7.15. Again most respondents indicate there would be a change for the worse if the organization reverted to manual record-keeping. The manual system is seen as superior by only one person in each of the following areas: program management, financial management and external reporting.

Slightly more than half (53 percent) of the respondents see computerization as bringing more benefits than costs in time and effort. One-fifth assess the costs and benefits as equal and a like proportion see more costs than benefits. In view of the staff's very positive assessment of the impact of computerization, we expected that fewer staff would feel computerization brings more costs than benefits. There is, then, a confusion of feelings

Table 7.10
Impacts of Computerization on Eight Areas of
Organizational Activities: STCC
(N = 30)

Rank	Area of Responsibility	Total (Percents)	Impact of Computerization		
			Positive	None	DNA* N/R
1	Internal statistical reporting	100	90	3	7
2	Client records	100	90	7	3
3	Case management	100	87	10	10
4	Program management	100	77	10	13
5	Supervision	100	54	27	19
6	Financial management	100	40	20	40
7	External reporting	100	33	10	34
8	Policy making	100	26	53	37

*This column includes those who did indicate that they could not rate the activity and those who did not respond to this question.

Table 7.11
State of Record and Statistics Keeping Pre and Post
Computerization: STCC

Descriptions	Status (Percents)									
	Excellent		Good		Fair		Poor		Very Poor	
	Pre	Post	Pre	Post	Pre	Post	Pre	Post	Pre	Post
Accuracy	—	3	10	40	45	50	30	7	10	—
Timeliness	—	3	10	30	25	33	40	27	15	3
Clarity	—	3	10	43	45	7	30	7	10	—
Comprehensiveness	—	3	10	27	20	60	50	7	15	3
Relevance	—	13	10	43	35	33	35	10	10	—

Pre-computer sample, N=20. This group comprises all those respondents who were employed prior to computerization.
Post-computer sample, N=30. This group comprises the total study population.

towards computers here, perhaps more aptly characterized as indifference than as dissensus.

Parkside Community Centre

In the last chapter, we found that the average factor scores for PCC were relatively highly dispersed in respect to efficiency, and relatively undispersed in respect to control, indicating little consensus on the first issue and greater consensus on the second. The average view was that computerization tended to increase control, but not efficiency. We now consider how these views are related to the actual effects of computerization on PCC's operation.

Table 7.12
Impact on Selected Aspects of Organization if Returned
to Manual System: STCC
(N = 30)

| Aspect of Organization | Total | Perceived Impact | | | |
| | | Better* | None | Worse* | NR |
			(Percents)		
Client records	100	0	20	80	0
Internal statistical reporting	100	0	7	93	0
Case management	100	0	23	74	3
Supervision	100	0	40	50	10
Program management	100	3	20	74	3
Financial management	99	3	23	43	30
External reporting	100	3	47	30	30
Policy making	100	0	57	23	20

*"Better" combines "somewhat better" and "much better," while "worse" combines "somewhat worse" and "much worse."

Impact on Staff

Several respondents in this small organization indicated they lacked enough information to assess the impact of computerization. It should be remembered that PCC's computer system is a tool used by and for management. As we reported in earlier chapters, only eight people fill out computer forms in this agency.

Seven respondents indicate they have had to learn new skills since the introduction of computers. Most of these are middle and upper managers (5 of 7). Only two of the seven feel these skills have had any impact on their job security; one staff member reports increased security and the other, decreased security.

There appears to have been little impact of computerization on productivity. Ten of 12 respondents see no change in their productivity while two see a moderate increase. These responses are consistent with the difficulties faced by the centre in computerizing. However, most of those responding (six of eight) indicate their paperwork has moderately increased with computerization. Despite an increase in paperwork, productivity has not increased very much, perhaps because paperwork is completed before information is put into the computer. Productivity would be most affected by access to output of computerized information. However, due to the difficulties in computerizing, output has not been consistently available for staff use. Thus, productivity has not increased despite a moderate increase in paperwork.

Two-thirds of the respondents do not feel the computer affects the discretion they can exercise in carrying out their responsibilities. Of the remaining five respondents, two report they have more discretion and three ''don't know.'' The situation is quite different with respect to the impact of computerization on the control staff exercise over their work. Of 12 respondents answering this question, two say they have more control, three that their control remains unchanged, while four report less control and three ''don't know.''

As Table 7.13 shows, computerization is seen by staff to have more costs than benefits for three of the five positions in the organization. Least benefit is seen to flow to support, direct service and supervisory staff.

Table 7.13
Appraisals of the Costs and Benefits of Computerization
for Staff, by Position: PCC

Position of Staff	More* Benefits	Equal Costs/ Benefits	More* Costs	NR**
Direct Service	1	4	3	7
Supervisors	1	3	3	8
Support Staff	1	3	2	9
Accounting and Fiscal Managers	5	2	0	8
Executive Director, Dept. Heads and Managers	4	2	1	8

*The ''more benefits'' category includes both ''many more benefits'' and ''some more benefits'' responses. Similarly the ''more costs'' category contains both ''some more costs'' and ''many more costs'' responses.

**Although 15 respondents answered the question some say they are not qualified to answer, or else indicate ''don't know'' or ''no response.'' These responses are combined in the NR column.

Impact on Clients

Most staff members express a general concern about ''the possible lack of confidentiality caused by storing client information on the computer'' (Table 7.14). This is not surprising since a majority of the PCC staff, like the STCC and DFCS staffs, also indicate a general concern that computers threaten clients' privacy (see the preceding chapter).

Only four respondents indicate ''no concern'' about this matter. However, the concern the respondents feel seems to be over access, not over the type of data stored. Only four respondents think some data should not be kept. These also tend to express ''a lot'' of concern about confidentiality in general. Those who feel ''some'' concern are divided as to whether or not there are data that should not be stored. By contrast, those expressing little or no concern (predictably) think there are no data that should not be stored. Yet eleven of 14 respondents (including several who are ''very concerned'' about confidentiality) do not know the Centre's confidentiality policy. There-

Table 7.14
Concern about Lack of Confidentiality of
Client Data in the Computer: PCC

Level of Concern	Number
Total	15
No concern	4
A little concern	2
Some concern	5
A lot of concern	4

fore, it seems confidentiality is a general or abstract concern to most staff members, and not a practical problem.

A sizable minority (40 percent) of the staff think computer technology discourages dealing with clients on an individual basis. Of the 15 respondents, two see considerable justification and four some justification for this concern. However, one-third do not see this as a problem at all. The remaining staff either take no position or choose not to answer the question.

Table 7.15
Level of Concern about Confidentiality that
Some Data Should Not Be Collected: PCC

Level of Concern About Confidentiality	Some Data Should Not Be Collected	
	Yes	No
Total	4	6
A lot	3	0
Some	1	1
A little	0	1
None	0	4

One-third of the respondents think computerization has no impact on service to clients, one-fifth see a positive impact, and six percent see a negative impact; 40 percent did not make an appraisal. Therefore, only one in four staff members says that computerization has either a negative or positive effect on the provision of services.

Impact on the Organization

Most staff members think computerization has had no effect on various records and activities within the centre, including such areas as case management, supervision, program management, external reporting, policy making and service to clients. However, opinions vary about the impact of computerization with respect to client records, internal reporting and financial management.

Where client records are concerned, six of eleven respondents see a positive result from computerization. However, some respondents indicate client records would remain unchanged (four say this) or become even better (five) if the centre reverted to a manual system (Table 7.16 and Table 7.17). Respondents who came to the centre after computerization tend to answer both questions consistently. On the other hand those who were with the organization before computerization tend to be split over the potential effect of reverting to a manual system.

Table 7.16
Staff Employed Prior to Computerization and Impact of
Computerization on Client Records: PCC

Employed Prior to Computerization	Perceived Impact on Client Records			
	Positive	No Impact	Negative	Don't Know
Total	6	4	1	4
Yes	4	1	1	0
No	2	3	0	4

While four of six who were with the organization prior to computerization think the impact has been positive, only three think reverting would have a negative impact. A further three think client records would be affected positively by reverting.

Table 7.17
Staff Employed Prior to Computerization and Impact of
Reversion to Manual System on Client Records: PCC

Employed Prior to Computerization	Perceived Impact on Client Records			
	Positive	No Impact	Negative	Don't Know
Total	5	4	3	3
Yes	3	0	3	0
No	2	4	0	3

Perceived effects on internal reporting are also affected by one's presence or absence prior to computerization. Five of eleven respondents feel internal reporting was positively affected by computerization. An additional five see no change. Six respondents think there would be no change if the centre reverted to a manual system, whereas four believe internal reporting would be worse. People tend to be consistent in their responses; but responses to both questions tend to vary depending upon whether or not the respondent was with the centre prior to computerization. Most (4 of 5) who came after computerization see no impact on internal reporting; and most (4 of 6) who were with the centre before computerization tend to see the impact as positive, as shown in Table 7.18 and Table 7.19. Similarly, most who were with the organization before computerization think reversion would cause no change or make reporting worse; while respondents who had joined later think no change would take place.

Responses regarding the impact of computerization on financial management are also split. Four of the nine respondents think the impact has been positive, while four others see no impact. With respect to the impact of reversion to a manual system, six of eleven think there would be no change while five think financial management would be worse. Again, responses to both questions are consistent; and responses tend to vary depending upon whether or not the respondent was with the agency prior to computerization.

Table 7.18

Staff Employed Prior to Computerization and Impact of
Computerization on Internal Reporting: PCC

Employed Prior to Computerization	Perceived Impact on Internal Reporting			
	Positive	No Impact	Negative	Don't Know
Total	5	5	1	4
Yes	4	1	1	0
No	1	4	0	4

Table 7.19

Staff Employed Prior to Computerization and Impact on Internal
Reporting if the Agency Reverted to a Manual System: PCC

Employed Prior to Computerization	Perceived Impact on Internal Reporting			
	Positive	No Impact	Negative	Don't Know
Total	1	6	5	3
Yes	1	2	3	0
No	0	4	2	3

Table 7.20

Employed at Agency Prior to Computerization by Perceived Impact
on Financial Management: PCC

Employed Prior to Computerization	Perceived Impact on Financial Management			
	Positive	No Impact	Negative	Don't Know
Total	4	4	1	6
Yes	4	1	1	0
No	0	3	0	6

As shown in Table 7.20 and Table 7.21, those who were present before computerization see the impact as positive (3 of 6) and reversion as having potentially negative effects (4 of 6). Those coming to the agency after computerization think there has been no impact and, for this reason, believe there would be no change if the agency reverted to a manual system.

Table 7.21
Perceived Effect on Financial Management if the Agency
Reverted to a Manual System: PCC

Employed Prior to Computerization	Perceived Effect on Financial Management			
	Positive	No Impact	Negative	Don't Know
Total	6	4	1	4
Yes	2	3	1	0
No	4	1	0	4

Table 7.22 presents the staff appraisals of records and statistics before and after computerization. The six staff employed before computerization rate the earlier record-keeping system as minimally satisfactory, with at least one person rating the system as poor or very poor in every category except for relevance. As Table 7.22 shows, computerization has only worsened an already poor record-keeping system. In every area the computerized system receives lower approval ratings than the old manual system.

Table 7.22
Appraisals of the Records and Statistics
Pre and Post Computerization: PCC

Description	Good*		Fair		Poor		Very Poor	
	Pre	Post	Pre	Post	Pre	Post	Pre	Post
Accuracy	3	4	1	1	1	4	1	3
Timeliness	2	3	3	2	—	5	1	2
Clarity	2	3	1	3	2	4	1	2
Comprehensiveness	1	3	3	2	1	5	1	2
Relevance	4	3	2	3	—	5	—	—

*There were no ratings of "excellent" in the pre or post period of computerization.

These ratings probably reflect the problems encountered in implementation, and indicate a considerable lack of confidence in the computer-processed data. Benefits of computerization have been mainly in the area of increased administrative control.

County Department of Social Services

In the last chapter, we found that the average factor scores for DCSS were relatively undispersed in respect to efficiency — indicating consensus on this issue — and highly dispersed in relation to control. The average view was that computerization tended to increase both efficiency and control. We now examine how these views are related to the actual effects of computerization on the organization.

Impact on Staff

Just over half (53 percent) of the respondents had to learn new skills following computerization. Of those, 17 percent think new skills have increased
their job security while 5 percent perceive a decrease in job security; but the
vast majority (78 percent) believe their new (computer) skills have had "no
effect" upon job security.

Only 14 percent have seen changes to their job descriptions due to computerization, and no clear patterns emerge to suggest which duties or staff
positions have been changed.

Staff who fill out computer forms have noticed a definite increase in
their "paperwork." More than three-fifths (61 percent) report an increase
since computerization, and more than a third (36 percent) describe the
increase as substantial. Only 4 percent of those who do computer-related
paperwork say it has decreased, while 17 percent say it has remained the
same.

The majority (63 percent) of respondents see no impact upon the
amount of "discretion" they exercise and twice as many (16 percent) feel
their discretion has increased, compared to those who feel it has declined (8
percent). Just four percent of the sample think their amount of discretion has
changed "a lot." These results are somewhat surprising since a majority of
CDSS staff cite loss of discretion as a concern in questions discussed in the
preceding chapter.

With respect to control and their own work, about half (48 percent) perceive an increase; a third (33 percent) see no difference; and fewer than one
in ten (9 percent) feels that control has diminished.

However, staff position tends to influence perceptions of these matters.
While only 5 percent of support staff and 10 percent of supervisors find their
"discretion" has been enhanced, 22 percent of direct service staff and 25
percent of managers report an increase. Even with respect to "control,"
where more respondents report an increase due to computerization, a similar
pattern emerges. Only two-fifths (41 percent) of the support staff and nearly
half of the direct service workers (46 percent) and supervisors consider their
exercise of control over their job has increased, while fully two-thirds of the
managers (63 percent) report such an increase. No sizable group of staff considers their exercise of discretion or control has seriously diminished due to
computerization. While all groups think they have gained more than lost
from computerization, the biggest winners are the managers. The support
staff, by their own assessment, have gained the least.

On the issue of "productivity," almost half (47 percent) of the respondents report an increase (12 percent a "substantial increase") owing to computerization, while only 5 percent report a decrease, and a third (34 percent)
indicate no change. Again, the benefits of computerization are unequally dis-

tributed. Approximately half of the direct service (49 percent) and support staff (53 percent), but three-fifths (60 percent) of the supervisors, and nearly all the managers (89 percent) report increased productivity.

Table 7.23
Self Appraisals of Costs and Benefits of Computerization
for Staff, by Position: CDSS
(N = 135)

Position of Staff	Total (Percents)	More* Benefits	Equal Ben./costs	More* Costs	NR**
Support Staff	100	43	10	7	40
Direct Service Staff	100	55	9	6	30
Supervisors	100	46	9	5	41
Accounting and Fiscal Managers	100	41	4	5	50
Department Heads and Managers	101	38	7	2	54

*The "more benefits" category includes both "many more benefits" and "some more benefit" responses. Similarly the "more costs" category contains both "some more costs" and "many more costs" responses.

**Of the 135 respondents some say they are not qualified to answer, or else indicate "don't know" or "no response." These responses are combined in the NR column.

All five occupational groups we studied see more benefits than costs in computerization (Table 7.23). Every group rates its net benefit highly in relation to the others, but senior occupational groups tend to rate the net benefit to junior occupational groups more highly than junior occupational groups rate it themselves.

Impact on Clients

A majority of the CDSS staff, like the staff at the three other advanced computer using organizations, indicated a general concern for the privacy of clients in the preceding chapter.

Thus it is not surprising that more than three-fifths (61 percent) of the CDSS respondents indicate at least "a little" concern about the threat to confidentiality posed by computers and 13 percent even expressed "a lot" of concern.

Although concern is expressed at every organizational level, attitudes vary by staff position. Fully four-fifths of the managers and almost two-thirds (65 percent) of the direct service staff express concern about breaches of confidentiality: understandably, since direct service staff are often the only ones to deal directly with clients, while managers may have to intervene (and take some responsibility) if serious breaches of confidentiality arise. By virtue of their roles, they may simply be more sensitive to the issue.

Concern about information stored in the computer centres on two themes, namely "personal data" and "access" to data. Twenty of 28 comments refer to concerns about personal information and six to concerns about data access; one mentions the storage of irrelevant data, and one objects to storing any data at all.

"Personal data" mentioned includes "demographic" or "identifying" data such as names, addresses, phone, OHIP and SIN numbers, etc. Other respondents object to storing "confidential" data which might include legal (i.e., criminal), medical, financial or social (i.e., family history) data. A subset of this group expresses concern about clinical data, such as "diagnostic" or "treatment" information, or even "reason for referral/service" data.

Expressions of concern about "access" have to do with the ease of gaining entry, or the extent to which data obtained legally may be shared. Very few (8 percent) respondents think there is any kind of client data that should not be stored in the computer after a case is closed. Of those who think otherwise, most object to retaining "personal" data, while others suggest imposing a "time limit."

Most staff (73 percent of respondents) believe that departmental policies protect client interests. Approximately one in four (27 percent) are not so sure, however, believing that present policies "may allow access by (outside) persons or organizations." Overall, only 19 percent say they are "not familiar with the present policies regarding access to client information"; but more than a third (35 percent) of the supervisory group are unfamiliar with these policies.

More than two thirds (69 percent) of respondents with an opinion see no justification for the fear that computer technology discourages dealing with clients as individuals. The following comment of a direct service staff member reflects the views of this group: "Social work still goes on, the computer has not really changed the nature of the interaction between the client and the worker." Only 4 percent claim "considerable justification" for this fear, while 27 percent see "some justification."

Curiously enough, those most concerned about the possible dehumanizing influence of computer technology are not the ones in closest contact with clients, the direct service workers, or their supervisors, but managers (60 percent), and to a lesser extent, the support staff (40 percent). Only 29 percent of direct service workers or their supervisors see any justification for concern about client de-individualization.

When the costs and benefits of computerization for clients are assessed by staff, 40 percent of the respondents report "more benefits," while only 8 percent report "more costs." Among those closest to the clients, direct service staff, the belief in a net benefit to clients is held even more widely than the departmental average (Table 7.24).

Table 7.24
Costs and Benefits of Computerization for
Clients as Assessed by Staff: CDSS
(N = 135)

Occupational Group	Total (Percents)	More* Benefits	Equal Ben./Costs	More* Costs	Not Qualified	NR
All Respondents	100	40	21	8	15	16
Direct Service Staff	100	44	22	8	13	13

*These include "many more" and "some more" categories combined.

Impact on the Organization

Global assessments of the impact of computerization on the organization are as follows: 54 percent believe computerization has brought more benefits than costs (24 percent see many more benefits); 14 percent believe benefits and costs are equal; 14 percent see more costs than benefits; and 18 percent did not make an assessment.

Respondents also rated the impact of computerization on selected organizational activities. Table 7.25 indicates that as the number of respondents indicating positive impacts diminishes, the number of respondents indicating "no impact," "does not apply," and/or no response, increases. This is probably because the survey sample is comprised largely of direct service staff, who know less about agency activities such as policy making and external reporting than they do about service to clients and client records. Many respondents may select the "no-impact" category, rather than disqualify themselves, even when they have little knowledge about the activity involved. Nevertheless, the following conclusions seem warranted:

a) Respondents are most positive about the impacts of computerization upon client records, service to clients, internal statistical reporting, case management, and financial management;
b) Respondents are least positive about the impacts of computers upon policy making, supervision, external reporting, and program management;
c) While perceptions of negative impact are few, they are highest in the areas of internal statistical reporting (10 percent) and supervision (8 percent).

Further examination shows that position influences respondent perceptions. For example, most support staff are positive only about the impact of computerization upon the first four areas of responsibility (i.e., they exclude financial management), while the majority of managers are positive about the computer's impact on all the areas listed. Except for ranking "client records" in first place, like everyone else, managers rank computer impacts quite differently from the norm. In order, managers feel most positively

Table 7.25
Impacts of Computerization on Nine Areas of Organizational
Activities: CDSS
(N = 135)

Rank	Activity	Total (Percents)	Impact of Computerization			
			Positive*	Negative*	None	DNR/NR*
1.	Client records	100	79	3	4	14
2.	Service to clients	100	63	3	15	19
3.	Internal statistical reporting	100	58	10	9	23
4.	Case management	100	54	3	21	22
5.	Financial management	100	52	3	13	32
6.	Program management	100	33	4	24	39
7.	External reporting	100	30	5	23	42
8.	Supervision	100	30	8	24	38
9.	Policy making	100	25	4	26	45

*Combined responses

about computer impacts upon client records and supervision (90 percent); program management, case management, and internal statistical reporting (80 percent); financial management (70 percent); policy making (60 percent); service to clients and external reporting (50 percent).

Respondents generally consider the impacts of computerization to be very positive with respect to client records and service. Many say they could not cope with existing high caseloads without the aid of the computer. Automation allows them to keep track of, and provide more efficient service to, their clients.

Accordingly, staff believe that reverting to a manual record-keeping system would be harmful, particularly with respect to client records (65 percent), internal statistical reporting (61 percent), service to clients (54 percent), and financial management (49 percent). Fewer than 10 percent of the respondents consider reversion to a manual system an improvement over the present one, for any of the activities listed; the largest group sees "no change" for activities such as case management (48 percent), external reporting (61 percent), program management (61 percent), supervision (64 percent), and/or policy making (68 percent). In other words, most staff think reverting to a manual system would have little effect on the performance of supervisory or management responsibilities. Supervisors and mangers, however, do not agree with that view.

Most respondents (particularly, direct service workers and support staff) may not appreciate the significance of computerized reports to their supervisors and managers. This may be due to a lack of communication between management and staff about the use of automated records and statistics. If

Table 7.26
Impacts of Reversion to a Manual Information System on
Nine Organizational Activities: CDSS
(N = 135)

Rank	Area of Responsibility		Better*	(Percents) Worse*	No Change	N/R
1.	Client records	100	7	65	13	15
2.	Service to clients	101	8	54	24	15
3.	Internal statistical reporting	100	9	61	12	18
4.	Case management	100	6	45	31	17
5.	Financial management	99	4	49	27	19
6.	Program management	100	5	34	41	20
7.	External reporting	99	4	34	39	22
8.	Supervision	100	7	29	42	22
9.	Policy making	100	3	28	46	22

*Combined responses

staff are not sure what the data are used for, they are likely to undervalue the computer. On the other hand, staff who see data being used in a threatening or controlling way might want to be rid of the computer.

On the subject of record quality, there is a strong consensus. For accuracy, timeliness, clarity, comprehensiveness and relevance, most respondents rate the computerized record system as good to excellent (Table 7.27). But it should be noted that approximately a quarter of the respondents rate the computerized system as only "fair" for each characteristic listed.

Table 7.27
Staff Appraisal of the Records and Statistics
Pre and Post Computerization: CDSS
(N = 135)

Description	Excellent		Good		Fair		Poor		Very Poor		NR	
	Pre	Post	Pre	Post	Pre	Post	Pre	Post	Pre	Post	Pre	Post
Accuracy	3	10	17	49	13	22	7	4	1	1	54	14
Timeliness	—	13	17	36	13	28	8	4	1	3	60	15
Clarity	1	15	21	40	13	24	6	5	1	1	59	15
Comprehensiveness	1	8	19	42	15	24	6	10	1	1	59	14
Relevance	—	12	23	45	12	23	5	4	—	1	60	15

Among respondents employed by the organization before computerization, ratings of the former (manual) system are lower, with most ratings in the "fair" to "good" range. Approximately 13 percent rate the manual system as "fair" for each of five characteristics listed.

Computerization is seen as a positive influence on the record-keeping system for each of the quality indicators examined. It is interesting to note, however, that the computerized system's strengths and weaknesses differ from those of the manual system. Data from the computerized system are rated as more "relevant" than data from the (former) manual system. But "accuracy" replaces "relevance" as the information system's best feature, while "comprehensiveness" replaces "timeliness" as its worst. Whether the position of "comprehensiveness" as last among the qualitative indicators implies comprehensiveness is a "problem," is not certain.

Summary

Table 7.28 summarizes the experiences of the four advanced computer using agencies we studied. The CDSS, largest of the four, has obviously had the most positive experience with computerization. Perhaps the fact that the CDSS was the first to computerize is a factor in their success – they have had longer to get the bugs out of their system and the staff has had more time to get used to working with computers.

PCC and the DFCS have had the least successful experiences. The computer system is under-utilized at both agencies, particularly so at PCC. As we saw earlier, this system was always intended to be a management tool at PCC, but management under-utilized it for a time, due to problems during the implementation period. At the DFCS, the second largest organization in our study, on the other hand, the under-utilization of the computer system by staff at lower levels is a disappointment to the management. Again, part of the problem may stem from difficulties during implementation. A lot of resentment was created early on when staff felt the system was installed without their being sufficiently consulted. This resentment increased when a work monitoring program seemed to imply that the staff were not very productive.

At the STCC, the computer system is viewed ambivalently. The staff seem to think computerization hasn't made a difference one way or the other; but they are certainly not anti-computer.

What is most striking about our results is that the philosophical or abstract concerns about computerization so prevalent in the literature – loss of discretion, the threat to privacy, de-individualization – appear to be relatively unimportant to the staffs we studied. For example, while many of the respondents believe that client privacy is a general problem with computerization, few are worried about breaches in client confidentiality at their own agencies. And, in many cases (CDSS was the exception), the majority of staff don't even know their agency's policy regarding access to client data.

Two other theoretical problems also turn out to be non-issues in our study – namely, job security and the use of computers to monitor staff. As

Table 7.28
Impact of Computerization on Advanced Computer-using Organizations

	DFCS	STCC	PCC	CDSS
The value of computer technology	net cost	slight net benefit	net cost	net benefit
Computerized record-keeping vs. manual	computerized system is better	computerized system is better	manual system was better	computer system is much better
Group most positive towards computerization	department heads and managers	supervisors and managers	upper managers	managers
Groups least positive towards computerization	direct service staff and support staff	support staff	direct service staff and supervisors	support staff
Activities most improved	internal statistics and client records	internal statistics and client records	client records and internal statistics	client records and service to clients
Activities least improved	policy making	policy making and external reporting	case management and supervision	policy making and supervision
Perceived impact on discretion	majority of staff no change	majority of staff no change	majority of staff no change	majority of staff no change
Perceived impact on control	more job control for supervisors and direct service staff	majority of staff no change	majority of staff no change	majority of staff no change
Perceived impact on productivity	greatest gains by managers	majority of staff no change	majority of staff no change	majority of staff no change
Staff assessment of accuracy of computerized records	majority rated accuracy as fair or poor	majority rated accuracy as fair, good or excellent	majority rated accuracy as poor or very poor	majority rated accuracy as good or excellent

mentioned earlier, the monitoring of the staff did become an issue briefly at
the DFCS, but tensions eased once a new system was instituted that showed
staff productivity in a more favourable light. Beyond that one example, the
computer's effect on job security and staff evaluations seems to have been
relatively benign.

So how can we explain the relatively poor approval ratings given to
computerization at three of these four organizations? This lukewarm reaction
to computers is even more puzzling when we remember that all the staffs
except PCC's conclude that computerized record-keeping is superior to a
manual system.

One possible explanation may lie in the way computers were implemented and used. Generally speaking, the computers were imposed from
above, to be used by and for management with only limited input (on their
uses) from the lower staff levels. Managers use computers in ways that are
often invisible to the rest of the organization — policy making, external
reporting etc. But before the managers can use the computer to generate
these "benefits," the lower levels (i.e., the support staff and direct service
staff) must first input the data. Thus a situation develops in which the lower
levels are doing more paperwork after computerization (all four organizations report an increase in paperwork) but only the upper levels are seeing
the (alleged) benefits. The social costs of dividing work into "headwork"
and "handwork" are certainly evident in this situation.

This is only a tentative explanation for the lack of enthusiasm for computerization we observed in most of the organizations. Judgement on this
will be reserved until after we look (in the next chapter) at the experiences of
the four organizations that are intermediate users of computers.

Chapter 8

Impact on Intermediate Computer Users

The last chapter examined the impacts of computerization on the staff, organization and clients of "advanced" computer users. There we found a wide variation in the actual extent of computer use across agencies, and within agencies, across positions. We found computer benefits to be greatest for managers and administrators, for whom the systems were typically designed; and costs to be greatest for those who had to do the paperwork and input data: namely, direct service and support staff. Below the managerial level, satisfaction with computerization was greatest among those affected least by the change.

At the same time, we discovered a disjuncture in many cases between people's ideal versions of computerization — its great potential for efficiency, or its great danger of violated confidentiality — and the actual experience of no significant impact on working conditions, job security, efficiency or confidentiality, among others.

In this chapter, we examine the same range of issues in four "intermediate user" agencies. Because computerization is less extensive or developed here, we expect to find similar but less marked patterns: like the same photograph printed on low-contrast rather than on high-contrast paper.

District Office/Correctional Services

In Chapter 6, we learned that the average factor scores for the staff of DOCS were relatively undispersed in respect to efficiency — indicating a consensus on this issue — but highly dispersed in respect to control. The average views were that computerization tended to increase control but not increase efficiency. We now examine how these views are related to the actual effects of computerization on this agency.

Impact on Staff
Of the 45 staff in this organization who completed questionnaires, 42 had been employed here before the introduction of computer technology. It is

149

therefore not surprising that 76 percent (34) had to learn new skills due to computerization. However, most (74 percent) of those who had to learn new skills report that learning them has had no effect on their job security. Only 16 percent report that computerization has changed their job descriptions. We learned, however, that the union has raised the following issues about the impact of computerization on staff: increased health risks from working at video display terminals; reduced job security for support staff; and a failure of management to change job descriptions to include computer tasks.

Table 8.1
Staff Assessment of the Impact of Computerization on
Amount of Paperwork and Productivity: DOCS

Impact	On Amount of Productivity (Percent) (N=18)	On Degree of Paperwork (Percent) (N=45)
Substantially increased	33	4
Moderately increased	39	38
Remained the same	22	44
Moderately decreased	5	9
Substantially decreased	–	2
No response	–	2

Only those respondents who fill out computer forms were asked about the impact of computerization on paperwork, whereas the total sample gave views on how computerization has affected productivity. The results in Table 8.1 indicate that while 17 out of 18 respondents (94 percent) think the amount of paperwork associated with computerization has remained the same or increased, only 5 out of 45 (11 percent) think computerization has decreased their paperwork. However, more than four out of ten respondents report computerization has had no impact on their productivity and a comparable proportion (42 percent) think productivity has increased. This seems to contradict the evidence from our factor analysis revealing relatively high consensus on the issue of efficiency.

Staff assessments of the impact of computerization on discretion and control, presented in Table 8.2, show the majority (69 percent) think computerization has had no impact. A minority (16 percent) see an increase in their discretion while one out of ten report having less discretion. With respect to the amount of control the respondents have over their work, the majority (58 percent) think computerization has had no impact. The remainder are more or less evenly split, with 20 percent indicating that computerization has increased their control over the work environment, and 22 percent indicating the opposite.

Table 8.2
Staff Assessment of the Impact of Computerization on
Staff Discretion and Control of Job: DOCS

Impact on Work Environment	Discretion (Percent)	Job Control (Percent)
		(N = 45)
A lot more	—	2
More	16	18
None	69	58
Less	11	18
A lot less	—	4
No response	4	—

The findings about productivity and discretion are consistent with comments made by the staff during interviews. Several say computer generated reports can be used to check the productivity of parole officers in quantitative terms, i.e., number of clients seen and time spent completing a community assessment report; but the computer is not programmed to evaluate the qualitative aspects of parole work, and, according to parole officers, this is where their real work is done. The parole officers do not think computerization has affected their discretion because discretion comes into play at the local level during consultations between the parole officer and the area manager/superintendent.

Respondents rated the benefits and costs of computerization for the different occupational groups in the district service. The ratings presented in Table 8.3 show that accounting and fiscal management personnel are seen to gain the most net benefits by computerization.

This finding is not surprising since financial procedures are being processed on FINCON, the only system at the agency that has had a relatively problem-free implementation. The support staff, who are responsible for inputting data, are least favourably disposed towards computerization, with 47 percent seeing net costs. The programs also receive a low approval rating from parole officers. During interviews, several comment that the information in the inmate/parolee data base is not comprehensive enough, there are delays in getting these data on-line, and some computerized data are out-of-date. As a result, parole officers receive a very sketchy inmate profile from computer generated reports.

For this reason, they continue to rely on hard copy records which are more detailed, accurate and current. Many parole officers say they have been promised more from computerization. As initially presented by the systems people, the PSS was expected to involve a total package of modules which would enable parole officers to work more efficiently. Because of financial

Table 8.3
Appraisals of Costs and Benefits of Computerization
for DOCS Staff: by Position
(N = 45)

Organizational Group	Total Percent	Perceived Benefits/Costs (Percents)			
		More Benefits	Equal Costs and Benefits	More Costs	NR*
Direct Service Staff	100	13	30	24	33
Supervisors	100	20	24	20	36
Support Staff	100	20	13	47	20
Accounting and Fiscal Managers	100	29	9	2	60
Executive Director, Department Heads, and Managers	100	16	18	8	58

*Includes also respondents who stated that they were not qualified to answer, or "don't know."

cut-backs the introduction of some modules has been delayed, and others are not being developed at all. Thus, for many workers, the computerization of parole offices has proved less effective and less efficient than expected. Some feel that head office never clearly addressed the issue of costs and, in particular, the human costs of computerization. Of all staff, the Case Documentation Clerks have received the fewest benefits from computerization. In the main, these are the workers who key in the data. Although the clerks were told computerization would streamline their work, for many it has had the opposite effect, as both manual and computer files are still being maintained. There was no increase in the complement of support workers to deal with this duplication, and the number of support workers may even be reduced.

Accordingly, some Case Documentation Clerks are worried that computerization might eventually cost them their jobs. Others are concerned because computer tasks have not been written into their job descriptions. Still others wonder why the organization does not institute training procedures for MUSE, the word-processing program. Instead, the very few workers who opt to use the program must rely on "hands-on" experience to gain familiarity with it. MUSE, the only program for which no training was provided, is the one program geared to meet the needs of the district rather than those of National and/or Regional Headquarters.

Impact on Clients

About one in five (22 percent) respondents indicate that they have no concern about the possibility of a breach of confidentiality resulting from unauthorized access to personal data stored in the computer (Table 8.4). The remaining three quarters indicate concerns ranging from "a lot" (18 percent) to "some" (31 percent). This level of concern over confidentiality is the highest found at any of the eight agencies we studied.

Table 8.4
Concern of Staff Re: Unauthorized Access
to Data Stored in the Computer: DOCS
(N = 45)

Level of Concern	Percent
A lot	18
Some	31
A little	29
None	22

Half the respondents think data of a personal nature — legal, criminal records, social histories — should not be kept after a case is closed. Others (22 percent) suggest that only research or statistical data should be retained.

Despite their level of concern over confidentiality, DOCS staff, like their counterparts at most of the other organizations we studied (CDSS was the exception) are often unaware of their organization's confidentiality rules. Thirty-eight percent don't know the present policies regarding access to client information. The same proportion of respondents say the policies are satisfactory, while 24 percent consider them unsatisfactory. Again, breaches of confidentiality are seen as a potential, rather than actual, problem.

When asked if they see any justification for the fear that computer use would discourage treating clients as individuals, the majority (56 percent) say they do not. However one-third take the opposite position, and one in ten respondents sees considerable justification for this worry.

These perceptions are reiterated in the interviews. For example, when asked if the values associated with the helping professions are at odds with the values associated with using computer technology, one staff member says she does not see a value conflict. In her opinion, the values associated with computerization, i.e., efficiency in processing information, may even facilitate the helping process. Yet more than half the respondents feel computerization has had no effect on service to clients. The proportion assessing the impact as positive is about one in six (18 percent). A small minority (4 percent) assesses the impact as negative.

Impact on the Organization

In their global assessment of the impact of computerization on the organization, only 28 percent see computerization bringing more benefits than costs to the organization. Thirty-four percent of the respondents believe computerization involves more costs than benefits and 24 percent regard the costs and benefits as equal.

It was anticipated that computerization would improve the quality of the agency's statistics and records. Table 8.5 shows the staff's assessment of the impact of computerization in this area.

Table 8.5
Staff Assessments of Records and Statistics Pre and Post
Computerization: DOCS
(N = 45)

| | Assessment (Percents) | | | | | | | | | |
| | Excellent | | Good | | Fair | | Poor | | Very Poor | |
Description	Pre	Post	Pre	Post	Pre	Post	Pre	Post	Pre	Post
Accuracy	15	4	42	49	37	36	5	4	—	—
Timeliness	12	2	32	38	32	27	17	18	5	11
Clarity	22	9	35	42	30	24	12	18	—	2
Comprehen-										
siveness	20	4	37	40	32	29	10	16	—	4
Relevance	15	7	55	31	17	42	7	9	5	4

Pre-computer sample, N=40. This group comprised all those respondents who were employed prior to computerization.
Post-computer sample, N=45. This group comprised the total sample.

The findings are decisive, suggesting computerization lowers the quality of record-keeping in all five designated areas. But it should be remembered that at the time of this survey, the computerized Supervision System had just become operational.

The respondents also assessed the impact of computerization on selected organizational activities, using a positive/negative scale. (See Table 8.6.) The staff clearly have more favourable perceptions of the impact of computerization in these areas than they do of its impact on records and statistics. As can be seen, the positive responses far outweigh negative ones for all activities. The highly positive appraisal of computerization's impact on the first three categories is unexpected, considering how harshly the computerized record-keeping procedures are judged.

Respondents also rated the potential impact on the same activities if the organization were to revert to a manual record-keeping system. These results, presented in Table 8.7, indicate that the great majority of respondents

Table 8.6
Staff Assessment of the Impact of Computers on Selected
Organizational Activities: DOCS
(N = 45)

Activity	Impact (Percents)			
	Positive*	None	Negative*	DN/DNA
Client Records	69	22	4	5
Internal Statistical Reporting	67	13	9	11
Case Management	42	33	11	19
Supervision	31	46	7	16
Program Management	33	24	2	41
Financial Management	40	22	–	35
External Reporting	35	26	7	32
Policy Making	11	38	7	49
Service to Clients	18	58	4	20

*The positive category includes both "Strongly positive" and "positive" responses. Similarly the negative category is made up of both "negative" and "strongly negative" responses.

Table 8.7
Impact on Organizational Activities: Staff Assessments of
the Organization if Reverted to Manual System: DOCS
(N = 45)

Activity	Impact (Percents)			
	Better*	None	Worse*	DN/DNA
Client Records	11	40	49	–
Internal Statistical Reporting	9	31	60	2
Case Management	7	64	24	5
Supervision	4	82	14	3
Program Management	–	44	42	14
Financial Management	2	38	44	16
External Reporting	4	44	40	12
Policy Making	–	53	33	24

*The better category includes both "much better" and "somewhat better" responses. Similarly the worse category is made up of both "somewhat worse" and "much worse" responses.

think there would be either no change, or a change for the worse if the organization reverted to manual record-keeping procedures.

The fact that computerized records and statistics can be judged so harshly, while computerization's overall effects on organizational activities are seen as positive, is difficult to explain. Perhaps it means that while the new computer system has brought new problems, the old system was also severely flawed. In the staff's global assessment, computerization is judged

to be a net cost to the organization. One explanation for this apparent inconsistency may be that, as a senior staff member observed, staff thinks that
computerization may be potentially helpful although it is a net cost to the
organization at present. The assessment that it is a net cost may also reflect
staff concerns, expressed in the interviews, concerning problems encountered in implementations, e.g., hardware breakdowns, delays, errors and
inadequate training procedures.

Urban Youth Counselling Service

In Chapter 6, we found the average factor scores for UYCS to be relatively
undispersed, reflecting a high consensus of opinion. The prevailing opinion
was that computerization neither increased efficiency nor control to any
marked degree. We now examine how that opinion is rooted in the actual
effects of computerization on the organization.

Impact on Staff

Of the 23 respondents who expressed their attitude towards computerization
in this organization, ten are very positive and 13 positive. Thus the staff are
supportive despite their limited involvement in the planning, implementation
and use of computer technology. A positive attitude also existed when computers were introduced, with only four staff reporting a "somewhat negative" attitude at that time.

Although more than half of the staff has had to learn new skills with the
introduction of computer technology, none feels job security has been diminished and only two indicate their job description has changed to reflect these
new skills.

Table 8.8 presents data on staff responses to changes resulting from
computerization in the amount of discretion they exercise on the job, job
control, and productivity.

Table 8.8
Impact of Computerization on Staff Assessment of the Staff
Discretion, Job Control and Productivity: UYCS

Area of Job Performance	Positive	Impact No Change	Negative
Amount of discretion exercised	—	25	—
Control over job	5	20	—
Productivity	10	14*	—

*1 no response

Although nobody sees computerization as a threat to the exercise of discretion and four out of five think it has had no impact on their ability to con-

trol their jobs, only two out of five think computerization has increased their productivity. Such increased productivity was probably intended by management and the Board of Directors. Staff were also asked if their paperwork has increased with computerization. Of nine staff members responding to this question, two report a moderate increase, six report it has stayed the same, and one thinks paperwork has decreased substantially.

In summary, computerization has had no substantial impact on staff in the day-to-day performance of their jobs. They have accommodated computerization with little or no disruption of their day-to-day job performance. This interpretation is supported by answers to the question, "Are you making more use of the computer today than when you first started using it in this organization?" Only eight people answer in the affirmative. Respondents, assessments of the benefits and costs to staff within the organization are shown in Table 8.9. Computerization is regarded as having been most beneficial to support staff and accounting and fiscal managers. The group seen as benefiting least are the supervisors and direct service staff.

Table 8.9
Appraisals of the Costs and Benefits of Computerization
for Staff, by Position: UYCS
(N=25)

| Staff | Total Percent | Benefits/Costs (Percents) | | |
		More Benefits*	Equal Benefits	More Costs*	NR**
Direct Service	100	36	40	4	20
Supervisors	100	28	20	—	52
Support Staff	100	60	12	—	28
Accounting and Fiscal Managers	100	52	12	—	64
Executive Director, Department Heads and Managers	100	44	8	—	48

*The "more benefits" category includes both "many more benefits" and "some more benefit" responses. Similarly the "more costs" category contains both "some more costs" and "many more costs" responses.

**Of the 25 respondents some say they are not qualified to answer, or else indicate "don't know" or "no response." These responses are combined in the NR column.

The staff assessment that computerization is most useful to support staff differs from the response in the other organizations where the groups seem to benefit most are the senior administrators and supervisors. The assistance and training given the support staff in learning to use the computer as a word-processor and for the entry and update of budgetary figures probably resulted in the perception of greater use of the technology by support staff than direct service staff and supervisors. This assessment was made despite the limited impact on most organizational administrators reported in Table 8.7. It should also be noted that only 1 staff member thought that there were more costs than benefits from computerization for any occupational group. As in other organizations, a substantial proportion of staff were unwilling or unable to assess the costs and benefits to the different levels of staff. However, when asked to rate the costs and benefits to the organization as a whole, 15 of the 25 respondents see more benefits than costs for the organizations, 8 assess costs and benefits as equal, and one sees more costs than benefits from computerization.

Impact on Clients

Our first question on confidentiality was, "To what degree are you concerned about the possible lack of confidentiality caused by storing client information on the computer?" We find 56 percent (14) of the respondents have some concerns, ranging from a little to a lot, about the possible loss of confidentiality resulting from computerization. We expected direct service staff to be most concerned about this issue. But Table 8.10 shows the direct service staff are less concerned about this issue than either the support or managerial and supervisory staff.

Table 8.10
Level of Concern About Lack of Confidentiality Resulting
from Storing Client Information on the Computer,
by Position of Staff: UYCS

| Position of Staff | Total | Level of Concern | | | |
		A Lot	Some	A Little	None
Total	25	4	7	3	11
Support	4	1	2	—	1
Direct Service	18	3	4	3	8
Management and Supervisory	3	—	1	—	2

This is surprising given that in their training, human service staff professionals are taught that the privacy of the client is inviolate. In this organization the staff involved in entering and retrieving data from the computer are the most concerned about possibilities of breaches in confidentiality. Perhaps if computerization were used more for case management and service to clients, the privacy issue might generate more concern among direct service staff.

The 14 staff voicing concerns about the confidentiality of client information identify five kinds of information that concern them most. These are: personal information which would identify the client (4); psychiatric information, diagnoses, etc. (4); all client information (1); confidential accounting information (1); and all information (1).

The staff were asked whether any kind of client data should not be stored in the computer after a case is closed. Eight of the 25 staff say "yes" and identify the following as information they feel should not be retained: personal information (name, etc.) which would identify clients (4); information relating to clients' problems (4); none, if there is another system of record keeping in use (1).

In view of these concerns about confidentiality and data storage, it is surprising that half (13) of the staff indicate they do not know their organization's policies regarding access to client information stored in the computer (Table 8.11). Of the 11 staff who reportedly know the UYCS policy in this area, ten feel it satisfactorily protects client confidentiality. Thus, as at the other agencies, breaches of confidentiality are seen as a potential or theoretical danger rather than an actual, present problem.

Table 8.11
Assessment of UYCS Policies Regarding Access to
Client Information, by Position

	Total*	Satisfactorily protect client confidentiality	Unsatisfactory as may allow access to unauthorized persons	Respondents do not know organization's policies
Staff	24	10	1	13
Direct Support	4	1	—	3
Management and Service	18	8	1	9
Supervisory	2	1	—	1

*(1 no response)

With respect to the impact on service to clients, 15 respondents report computerization has resulted in no change while six report a positive impact. When asked about the benefits and costs to clients, 11 report equal benefits and costs, four more benefits than costs, and four more costs than benefits. This finding is consistent with the perception that computerization has been most useful for administrative purposes, not service to clients. One staff member observes: "The present computer system is purely an administrative tool that has no effect directly on clinical work. . . . The computer provides no benefit to clients." However, another staff member feels that, although the clients are unaware of the computer, they benefit from it: the computer speeds up the whole system so the client is dealt with faster, and the case worker has more time to deal directly with the client. This latter view of an indirect gain by the clients may be an accurate appraisal of the situation.

Impact on the Organization

Staff assessments of the effects of computerization on records and statistics, with respect to accuracy, timeliness, clarity, comprehensiveness and relevance, are presented in Table 8.12. Accuracy is rated as "good" or "excellent" by most (17) of the 21 respondents answering this question. In only two areas, comprehensiveness and relevance, do fewer than half the respondents assess the computerized records as either "good" or "excellent." In no area does more than one respondent rate the records as "poor." When staff use the same criteria to rate the records and statistics as they existed before computerization, the most commonly chosen rating, for every category, is "fair." The staff sees computerization as having improved the quality of records, raising their overall ratings from "fair/good" to "good/excellent" in all five aspects.

Table 8.12

Staff Assessment of Selected Characteristics of Computerized
Records and Statistics in the Organization: UYCS

Characteristics of Records and Statistics	State of Records and Statistics				
	Excellent	Good	Fair	Poor	Very Poor
1) Accuracy	3	14	4	–	–
2) Timeliness	3	11	6	1	–
3) Clarity	3	12	5	1	–
4) Comprehensiveness	3	8	8	1	1
5) Relevance	3	9	8	1	–

Table 8.13 summarizes the staff's assessments of the impact of computerization on eight organizational activities.

In two areas, case management and supervision, more than half (14) of the respondents report computerization has had no impact. Slightly less than half (12) report no impact on client records. The most positive assessments are for internal statistical reporting and financial management. This is consistent with staff assessments given in the interviews, where a consensus is expressed that computerization has been most useful and productive in accounting and administration.

The staff of UYCS are very positive about the benefits expected to accrue to the organization from computerization. There is no evidence of widespread negative attitudes or resistance to the introduction of computer technology. At the same time the lack of involvement of staff and distancing of themselves from the day-to-day operation would suggest that their answers probably reflected their positive feelings about the potential values of computerization for the organization. This view is supported by the finding that despite the favourable organizational environment for computeri-

Table 8.13
Staff Assessment of the Impact of Computerization
on Selected Organizational Activities: UYCS

| Activity | Assessment of Impact | | | |
	Strongly Positive	Positive	None	Negative
Client records	–	7	12	–
Internal statistical reporting	3	11	–	4
Case management	–	3	14	–
Supervision	–	1	14	–
Program management	–	5	10	–
Financial management	4	11	4	–
External reporting	–	8	7	–
Policy making	–	3	10	–

zation the initial momentum is not maintained and the level of use remains very low. One reason for the current low level of use is the failure of the organization to provide the ongoing operational support and expertise necessary for the organization to move from the most elementary use of the technology.

Immigrant Aid

In Chapter 6, we found that the average factor scores for IA were highly dispersed on both factors, indicating little consensus of opinion. However the average view was that computerization tended to increase both efficiency and control to a marked degree. We now examine the ways that view is connected to actual effects of computerization on the organization.

Impact on Staff

Nineteen of the 25 staff members completing the questionnaire were employed before the organization introduced computers. It is surprising that none of the 19 report they have had to learn new skills as the result of computerization. Of the six who were employed after computerization all reported that they did have to learn new skills, only one thinks this has affected (increased) job security. More than four out of five respondents thinks computerization has not resulted in a change in their job description.

The effects of computerization on discretion and control exercised in the workplace are shown in Table 8.14. Of 21 responding, the majority indicate computerization has either had no impact (13) or has increased the amount of their discretion (7). With respect to the amount of control respondents have over their work, almost all (19 out of 21) think computerization has had no effect (10) or else has increased their control over the work envi-

Table 8.14
Staff Assessment of the Impact of Computerization on Discretion
and Job Control: IA

Discretion and Impact	Staff Discretion	Job Control
A lot more	3	5
More	4	4
None	13	10
Less	—	2
A lot less	—	—
Don't know	1	—
Total	21	21

ronment (9). Only two out of 21 indicate their control has decreased due to computerization.

Only staff members who fill out computer forms were directed to answer the question about paperwork; but all staff members could respond to the question on productivity. While 9 out of 11 respondents think the amount of paperwork associated with computerization has either increased or remained the same, only 1 out of 21 respondents thinks computerization has (moderately) decreased her/his productivity.

Table 8.15
Staff Assessment of the Impact of Computerization
on Paperwork and Productivity: IA

Impact	Paperwork	Productivity
Substantially increased	3	6
Moderately increased	3	4
Remained the same	3	10
Moderately decreased	2	1
Substantially decreased	—	—
Total	11	21

The global assessment of almost one-half of the respondents is that computerization has yielded more benefits than costs for the organization. A minority, 20 percent, report more costs than benefits and 12 percent, equal costs and benefits.

The direct staff are the only group in which a sizable minority (28 percent of the staff) conclude the costs of computerization outweigh the benefits (see Table 8.16). It should be noted that from 32 to 64 percent of the staff did not assess costs and benefits of computerization for the various levels. Staff are particularly reluctant to assess the benefits and costs for accounting and managerial staff. However, those who rate the value of computerization for

Table 8.16
Appraisals of the Costs and Benefits of Computerization
of IA Staff, by Position
(N = 25)

	Total	Benefits/Costs (Percents)			
		More* Benefits	Equal Benefits and Costs	More* Costs	NR**
Direct Service Staff	100	28	12	28	32
Supervisors	100	32	8	4	56
Support Staff	100	24	24	4	48
Accounting and Fiscal Managers	100	28	4	4	64
Executive Director, Department Heads and Managers	100	12	4	4	64

*The "more benefits" category includes both "many more benefits" and "some more benefit" responses. Similarly the "more costs" category contains both "some more costs" and "many more costs" responses.

**Of the 25 respondents some say they are not qualified to answer, or else indicate "don't know" or "no response." These responses are combined in the NR column.

their own group, for the most part regard computerization as beneficial.

Impact on Clients

Table 8.17 shows that 17 of 24 staff feel some concern about the threat to client confidentiality posed by computerization.

Table 8.17
Concern about Lack of Confidentiality
Resulting from Storing Client
Information on the Computer: IA

Level of Concern	No.
A lot	3
Some	9
A little	5
None	7
Total	24

Five out of seven respondents feel that client data of a psychosocial nature should not be retained after a case was closed.

The attitude of the staff of IA towards confidentiality is very similar to that of staffs at other agencies we studied. Only one half of the respondents indicate they are familiar with their organization's present policies regarding access to client information. Of those familiar with the policies, nine say they are satisfactory, while two think them unsatisfactory because they might allow access to outside persons or organizations. Again, confidentiality is a theoretical rather then actual concern.

The findings with respect to client confidentiality support statements made by staff during the interviews. Because 60 percent of the client population at IA are refugees, staff are concerned about the confidentiality of client records. However, one staff member commented during an interview that due to the large number of clients handled (6,000 new cases in one year) there is very little documentation on any given person. Another staff member points out that not much in the files can be identified by an outside person, due to the cross-referencing of names and numbers.

Staff were presented with the following statement on the survey and asked if they thought there was any justification for this fear, given their experience at IA: ''One of the fears expressed about the use of computer technology in human service organizations is that it discourages dealing with the client as an individual.'' Sixteen out of 24 report some justification and three of those 16 considerable justification for this fear.

Impact on Organization

The respondents' assessments of the impact of computerization on selected activities of the organization are summarized in Table 8.18. For every activity, more staff assesses the impact as positive than negative; and for five of the eight activities, there are no negative assessments at all.

The respondents then rated the potential impact on the same activities if the organization were to revert to manual record-keeping. These results, plotted on a better/worse scale, are shown in Table 8.19. The answers slightly favour computerization, as in most instances about half the staff indicate reversion would hinder carrying out these activities. However, a sizable group indicates there would be no change with reversion to the manual record-keeping system. Also, more than 4 out of 5 staff think that reverting to a manual system would result in better service to clients. The assessment of two-thirds of staff that the impact of computerization on ''service to clients'' is positive and yet would supposedly improve if a manual system were reintroduced, is puzzling. Perhaps computers may be more useful than the manual system in providing information; but the old system may have been more useful in supporting counselling activities.

Another reason for apparent inconsistencies in the two assessments may be that from 4 to 32 percent of the staff offer no assessment of the impact of computerization on the various activities.

Table 8.20 presents the respondents' ratings of various facets of records and statistics keeping before and since computer implementation. It seems computerization has improved records and statistics-keeping in three of the

Table 8.18
Staff Assessment of the Impact of Computerization
on Selected Organizational Activities: IA

		Impact		
Activity	Positive*	None	Negative	NR
Client records	21	1	—	1
Internal statistical reporting	19	1	—	2
Case management	11	4	—	6
Supervision	8	5	1	7
Program management	8	5	1	7
Financial management	8	4	1	8
External reporting	13	4	—	4
Policy making	9	6	—	6
Service to clients	15	2	2	3

*The positive category includes both "strongly positive" and "positive" responses.

Table 8.19
Staff Assessment of the Impact on Selected Activities
of the Organization if it Reverted to a Manual
System of Record Keeping: IA

		Impact	
Activity	Better*	None	Worse*
Client records	6	4	11
Internal statistical reporting	7	1	11
Case management	4	6	9
Supervision	4	8	7
Program management	5	5	8
Financial management	3	7	8
External reporting	4	4	10
Policy making	2	6	9
Service to clients	9	4	8

*The better category included both "much better" and "somewhat better" responses. Similarly the worse category is made up of both "somewhat worse" and "much worse" responses.

five areas. With respect to timeliness and comprehensiveness, staff who were employed after computerization were split in their ratings. Three staff assessed the quality of records as excellent in the post-computerization period and a like number assessed it as very poor. A similar situation prevails with respect to comprehensiveness with 2 staff rating it as excellent and 3 as

Table 8.20
Staff Assessing of Record and Statistics Keeping
Pre and Post Computerization: IA

Description	Excellent Pre	Excellent Post	Good Pre	Good Post	Fair Pre	Fair Post	Poor Pre	Poor Post	Very Poor Pre	Very Poor Post	NR Pre	NR Post
Accuracy	—	3	5	6	2	9	2	2	1	—	—	1
Timeliness	—	3	4	8	5	6	—	3	1	3	—	1
Clarity	1	2	3	5	3	10	2	3	1	—	—	1
Comprehensiveness	1	2	3	8	2	6	2	4	2	3	—	1
Relevance	1	2	3	8	4	8	1	2	2	—	1	—

Pre-computer sample, N=11. This group comprises all those respondents who were employed prior to computerization.
Post-computer sample, N=21.

very poor in the post-computerization period. This is not surprising as 28 percent (7) of the staff reported that internal statistical reporting would be better if the organization reverted to a normal system. This view is consistent with the view of the programmer responsible for processing the data. He stated that the validity of the data collected was suspect because the criteria were suspect. More specifically, "do the forms used (to collect data) address the correct questions?" Another observation was that the training of staff with respect to completing forms for collection of data is inadequate.

Data from IA are processed on a mainframe computer off the premises. The data is sent for processing once a month and is returned to the organization a month or 6 weeks late. Staff feels that they often receive the data when it is out of date with limited usefulness. The staff has been attempting, with no success, to get microcomputers which would give the organization more control over the data. Staff dissatisfaction with present arrangements may account for their ambivalence concerning the usefulness and quality of the data.

United Family and Child Services

In Chapter 6, we found that the average factor scores for UFCS were relatively undispersed, indicating a high consensus of opinion. The prevailing opinion was that computerization neither increased efficiency nor control to any marked degree. We now examine how that view is related to actual effects of computerization on the organization.

Impact on Staff

Most respondents (58 percent) did not have to learn new skills when the computer system was implemented. Most of those who have had to learn new skills are support staff, supervisors and managers. However, job security is not seen to have been affected. During interviews we learned that the new skills learned do not relate to operating the computer but rather to completing forms accurately and interpreting computerized information. Had the staff been required to learn operating skills, worries over job security might have been less, especially for support staff, as they would have acquired new skills.

Since the computer system is a management tool (i.e., used to direct agency policy and resources) rather than a direct service tool (i.e., used to make case management decisions), we expected that most respondents would not feel their amount of discretion and control over their jobs had been changed by computerization. We also thought supervisory and management staff would gain more control and possibly more discretion from computerization. In fact, few respondents indicate any change in control and discretion; but those who do indicate changes in discretion and control occupy positions spread throughout the agency. This is probably because management at UFCS uses computer information to assist in decision-making; but computerized data are supplemented by information from staff, clients and others. Information gathered in interviews supports this view. Since decisions made using computerized data are supplemented by up-to-date information gathered from managers, supervisors and direct service staff, managers do not find their control of their work and discretion much changed by computerization.

As at all the other organizations we studied, computerization at the UFCS has meant more paperwork. Two-thirds of the respondents report their paperwork has increased due to computerization, with 18 percent reporting a substantial increase. With respect to overall productivity, more than four out of ten (42 percent) find their level of production has remained the same. Almost one-third (32 percent) of the respondents think their productivity has increased moderately while a few (8 percent) see a moderate decrease. Position was not a statistically significant factor in determining one's view of the change in productivity, but those seeing a moderate decrease are all support and direct service staff. Thus, although the amount of paperwork has increased, the level of productivity has remained the same or only moderately increased. This suggests the computer system has had a positive impact at a higher organizational level than the information inputting stage.

Those reporting a moderate decrease in productivity are all direct service and support staff. Although few in number, this group is responsible for completing computer forms (paperwork). While burdened with more paperwork, direct service and support staff are unable to fully use the computer's output. This finding tends to support the hypothesis made at the end of the previous chapter, that those who bear the costs of computerization are not usually those who reap the benefits.

Using a computer system requires staff to classify clients according to forced-choice categories. Most respondents (61 percent) find forced-choice classification poses a problem for them, but only a slight one. The extent of the problem posed does not appear to vary by staff position but does vary by the level of social work education. Generally, the lower the level of social work education, the more likely one is to find forced-choice classification a serious problem. However, the small number of respondents in this agency does not allow for statistical testing of this generalization.

Two major concerns about forced-choice classification of data are expressed in interviews. The first deals with the difficulty social workers have in "seeing all their work brought down to a couple of pages of computer printouts because social workers are 'human-oriented.'" The second deals with the validity of statistics gathered, given forced-choice classification. Some workers think classifying clients for the computer system interferes with seeing the client as an individual. Because the client is viewed as an individual by social workers, "in some cases, it's hard to find a category that fits." Further, some state that the categories were made by computer specialists rather than social workers and lack a social worker's perspective.

Impact on Clients

Confidentiality is not a major concern at the UFCS. As indicated in Table 8.21, half of the respondents feel no concern whatever about the confidentiality of computer records.

Table 8.21
Level of Concern about Lack of Confidentiality
Resulting from Storing Client Information
on the Computer: UFCS
(N = 38)

Level of Concern	Percent
None	50
A little	18
Some	18
A lot	13

Of those concerned about confidentiality, almost 3 out of 5 (58 percent) think some data — personal identifying information such as social insurance numbers — should not be stored in the computer. However, as at other organizations most respondents (this time more than two-thirds, 68 percent) are unfamiliar with their organization's policies regarding confidentiality. A further 29 percent are satisfied with the confidentiality procedures.

Those interviewed indicate their concerns about confidentiality centre more on the type of information collected than on the security of access. Most think highly personal information (social insurance numbers, case recordings) should not be stored. However, all believe the information stored at UCFS is secure. The computer system is said to be no less secure than the old system, since "anybody can go into a file and get some information." However, it is also said that some information is locked in desks or vaults. Again, no great concern about confidentiality is apparent in this agency.

When asked if there is any justification for the notion that computer use dehumanizes clients, almost nine out of ten (87 percent) respondents say "no." Almost half (45 percent) of the respondents deny computerization has had any impact on service to clients. Another thirty-four (34 percent) think computerization has had a positive impact on service, while only 5 percent report a negative impact.

Impact on the Organization

Respondents evaluate the current computerized records with respect to accuracy, timeliness, clarity, comprehensiveness and relevance. Overall, the records are judged to be in good order, as indicated in Table 8.22. However, timeliness and relevance of the records are rated only fair to poor. When compared with record-keeping before computerization, computerized records are rated more highly except with respect to timeliness and relevance. Not all records are computerized yet and, therefore, the computerized records are less relevant overall than the previous manual records, which were complete. In addition, under the computerized system, staff do not receive printouts of information until as much as one month after an information form has been completed. Under the manual system, information on a given case could be retrieved immediately.

Interview data also indicate dissatisfaction with the timeliness of data. Most direct service and support staff maintain manual files because the printouts they receive are outdated. At the management level, the delay of information is somewhat less; managers also receive information directly from supervisors, other managers and staff.

Computerized records are judged to be generally superior to manual records. The perceived impact of computerization depends upon whether the activity in question is of an administrative or clinical nature. This distinction also applies to perceived organizational costs and benefits. Predominantly administrative tasks are seen to benefit most from computerization, whereas perceptions are split in regard to the usefulness of computerized data for clinical tasks.

Staff assessments of the impact of computerization on various activities are shown in Table 8.23. Generally, the impact is described as positive by

Table 8.22
Ratings of Manual and Computerized Records: UFCS
(N = 38)

	Excellent		Good		Fair		Poor		Very Poor	
	M*	C*	M	C	M	C	M	C	M	C
					(Percents)					
Accuracy	0	11	45	54	35	24	15	5	5	5
Timeliness	0	11	35	27	40	38	20	11	5	14
Clarity	0	11	35	47	45	28	15	11	5	3
Comprehen- siveness	0	20	30	43	45	31	15	14	5	6
Relevance	0	9	35	43	60	17	0	31	5	—

*M = manual; C = computer

more than half of the respondents for 5 of the 8 activities. More specifically, a majority of the staff assessed the impact as positive for client records, internal statistical reporting, policy making, case management, and financial management. Supervision, program management, and external reporting were assessed as positive by between 40 and 44 percent of the respondents.

Table 8.23
Staff Assessment of the Impact of Computerization
on Selected Activities of the Organization: UFCS
(N=38)

Aspect of Functioning	Perceived Impact (Percents)			
	Strongly Positive	Positive	No Impact	Negative
Client records	19	52	7	10
Internal statistical reporting	15	70	9	6
Case management	6	58	33	3
Supervision	0	43	53	3
Program management	—	44	56	—
Financial management	24	40	36	—
External reporting	4	37	58	—
Policy making	—	56	44	—

The activities seen to be most positively affected by computerization tend to involve administrative work. Designed as a tool to assist management in case management and other administrative tasks, the computer system is seen to have had positive effects where intended. The system was not designed to aid clinical case work. Therefore, the fact that respondents assess the impact as less positive for supervision is not unexpected, since it may involve clinical analyses, evaluations and judgements not programmed into the computer system. By contrast, both external reporting and program management are administrative tasks the computer system was designed to do. However, the perceived impact of computerization access on the eight activities is very positive in this organization, ranging from 10 percent for client records to 3 percent for case management and supervision; in only half of the activities was there any assessment that the impact was negative. More than half of the respondents reported no impact on supervision (53 percent), program management (55 percent), and external reporting (58 percent). Less than 10 percent of the respondents think computerization had no impact on client records (7 percent) and internal statistical reporting (9 percent). To summarize, there is a consensus that if the computerization did impact the eight activities, the impact was positive.

Respondents may not view program management as being significantly affected because managers use computerized information only as a supportive tool for this purpose. In managing programs, computerized information is always supplemented with more immediate information (as indicated earlier, the system's records are not viewed as 'timely') from supervisory and direct service staff. Therefore, the effect of computerization on program management would be seen as more limited than the effect on other administrative tasks.

Finally, external reporting is not seen to have been affected by computerization. Respondents' position within the agency does not seem to influence perceived effects of computerization on external reporting. The Ministry of Community and Social Services has never required the amount of statistical detail the agency's computer system provides. Statistics needed for funding reports are easily accessible through the computer system, but an agency does not need to have a computer system in order to complete such reports. Therefore, the agency's computer system may be seen as having no impact on external reporting because it is unnecessary for this task.

Table 8.24
Appraisals of Costs and Benefits, by Position: UFCS
(N = 38)

Position of Staff	Perceived Benefits/Costs (Percents)			
	More Benefits	Equal Costs/Benefits	More Costs	NR
Direct Service	30	8	27	35
Supervision	33	14	5	48
Support Staff	38	17	3	42
Accounting and Fiscal Managers	49	3	3	45
Executive Director, Department Heads and Managers	42	3	3	52

Table 8.24 summarizes the perceived costs and benefits to the organization as a whole, and to various positions within the agency.

Overall, respondents indicate split perceptions about the costs and benefits of computers to the whole organization. However, a more detailed examination of costs and benefits to various positions in UFCS explains this split. Computerization is perceived to be of most benefit in positions carrying out administrative/clerical tasks. Given the use of the computer system as an administrative tool, here, this is not surprising. Interestingly, although supervision is not seen to have been affected by computerization, supervisors are seen as having gained more benefits than costs. While supervision deals with clinical aspects of cases, but also fulfils administrative responsibilities, this explains why supervisors benefit from computerization. Direct service staff are seen to be split between benefits and costs. Some aspects of the direct service worker's job are affected positively by computerization (client records, internal reporting and case management), while the major part of their job, involving clinical work, is unaffected. Given the two aspects of a direct service worker's job, administrative and clinical, the former affected by computerization and the latter not greatly, we can understand why direct service workers have mixed views about the costs and benefits of computerization.

However, as in other organizations a substantial proportion (from 35 to 52 percent) of staff did not make an appraisal for each position.

This organization experienced few problems in introducing computer technology. The computer system, developed by a computer service organization, was introduced as a management system that did not change the content of the existing manual information system. The attitudes of staff were generally positive toward the introduction of computer technology thus there was little overt resistance to computerization. The use of computerization to collect and process administrative and management data did not threaten the clinical aspects of direct service workers and supervisors jobs. In this organization computerization was strongly supported by a senior staff member with knowledge of the potential and limitations of computer technology, particularly for fiscal management.

This organization, unlike some others participating in this research, had adequate continuing funding to implement, maintain and expand computerization.

Summary

As expected, the organizations that are intermediate users of computers prove to be similar in many respects to advanced user agencies. Table 8.25 summarizes the impact of computerization on these four organizations.

Table 8.25

Impact of Computer Technology on Intermediate Users of Computers

	DOCS	UYCS	IA	UFCS
The value of computer technology	net cost	little impact on day-to-day work	net benefit	equal costs and benefits
Most positive towards computerization	accounting and fiscal managers	support staff and managers	supervisors and managers	accounting and fiscal manager
Computerized record-keeping vs. manual system	both systems are bad	computerized system is better	computerized system is better	computerized system is better
Activities most improved	internal statistics and client records	internal statistics and financial management	client records and internal statistics	client records and internal statistics
Activities least improved	policy making and service to clients	supervision, policy making and program management	supervision, program management and financial management	internal statistics and client records
Perceived impact on discretion	majority of staff no change	all staff no change	majority of staff no change	majority of staff no change
Perceived impact on job control	majority of staff no change	majority of staff no change	divided between no change and more control	majority of staff no change
Perceived impact on productivity	divided between no change and increased productivity	divided between no change and increased productivity	divided between no change and increased productivity	divided between no change and increased productivity
Staff assessment of computerized records	good or excellent	good or excellent	fair, good, or excellent	good or excellent

The major differences in the impact of computerization on the organizations are:

1. Staff in the advanced computer use organizations more often perceive computerization as giving them more control over their jobs;

2. Staff in intermediate use organizations more often report that productivity increased following computerization; and

3. Staff in intermediate computer use organizations assessed the accuracy of computerized records more positively than staff in advanced use organizations.

Among the intermediate use organizations, staff of IA are the most positive in their perception of the impact of computerization. However, this organization has made very limited use of computer technology. DOCS is the intermediate user with the least positive staff perceptions of the impact of computerization. This organization has introduced computer technology very recently. Although in both organizations pressure for computerization came from external sources the system at DOCS was more complicated with continuing accountability to the central office.

In the next and final chapter, we attempt to pull together our findings and draw some conclusions about successful and unsuccessful computerization.

Chapter 9

False Alarms: Conclusions and Implications

The literature reviewed earlier indicated a lot of anxiety in the social welfare community about the possible negative impact of computer technology on social welfare organizations and their staff. Many observers predicted that the introduction of computer technology in social welfare organizations is inevitable, but the price may well be dramatic and far-reaching changes that would adversely affect the staff and ultimately the delivery of service. Despite little empirical research to test this prediction of the dire consequences of computerization for these organizations, the predictions have been widely accepted and sometimes used to block or delay computerization.

We have tested many of the predictions in this research. The organizations we studied varied in three dimensions — size, level of computer use, and anticipated outcome of service provided — that the literature suggested would explain different uses of computer technology and reactions to it. Our overall findings are that, in the organizations studied, despite positive and favourable attitudes of staff to computerization the impact has been considerably less than anticipated. Staff response has been mixed, ranging from indifference and inertia to enthusiasm.

In this chapter we will review the anticipated and actual differences among organizations, according to the type of organization (people-processing and people-changing), size, and level of use of computer technology; examine the overall impact of computerization on organizations and staff; and state the implications of our findings for further research and application.

People-Processing and People-Changing Organizations
The literature anticipated that staff in people-changing organizations would, more than staff in people-processing organizations, fear that the introduction of computer technology would replace humanistic with technical concerns. A related fear is that computerization would result in an over-emphasis on the use of empirical data in decision-making about service and programs. Many today hold the view that computer technology will have a negative and

175

destructive impact on professional discretion and autonomy, confidentiality, and the worker-client relationship.

Accordingly, we expected that social work values and ideology would be stronger in people-changing than in people-processing organizations. The former, with a higher proportion of professionally trained staff, would resist computers more and perceive computer use more negatively. On the other hand, we anticipated that staff in people-processing organizations would be concerned, though less so than staff in people-changing organizations, about the impact of computer technology, but agree less about the extent of its negative impact.

Yet staff in the people-changing organizations proved no more likely to report that computerization had affected their exercise of discretion than staff in people-processing organizations. In the latter organizations a substantial minority of staff feel that since computerization they have enjoyed more discretion in decision-making. On the related issue of job control, staff in people-processing organizations more often report that computerization has positively affected their control of their jobs than staff in people-changing organizations. Further, in three of the four people-processing organizations the computer is perceived to be controlling. Staff there also perceive that computerization results in greater efficiency than the staff in people-changing organizations do.

This lack of concern among staff in people-processing organizations about the impact of computer technology on their exercise of discretion in decision-making and on the control of their jobs is not consistent with the literature reviewed earlier. A threat to the professionalism of the social work staff is widely supposed in the computerization literature, and the expected results are loss of discretion and job control, two outcomes that would impact directly on the effectiveness of professional staff. Many observers also fear a threat to the traditional relationship of worker and client, a relationship that rests on the proposition that each case is unique.

The literature is full of predictions that computerization will dehumanize clients, e.g., treat them as numbers rather than individuals. We expected to find more of this concern in the people-changing organizations where computerization should pose the greatest threat to, or infringement on, the worker-client relationship that is the vehicle for delivering service. Accordingly we asked respondents whether they thought the fear that computer technology would discourage dealing with clients as individuals was justified. Staff of the people-changing organizations were much more agreed than staff of the people-processing organizations that the fear was not justified.

This finding does not support the view, commonly expressed in the literature, that a likely result of computerization is the dehumanization and/or depersonalization of clients. Surprisingly, staff of people-changing organizations expressed less concern about effects on the delivery of service based on the needs of individual clients than did staff in people-processing organizations.

Staff in the people-processing organizations on the other hand were more concerned about the risk of unauthorized access to records than the staff in people-changing organizations. This is consistent with their justified perception that computer technology will result in greater control. Given the literature's extensive discussion of the importance of protecting client records against unauthorized access in a computerized system, the lack of concern about, or interest in, this issue among staff in both types of organization is unexpected.

In three of the four people-changing organizations we studied, staff felt that computerization increases neither efficiency nor control. In the four people-processing organizations, we found no consensus on these issues. A claim made consistently in proponents' literature is that computerization will result in more efficient operation. The assessments of staff in people-processing organizations provide some support for this claim, but there is very little support for it in people-changing organizations. With the limited use made of computer technology by staff in the latter type of organizations to assist them in delivering services, their perception of little or no impact on efficiency is probably based in reality.

In conclusion, when the two types of organizations are compared with respect to the impact of computer technology on discretion, control, confidentiality and the individuality of clients, staff in the people-processing organizations show more concern than staff in people-changing organizations. The majority of staff in people-changing organizations, and a substantial minority of those in people-processing organizations studied do not find computerization a threat to their discretion, autonomy, or relations with clients. The predictions made in these areas have not been borne out by our study.

Our findings suggest the literature has overestimated the strength and pervasiveness of the value base and ideology of social work among the staff of social welfare organizations. Staff appear pragmatic in their response to computerization. Their perceptions and assessments are based on ''what is,'' since they have not yet had to face what ''might be'' considered challenges or threats to their pattern of work or the values underlying it.

Size of Organizations

Size was a second variable used to select organizations in this research. The literature anticipated that large organizations would have more difficulty than small ones in implementing a computerized system. This difficulty was expected to result from hierarchical and bureaucratic features of large organizations that tend to resist change. In large organizations staff relationships are characterized by specialization, well-established lines of authority, and decentralization, all of which may be challenged by the introduction of computer technology. Consequently, implementation of computer technology in most large organizations should be more difficult and time consuming than in small organizations. On the other hand, large organizations typically have more resources and often use a management-oriented computer system for accounting and processing client data, thus achieving greater economies of scale.

Resources made available to implement computerization in both the large and small organizations we studied were primarily used to purchase hardware and/or software. Little money was left over to train staff or hire additional technicians to operate the computer. In the large organizations we studied senior management were committed to computerization, but only one of these made provisions to monitor the use of computer technology continuously. Computer use was evenly divided between service and housekeeping data, at least in the beginning.

The four smaller organizations reported that a lack of resources led to problems in implementing computerization. All experienced problems with software. Three hired temporary programmers on contract to develop their programs; however, these experts were rarely or never available to deal with problems as they arose. Staff and management offered more support for computerization in these organizations than in the larger organizations; but the lack of an implementation plan and insufficient resources restricted the uses made of the computer. In two of the small organizations, computer use patterns went unchanged for nearly three years after computers were introduced.

We found that staff was less supportive of computerization in large organizations using mainframe computers than in small organizations with microcomputers. Though large organizations have more resources for implementation, the resources have not been used to staff the computer operation. Size did not prove to influence the way computer technology was used; in all organizations, data on clients and data for the internal statistical system were computerized first. Further, size is not an important variable in predicting staff perceptions of efficiency and control. Perceptions of computer efficiency and control vary indistinguishably among staff in the large and small organizations.

Our evidence does not support the proposition that staff in large social welfare organizations are more resistant to implementing computer use than staff in small organizations. Nor is there evidence that the complexity of large organizations creates a less favourable environment for the introduction of computer technology. The lack of resources for implementation was a greater problem for the small organizations we studied but, despite this, large and small organizations differed very little in their levels of use of computer technology. However, in two areas we did find minor differences between the small and the large organizations. First, staff support for the introduction of computer technology was greater in smaller organizations. Second, large organizations made greater use of mainframe computers and in-house programmers. But neither of these differences resulted in distinctive patterns of use or distinctive views about efficiency and control.

Although we found little overt staff resistance to computerization in either large or small organizations some staff, particularly direct service staff, avoided using the computer outputs, or continued to work in their usual way as if the system were not in place. Trute, Tonn and Ford (n.d., p. 7) found a similar response in their research on computerization in Health Centres: "These staff (direct caregivers) may insure that the form of a new system is carried out, in order to appease higher level management, but may also basically ignore its content." Bronson reported that the results after research were inconclusive with respect to the "relationship between the costs and benefits of computerization and reported satisfaction with the system for client service workers" (Bronson, 1986, p. 79).

Level of Use

Chapter 8 noted that the impact of computer technology on organizations classified as intermediate or advanced users was very similar. In each group, one organization's staff responded unfavourably. In each group, direct service staff were little involved in planning for the introduction of computers or assessing their use.

Though generally positive, staff in each group felt that changes were needed in their computer system. The changes most often mentioned by staff in both types of organizations were: increased uses of the data; improved quality (accuracy and completeness) of the data; and improved access to data through computer terminals.

Direct service staff in both types of organization deny they have benefited very much from computerization. This reaction is slightly stronger in the organizations that are intermediate computer users, where the direct service staff have been put under less obligation to use the system. In both types of organizations, staff are favourably inclined towards computer technology but few appear to have any interest or investment in insuring that it succeeds.

Whatever the level of use, advanced or intermediate, staff without administrative or managerial responsibilities regard the technology as just another management tool; they support it so long as it does not impinge on their day-to-day work. Indeed, it may be as Glastonbury (1985, p. 8) reports, that most staff first deal with computers when providing information to management; they do not expect to benefit themselves. Through avoidance, staff reach an accommodation with the system; this accommodation meets their own needs but contributes to under-utilization of the technology. Management may permit this situation to continue because they too see the usefulness of computer technology as limited to administrative and managerial matters; or they are unwilling to introduce changes that they think will be unacceptable to direct service staff.

Impact on Organizations and Staff

One result of computerization anticipated in the literature is an increase in social control resulting from a shift in the distribution of power and its impact on decision-making. Since it is used primarily for administrative purposes, computer technology gives management quick and continuing access to information useful in monitoring work performance. Such use of computer technology gives supervisors and managers more control over staff and, indirectly, over clients. However, in none of the organizations we studied are the administrative data that have been computerized more complete than data already available through the manual system.

The majority of staff in supervisory and managerial positions report that computerization has affected supervsion positively. By contrast, a majority of support and direct service staff feel that computerization has had little or no impact on supervision. There is no evidence of a change in the traditional supervisory practice in the organizations studied; yet computerization has increased management's potential to monitor worker performance continuously. It is this potential which increases their control over all staff below the management level.

More than half of the managers and 40 percent of supervisors reported that, with computerization, they have more control over their work. On the other hand, fewer than half of the direct service and support staff report a change in the control over their jobs due to computerization. Our findings suggest that some supervisory and managerial staff use computerized data to monitor staff performance; but such use is uneven and it is not perceived as a threat by most junior staff.

In the organizations we studied, computerization has neither resulted in a centralization of power nor in major structural changes to accommodate the new technology. However, given the emphasis on the use of the computer for administrative purposes, management will probably make greater use of computerized data to control staff and the delivery of service as the systems continue in place for a longer time. Organizations introduced computers believing that they would provide greater efficiency. We found no evidence that the promise of greater efficiency has been realized in any of the eight organizations we studied. Staff in six of the eight organizations expressed this view in responses to the attitude scale and in stating that productivity, the quality of data available from the computerized system, and the delivery of service to clients had all gone unchanged by computerization.

Although staff perceptions of the accuracy of data vary considerably from one organization to another, almost half of all respondents rated the accuracy of the computerized records as fair or poor. In fact, more than half of all supervisors, support staff and direct service staff felt that the organizations' statistics were less accurate after computerization than before. Direct service and support staff, who are responsible for virtually all of the input to the system, perceive the accuracy of the records more positively than supervisory or managerial staff, who make the most use of the data. One explanation may be the former group's lack of understanding of, and investment in, the information system. Senior staff would naturally be much more disturbed by unresolved questions about the accuracy of the data; yet uncertainty about accuracy may explain why so few managers report that they use the data to monitor or assess the performance of staff.

Despite their unease about the accuracy of the data, few staff members are prepared to recommend a return to the manual system. More than half recommended improving the system by improving the accuracy and completeness of the data. One of the factor probably contributing to the perception of problems with the accuracy of the data is the shortage (in most organizations) of staff who can deal with software problems as they arise. Competent staff were available in only two of the four large organizations, both advanced users of computer technology. Other factors may be the failure to reduce errors before the system was implemented and difficulties encountered in setting up computer systems, trying to make them accurate, and debugging the software.

In none of the organizations studied did a majority of respondents think that computer technology had helped to improve the delivery of service to clients. This is not surprising, since these organizations had as their primary, usually unstated, goal improving the accessibility and use of records for administrative purposes. Managers may envision that the system will eventually expand to provide data for use by the direct service staff. As yet there has been little or no movement in this direction, though most of these organizations have been using computer technology for several years. In fact, all of these organizations had continued to maintain both manual and computerized files. Glastonbury (1985, p. 107) points out that while this duplication involves extra work, it is the "price of having tailor-made systems for both managers and practitioners."

Thus, the organizational impact of computerization has been less than expected, for several reasons. Most of these organizations have computerized without clear goals. They did not know what to expect and had not clearly identified potential users and their needs. They had not involved staff in planning or implementing the new system. Senior staff often failed to give leadership and on-going direction to the implementation. There were few rewards, either external or internal, for extending the use of computer technology: some external pressure to introduce computer technology, perhaps, but no pressure to develop a wide range of uses. Organizations were unwilling to use the technology in ways that could be perceived as changing established procedures, staff relationships, or organizational structure. This unwillingness is reflected in the staff's lack of concern that computerization would eliminate jobs, deskill jobs, or realign responsibilities. Finally, these organizations have not transferred resources away from direct client service to aid computerization; nor is there evidence that they have campaigned vigorously for additional funds to extend the use of computer technology.

Most staff who participated in our research are favourably inclined towards using computer technology in their organization. Managers express the most favourable attitudes and direct service staff, the least favourable. Positive, favourable attitudes persist despite unresolved problems surfacing with the implementation of computers that might be expected to dampen the staff's enthusiasm. To reiterate, the following problems and issues mentioned most frequently by staff are: (1) A lack of confidence in the accuracy of computer generated data; (2) The failure of computerization to increase productivity; (3) The increase in paperwork associated with the computerization; (4) Additional costs of computerization to the organization; and (5) Limited participation of direct service and support staff in planning for and implementing computerization.

At first blush the response of staff to computerization would appear inconsistent with what is really happening in the organization. Staff are favourable to a technology they characterize as costly, inaccurate, unproductive, bothersome, and imposed from above. This contradiction suggests that people do not see things for what they are, but rather for what they want, or need, to see, given their values, emotions and past experience. In this case staff perceptions reflect a widely held view that computerization will benefit the organization through improved efficiency, though it hasn't yet. Holbrook's observation on this point validly accounts for the perceptions of staff:

Computer information is no more reliable than the humans who make the decisions and operate the machines, but the imposition of new technology seems to have given new value to computerized information. Computers reinforce the perception of reality shared by those on the front line and at the top of social service organizations. Imbued with the naive faith of millions of Americans in the accuracy of records, the inevitability of progress, and the inherent benefits of technology, there seems to be little opposition (Holbrook, 1986, p. 106).

A related factor is more rooted in reality: the introduction of computer technology has not (yet) disturbed or seriously challenged established patterns of work, staff relationships, or formal and informal structures within the organizations.

One explanation of this is offered by Glastonbury (1986, p. 11), who observed that social service departments have "shuffled rather slowly into computing over the last decade," and this pace has allayed many of the fears of staff. Lacking a clear and present threat to their status, job security or power in the organization, staff can afford to overlook or minimize the negative effects of computerization. The computer is a toothless enemy, at least so far.

To conclude, fears about the harmful impacts of computerization have thus far proved groundless: mere false alarms. True, the potential for "dangerous" uses is there, and what commentators in the literature have most worried about may yet come to pass. But for the time being, computer use is limited and easily avoided within the organizations we studied. The computer has had little impact, either positive or negative. For most, it is a gadget, a new toy that adorns the organization without hurting or helping. The motivation to make it more than that is, apparently, lacking at all levels of the organization.

Whether the computer, swallowed whole like a stone, will pass through the system leaving it unchanged or instead disrupt its functioning in serious ways, remains to be seen.

Implications

Our sample was selected to test theories about particular kinds of organizations. Since agencies were not selected to represent all social welfare organizations, we cannot claim that our findings describe the general state of affairs in social welfare. However, the agencies we chose were intended to represent particular kinds of organizations, and in this respect our findings are generalizable to other, similar organizations. There is no reason to think our findings are in any way biased, one-sided or inappropriate to the theories tested.

What, then, are the implications of our findings for other organizations of similar size, function and computer complexity? First, our research has raised some doubts that much can be learned about organizations merely by analysing staff attitudes towards computerization. We have seen that a great many respondents maintained general attitudes towards computers and computerization that bore little relation to computer experiences in their own organization.

Because we had obtained data by direct observation as well as attitudinal data, we could see where the two types of evidence converged and diverged. Research relying on attitudinal data alone might easily fall into the trap of thinking that these adequately described the effects of computerization on an organization. They described a psychic reality, perhaps, but not the daily experience or reaction to computers on the job.

Subjective measures also tend to obscure the organizational processes leading to computer adoption and implementation. Subjective realities are not lesser realities, since what people believe to be true will, in many cases, become true as "self-fulfilling prophecies." But things that people say and feel about computers tend to reflect values and ideologies, hopes and fears, that bear a distant and (at this point, at least) somewhat mysterious relationship to what computers are actually doing in the organization.

Whether a similar problem arises in all organizations, or only in social welfare organizations — which tend to greater innocence about numbers, technology and accountability — can only be determined by a comparative study of welfare and other organizations. We have not been able to make this comparison here. Many contend in the literature that welfare organizations are unique and their reactions to computerization will be qualitatively or quantitatively different. This is an intereting conjecture but not one that has so far been validated.

Future research comparing human service and commercial organizations will be very useful, then. Comparative research will provide an empirical test of the hypothesis that the problems encountered by social welfare organizations in implementing computer technology are different from those encountered in business organizations. There are good reasons for expecting this is so, chief among them the different types of people who are recruited for social service and business work, and the different kinds of education each receives. But our findings add little to this debate and, if anything, point in the other direction.

Our findings are also inconclusive about the effects of computerization on social control over clients and staff; this is another area where further research is needed. We saw no evidence that computerization had changed control patterns in significant ways, though in one or two organizations control may have tightened somewhat. But what we saw was far from the drastic fears of totalitarian management hinted at in the social welfare literature.

To say that we didn't see it, is not to prove that it didn't happen, although we did look very carefully for signs. Moreover, to say it hasn't happened yet is not to prove that it cannot ever happen. Perhaps people's worst fears will be realized in due course. Doubtless, changes in social control through computerization need to be watched for carefully, both by researchers and by citizens. These issues will become even more important as management extends its use of computer data in new and innovative ways.

Further research is needed on the ways computerization affects the quality of data in an information system, and overall organizational productivity. We had to base our assessments of these on staff perceptions, and staff perceptions about computerization's effects varied considerably both between and within organizations. We can feel more certain that assessments of the computer reflected social, organizational and perhaps even psychological characteristics of the respondent than that they reported realistically.

There was less variation in staff assessments of the impact of computers on productivity and here the majority perceived no impact whatever. This perception, however valid or invalid, has allowed some staff to rationalize avoiding the use of computer technology and computerized data. It is important for researchers, and managers, to get independent believable assessments of the quality of computerized data and changes in productivity, in order to determine the true extent of their data and productivity problem. We were not allowed a close, first-hand look at either, probably for good reason.

The literature led us to expect that the demands by government and private funding bodies for greater accountability would compel social welfare organizations to computerize. Yet we found that such external pressure was only a minor influence in the decision organizations made to computerize. This fact further supports our view that the differential use of computers in social welfare organizations must be explained by the dynamics of the organization itself. Computerization is an internally generated initiative, typically. Its successes and failures are also, typically, ascribable to intra-organizational strengths and weaknesses. Exploring these further should be a priority in future research.

What we learned in this research holds implications for all organizations planning to implement computer technology, as well as for organizations that have already computerized. We have identified three important such implications having to do with:

1. planning and staff involvement,
2. resource allocation, and
3. resistance to computerization.

These conclusions are not entirely novel: they can be found in the literature already. But given the large amount of published writing we found to be simply erroneous or ill-conceived, we may be forgiven for affirming what we have found in the literature to be valid.

First, one cannot overestimate the importance of planning. Despite some awareness of its importance, organizations often fail to make an implementation plan before computers are introduced. Making such a plan provides an opportunity to realistically appraise what staff can expect from the technology. It identifies specific long-term and short-term goals and potential benefits for staff and clients. If nothing else, this planning process forces the organization to think more clearly about what it is doing generally, and by what means.

Beyond that, the planning process provides a forum for intra-organizational communication that may enhance organizational functioning whether computers are, ultimately, introduced or not. Administrators who fail to involve staff in planning for the introduction of computers do so at great risk of failure. At best, they will generate indifference, avoidance and resentment. At worst, they may create stolid opposition and subterfuge.

Often administrators feel that staff shortages prevent involving the staff in such planning, as involvement would reduce the delivery of service to clients. Administrators holding this view should postpone introducing computer technology until they have been able to hire enough additional staff so that cooperative planning is feasible.

Second, many of the problems organizations experience when computerizing are due to a failure to allocate enough financial and human resources to train staff, continue to monitor and upgrade the system, and generally evaluate its performance. Many problems that arise reflect the failure to ensure that expert staff or consultants would work with and learn from the potential users of the computer output. Administrators and board members too often fail to sustain their interest in the technology after purchasing the hardware. As problem after problem arises, they prove unwilling to commit the resources needed to continue upgrading the staff and system.

This fact also underscores the importance of a long-range plan at the time of adoption. Often the hardware proves the least expensive part of the implementation, the thin edge of the wedge. Software acquisition, staff training, expert consultation, and managerial time spent in thinking (and rethinking) about computerizable processes are far costlier. No organization should begin computerization without having realistically assessed whether and how it can meet all of the costs that will predictably (and unpredictably) arise.

Third, covert staff resistance to computerization — apparently more common than overt resistance — is not necessarily to be preferred. Staff avoidance of computer generated data, and general non-involvement, are forms of covert resistance that are difficult to detect and therefore more difficult to remedy than overt resistance. There is also the chance that hidden opposition will explode unexpectedly if and when computers are used for monitoring staff performance or ensuring accountability.

It is probably safest for a manager implementing computerization to assume that covert resistance will occur unless prevented and will continue until remedied. The way to prevent it is through cooperative planning and full and open discussion of the consequences of the new technology for every aspect of work. Assume that what is not discussed openly will be discussed secretly or, at least, feared in private. Probably prevention is better than remedy and may be the sane course to take: namely, open discussion and a genuine willingness to accept input from all levels of staff.

Initial uses of computers for management and administration tend to let direct service staff imagine that computer technology has little value for their day-to-day work. Once computers are identified as no more than management tools, staff will show little interest in looking for and undertaking other, more creative uses. Organizations should simultaneously implement technology that will meet some information needs of all levels of staff.

Like all technology, the computer and its uses must be understood in its human context. This means that the fears and fantasies people have about comptuers are just as real in their consequences as silicon chips and management memos. Since the technology cannot use itself, we now need to better understand the organizational mechanisms that make computers useful or useless, objects of fear and avoidance or tools for serving clients better. We have made a small start in that direction.

APPENDIX

This questionnaire is being administered as part of a larger study on the use of computers in human service organizations. The first part asks for your opinions about computers. The second part asks some questions about your experience with computers at your place of work. In order to analyse these responses we need some personal information. This is collected in the third part of the questionnaire. Your responses to all the questions will be kept confidential, and the questionnaire will be seen only by the researchers.

189

A. <u>OPINIONS ABOUT COMPUTERS</u>: Here are a number of statements about computers. We would like to get <u>your opinions</u> about these statements. Please respond to each one; there are no right or wrong answers. Using the following code, <u>please circle the</u> <u>number</u> to the right of each statement that indicates the extent to which you agree or disagree with it.

1 STRONGLY AGREE   2 AGREE   3 DISAGREE   4 STRONGLY DISAGREE

(Please circle)

A1. Computerization results in more rational
     decision making within an organization.   1   2   3   4

A2. Computerization in human service organ-
     izations reduces the amount of discretion
     exercised by staff working with clients.   1   2   3   4

A3. Computerization results in improved
     delivery of service to clients.   1   2   3   4

A4. Computerization upsets good relations
     between managers and workers.   1   2   3   4

A5. People place more value on conclusions
     arrived at by computer analysis than by
     human evaluations.   1   2   3   4

A6. Computerization fosters the sharing of
     information in an organization.   1   2   3   4

A7. Computer use forces client data into
     artificial categories.   1   2   3   4

A8. A well organized computer system improves
     the overall efficiency of an organization.   1   2   3   4

A9. Computerization decreases the flow of infor-
     mal communication within an organization.   1   2   3   4

A10. Computerization poses a threat to the
     autonomy of staff working with clients
     in a human service organization.   1   2   3   4

A11. Computers are the best means of distrib-
     uting information in an organization.   1   2   3   4

A12. Computerization will not improve the
     quality of service provided by an
     organization.   1   2   3   4

A13. Computerization helps to clarify the tasks
     and the responsibilities of staff.   1   2   3   4

A14. Computerization reduces the amount of
     social interaction on the job.   1   2   3   4

A15. Computerization dehumanizes the clients by
     treating them as numbers.   1   2   3   4

A16. Computerization will result in more
     co-operation between organizations
     providing similar services.   1   2   3   4

A17. Computer technology threatens the privacy
     of clients.   1   2   3   4

A18. Computerization will result in more co-
     ordination of services in an organization.   1   2   3   4

B. <u>COMPUTER USE IN YOUR ORGANIZATION.</u>

B1. Which of the following best describes your main activity in this organization? (Please check only <u>one</u>.)
    a) support staff   ____
    b) provision of service to clients   ____
    c) supervision of staff providing service
       to clients   ____
    d) manager or department head   ____
    e) branch, agency director   ____
    f) other (please specify) _____

B2. How long have you worked in this organization?
    years ____ months ____

B3. How long have you worked in your current position?
    same as (B2) above ____
    if different from B2; years ____ months ____

B4. Was computerization implemented before you joined this organization? yes ____ no ____

B5. Have you had to learn new skills due to computerization in this organization?
    yes ____ no ____

If yes, how has learning these new skills affected your job security?
    increased security ____
    no effect ____
    decreased security ____

B6. Has computerization in this organization changed the job description of the position you now occupy? yes ____ no ____

If yes, how?_____
_____
_____

B7. In your view, how has <u>computerization</u> of this organization affected the following:

a) the amount of discretion your job allows you to exercise in making decisions
    a lot more ____
    more ____
    none ____
    less ____
    a lot less ____

b) the amount of control you have over your work
    a lot more ____
    more ____
    none ____
    less ____
    a lot less ____

B8. In general, to what degree do you approve of the following? (Please respond to <u>each</u> item with a check.)

	Strongly approve	Approve	Disapprove	Strongly disapprove
a) current use of computers by this organization	____	____	____	____
b) planned use of computers by this organization	____	____	____	____

B9. How do you regard the present state of computerized records and statistics in this organization? (Please respond to <u>each</u> item with a check.)

	Excellent	Good	Fair	Poor	Very poor
a) accuracy	___	___	___	___	___
b) timeliness	___	___	___	___	___
c) clarity	___	___	___	___	___
d) comprehensiveness	___	___	___	___	___
e) relevance	___	___	___	___	___

B10. Were you employed here prior to computerization?

yes ____   no ____   (If <u>no</u>, please proceed to Question B13.)

B11. How did you regard the state of records and statistics prior to the introduction of the computer system? (Please respond to <u>each</u> item with a check.)

	Excellent	Good	Fair	Poor	Very poor
a) accuracy	___	___	___	___	___
b) timeliness	___	___	___	___	___
c) clarity	___	___	___	___	___
d) comprehensiveness	___	___	___	___	___
e) relevance	___	___	___	___	___

B12. Were you consulted about the introduction of the computer?
     yes ____   no ____

     If no, do you think you should have been consulted?
     yes ____   no ____

B13. Have you been consulted about the kinds of computer programmes now being used?
     yes ____   no ____

     If no, do you think you should have been consulted?
     yes ____   no ____

B14. Have you been consulted about the types of computer reports now being generated?
     yes ____   no ____

     If no, do you think you should have been consulted?
     yes ____   no ____

B15. Do you complete forms for the computerized system as part
of your job?
yes _____ no _____ (If <u>no</u>, please proceed to Question B16.)

If yes, please answer the following:
a) How often do you fill in these forms? (Check the most
appropriate response.)
   i) daily
  ii) weekly _____
 iii) monthly _____
  iv) quarterly _____
   v) other (specify) _____

b) What types of computer information forms do you complete?
(Check as many as apply)
   i) accounting forms
  ii) time management forms (log of daily
     activities) _____
 iii) case management forms (i.e. case recordings) _____
  iv) client profiles (i.e. age, sex, place of
               residence) _____
   v) other (specify) _____

c) Computerization requires forced choice classification of
data. To what degree, if any, does this present a
problem in coding data?
   i) serious problem _____
  ii) slight problem _____
 iii) no problem _____

d) Since you joined the staff, how has computerization changed
the amount of 'paperwork' you are required to complete?
   i) substantially increased _____
  ii) moderately increased _____
 iii) remained the same _____
  iv) moderately decreased _____
   v) substantially decreased _____

B16. Do you enter or retrieve (call up) data from the computer?
yes _____ no _____ (If <u>no</u>, please proceed to Question B17.)

If yes, please answer the following:

a) How frequently do you enter or retrieve data?

	Daily	Weekly	Monthly	Not Applicable
i) enter data	_____	_____	_____	_____
ii) retrieve data	_____	_____	_____	_____

b) How long have you been entering or retrieving data?
years _____ months _____

c) If you were here prior to computerization, how do
you think the present system compares to the previous
method of record keeping?

	Much easier	Remained the same	Much more difficult	Not Applicable
i) data entry	_____	_____	_____	_____
ii) data retrieval	_____	_____	_____	_____

B17. Do you use computer generated output for any purposes?
         yes ____   no _____   (If <u>no</u>, please proceed to Question B18.)

If yes, how often do you use computer generated output to
<u>assist</u> in any of the following activities? (Please
check appropriate column for <u>each</u> item.)

		Usually	Sometimes	Never	Not Applicable
a)	to budget and manage resources	____	____	____	____
b)	to monitor client service data	____	____	____	____
c)	to develop new services/ programmes	____	____	____	____
d)	to revise existing services/ programmes	____	____	____	____
e)	to refer clients to other departments or agencies	____	____	____	____
f)	to monitor staff performance	____	____	____	____
g)	to conduct research	____	____	____	____
h)	to formulate policy	____	____	____	____
i)	to determine eligibility for agency service	____	____	____	____
j)	to determine amount of financial assistance	____	____	____	____
k)	other - specify	_____			

B18. Are you making more use of the computer system today than
when you first started using it in this organization?
         yes ____   no ____

If yes, to what do you attribute the change? (Please check as
many as apply.)

          i)   job requirement   ____
         ii)   experience in using computers   ____
        iii)   system is easier to use   ____
         iv)   faster response time   ____
          v)   wider range of applications   ____
         vi)   formal training   ____
        vii)   other (please specify)   _____

B19. Which of the following most closely describes the impact of
the computer on your productivity at work?
         a)   substantially increased   ____
         b)   moderately increased   ____
         c)   remained the same   ____
         d)   moderately decreased   ____
         e)   substantially decreased   ____

B20. In your view, what has been the impact of computerization on
     each of the following aspects of the organization? (Please
     respond to each item with a check.)

	Strongly positive	Positive	None	Negative	Strongly negative	Does not apply
a) client records	___	___	___	___	___	___
b) internal statistical reporting	___	___	___	___	___	___
c) case management	___	___	___	___	___	___
d) supervision	___	___	___	___	___	___
e) program management	___	___	___	___	___	___
f) financial management	___	___	___	___	___	___
g) external reporting	___	___	___	___	___	___
h) policy making	___	___	___	___	___	___
i) service to clients	___	___	___	___	___	___

B21. a) To what degree are you concerned about the possible lack of
     confidentiality caused by storing client information on the
     computer?
                a lot   ___
                some   ___
                a little ___
                none   ___

     b) If you are concerned about the kinds of information stored on
     computer, which kinds concern you the most?_____
     _____
     _____
     _____

B22. Is there any kind of client data which should not be
     stored in the computer after the case is closed?
            yes ___   no ___
     If yes, please specify _____
     _____
     _____
     _____

B23. What is your opinion on this organization's policies
     regarding access to client information that is stored in
     the computer? (Please check only <u>one</u> statement.)

     a) Present policies controlling access to information
        on clients satisfactorily protect client confidentiality.   ____

     b) Present policies for security of client data stored in
        the computer are unsatisfactory as they may allow access
        to persons or organizations outside our organization.   ____

     c) I am not familiar with the present policies regarding
        access to client information.   ____

B24. In your opinion, if this organization were to revert to a
     manual record-keeping system, in what ways would the following
     change? (Please respond to <u>each</u> item with a check.)

	Much better	Somewhat better	No change	Somewhat worse	Much worse
a) client records	____	____	____	____	____
b) internal statis- tical reporting	____	____	____	____	____
c) case management	____	____	____	____	____
d) supervision	____	____	____	____	____
e) programme management	____	____	____	____	____
f) financial management	____	____	____	____	____
g) external reporting	____	____	____	____	____
h) policy making	____	____	____	____	____
i) service to clients	____	____	____	____	____

B25. One of the fears expressed about the use of computer technology
     in human service organizations is that it discourages dealing
     with the client as an individual. On the basis of your experience
     with this organization, do you think there is any justification
     for this fear? (Please check only <u>one</u> answer.)

     Considerable   Some   No
     justification ____   justification ____   justification ____

B26. Which of the following best describes your <u>present attitude</u>
     toward the use of computers in this organisation?
                  very positive   ____
                  positive   ____
                  negative   ____
                  very negative   ____

B27. Which of the following best describes your <u>attitude</u> toward the
     use of computers in this organization <u>when you first started</u>
     using them here?
          very positive   ____
          somewhat positive   ____
          somewhat negative   ____
          very negative   ____

B28. From your perspective, has computerization brought about more
     benefits or more costs in terms of time and effort in this
     organization? (Please check only <u>one</u> response.)

Many more benefits than costs	Some more benefits than costs	Equal benefits and costs	Some more costs than benefits	Many more costs than benefits
____	____	____	____	____

B29. From your perspective, how do the benefits/costs of computerization
     vary for each of the following groups within this organization?
     (Please respond to <u>each</u> item with a check.)

	Many more benefits than costs	Some more benefits than costs	Equal benefits and costs	Some more costs than benefits	Many more costs than benefits	Not qual- ified to answer

a) Direct
   service
   staff
	____	____	____	____	____	____

b) Super- visors	____	____	____	____	____	____
c) Support Staff	____	____	____	____	____	____

d) Account-
   ing and
   Fiscal
   Managers
	____	____	____	____	____	____

e) Execut-
   ive
   Director,
   Department
   Heads and
   Managers
	____	____	____	____	____	____

f) Clients	____	____	____	____	____	____
g) Board of Directors	____	____	____	____	____	____

C. PERSONAL CHARACTERISTICS

C1. Male _____   Female _____

C2. Please check the age group to which you belong:
          under 20 years   _____   40 to 44 years   _____
          20 to 24 years   _____   45 to 49 years   _____
          25 to 29 years   _____   50 to 54 years   _____
          30 to 34 years   _____   55 to 59 years   _____
          35 to 39 years   _____   60 years and over _____

C3. Which of the following describes your highest level of
education? (Please check only one.)
        a) some high school   _____
        b) high school graduate   _____
        c) some community college   _____
        d) community college graduate   _____
        e) some university   _____
        f) undergraduate degree   _____
        g) some graduate study   _____
        h) graduate degree   _____
        i) other (specify)   _____

C4. Do you have professional qualifications in an area other
than social work? yes _____   no _____

If yes, please specify _____

C5. If you have professional qualifications in social work, please
indicate your highest level of social work education. (Please
check only one.)
        community college diploma   _____
        undergraduate degree (B.S.W.)   _____
        graduate degree (M.S.W. or M.A.-Social Policy) _____
        postgraduate degree (D.S.W./Ph.D)   _____
        other (specify) _____
        does not apply   _____

C6. Do you belong to one or more professional associations?
        yes _____   no _____

If yes, please list them _____
_____

C7. Have you used computers outside of or prior to this job?
        yes _____   no _____

If yes, how long have you been using computers?
        years _____   months _____

C8. Do you own and use a home computer? yes _____   no _____

C9. Have you had training in the use of computers outside of or
prior to this job?
        yes _____   no _____

C10. If you were setting out to improve this organization's computer
     system, what changes would you make? (Check as many as apply.)
     a) increase the amount of data collected   ____
     b) reduce the amount of data collected   ____
     c) collect different types of data   ____
     d) improve data quality (accuracy, completeness) ____
     e) improve access to computer terminals   ____
     f) improve the response time for data processing ____
     g) expand the uses to which data is put   ____
     h) increase the number of reports printed   ____
     i) reduce the number of reports printed   ____
     j) automate functions now performed manually   ____
     k) other, specify _____

C11. Do you have any comments on the use of computers in human
     service organizations that have not been covered in this
     questionnaire?
     Please specify _____
     _____
     _____
     _____
     _____

C12. Do you have any other comments about this questionnaire? Please
     specify _____
     _____
     _____
     _____

     Thank you very much for your participation in this study.

BIBLIOGRAPHY

Abels, P. (1972). "Can Computers Do Social Work?" *Social Work* 17:5, 5-11.

Abels, S.L., Abels, P. and Richmond, S.A. (1974). "Ethics Shock: Technology, Life Styles and Future Practice." *Journal of Sociology and Social Welfare* 2:2, 140-54.

Ackoff, Russel L. (1967). "Management Misinformation Systems." *Management Science* 14:4, B147-56.

Adler, Michael and du Feu, David (1977). "Technical Solutions to Social Problems: Some Implications of a Computer-Based Welfare Benefits Information System." *Journal of Social Policy* 6:4, 431-47.

Anthony, Robert (1965). *Planning and Control Systems: A Framework for Analysis.* Boston: Harvard University Press.

Association of Minnesota Counties (1977). *Process for the Development of New Human Service Programs: A Guide for Human Service Agencies.* St. Paul: Association of Minnesota Counties.

Attewell, Paul and Rule, James (1984). "Computing and Organizations: What We Know and What We Don't Know." *Communications of the ACM* 27:12, 1184-92 (December).

Baier, Kurt and Rescher, Nicholas (1969). *Values and the Future.* New York: The Free Press.

Barker, Narviar (1986). "The Implications of Computer Technology in the Delivery of Human Services." *Journal of Sociology and Social Welfare* 8:1, 56-63.

Baskin, David and Seiffer, Samuel (n.d.). "A Nationwide Survey of Computer Utilization in Community Mental Health Centers." Albert Einstein College of Medicine/Sound View-Throgs Neck CMHC, Bronx, New York. Mimeo.

Beam, Paul (1982). "Telidon and Computer Aided Learning." *Proceedings from a Forum, The Social Impacts of Computerization.* University of Waterloo, January 14-16.

Bell, Daniel (1973). *The Coming of Post-Industrial Society.* New York: Basic Books.

Bellerby, Linda J. and Goslin, Lewis N. (1981). "Managing for Success: Assessing the Balanced MIS Environment." *Administration in Social Work* 5:3-4, 69-82.

Betcherman, G. and McMullen, K. (1986). *Working With Technology: A Survey of Automation in Canada.* Ottawa: Economic Council of Canada.

Birmingham, Michael (1981). "Computerized Management Information Systems in

Human Services: An Application in Mental Health.'' Unpublished M.S.W. practicum report, University of Manitoba.

Black, John (1982). ''Telidon: Social Aspects.'' *Proceedings from a Forum: The Social Impacts of Computerization*. University of Waterloo, January 14-16.

Blacklock, Wilma M. (1982). ''The Byte Bandwagon: A Case Study of Word Processing as Innovation.'' Mimeo.

Boden, Margaret A. (1982). ''Artificial Intelligence and Social Forecasting.'' *Proceedings from a Workshop, Microelectronics — Information Technology and Canadian Society*. Queen's University, Kingston, Ontario, May 5-7.

Bowers, Gary E. and Bowers, Margaret R. (1978). *The Elusive Unit of Service*. Washington, D.C.: U.S. Department of Health, Education and Welfare, Project SHARE, Human Service Monograph Series No. 5.

Boyd, Lawrence, Jr., Hylton, John H. and Price, Steven V. (1978). ''Computers in Social Work Practice and Review.'' *Social Work* 23:3, 368-71.

————, Pruger, Robert *et al.* (1982). ''A Decision Support System to Increase Equity.'' *Administration in Social Work* 5:3-4, 83-96.

Boyd, N. Kent and Silver, Evelyn Stern (1975). *Factors Affecting the Development and Implementation of Information Systems for Social Services: A Summary Report*. Washington, D.C.: Department of Health, Education and Welfare.

Brady, Terri (1983). ''The Rationalization and Routinization of Child Welfare: A Study of Service Delivery Patterns in Foster Care in the City of New York.'' S.U.N.Y. College at Old Westbury, St. Christopher's Home, October 15. Mimeo.

Bronson, Ellen (1986). ''Implementing Computer Systems for Social Service Agencies: An Analysis of Costs and Benefits for the Direct Service Staff.'' Unpublished Ph.D. dissertation, University of Michigan.

Brooker, W.M.A. (1965). ''The Total Systems Myth.'' *Systems and Procedures Journal* 16:2, 28-32.

Burnett, J. Dale (1982). ''Microelectronics and the Implicit School Curriculum.'' *Proceedings from a Workshop, Microelectronics — Information Technology and Canadian Society*. Queen's University, Kingston, Ontario, May 5-7.

Butterfield, William H. (1986). ''Computers In Social Work and Social Welfare, Issues and Perspectives.'' *Journal of Sociology and Social Work* 8:1, 5-26.

Campbell, Marie L. (1982). ''The Codification of Caring: Canadian Hospital Nursing in Transition.'' Mimeo.

Cannon, S., Krapfl, J.E. *et al.* (1976). ''Developing a Management Information System in a State Institution.'' Paper presented at the Midwestern Association of Behaviour Analysis, Chicago, May.

Catherwood, H.R. (1978). ''A Management Information System for Social Services,'' pp. 493-505 in Simon Slavin (ed.), *Social Administration: The Management of the Social Services*. New York: The Haworth Press.

Clement, Andrew (1986). ''Managerial Control and On-Line Processing at a Large Insurance Firm.'' Unpublished Ph.D. thesis, University of Toronto.

Cobb, C.W. (1976-1977). ''Problems and Principles in the Development of Management Information Systems.'' *International Journal of Mental Health* 5, 103-20.

Cohen, Stanley H., Noah, James C. and Pauley, Ann (1979). ''New Ways of Looking at Management Information Systems in Human Service Delivery.'' *Evalu-*

ation and Program Planning 2:1, 49-58.

Cordell, Arthur (1985). *The Uneasy Eighties — The Transition to an Information Society.* Ottawa: Science Council of Canada.

Cotter, Barbara (1981). *Planning and Implementing Social Service Information Systems: A Guide for Management and Users.* Washington, D.C.: U.S. Department of Health, Education and Welfare, Project SHARE, Human Service Monograph Series No. 25.

Danziger, James N. (1985). "Social Science and the Social Impacts of Computer Technology." *Social Science Quarterly* 66:1 (March), 3-21.

———— and Kraemer, K. (1986). *People and Computers — The Impact of Computing on End Users in Organizations.* New York: Columbia University Press.

Davidson, J.H. (1987). "Tech Change: Boom or Bane For Professionals, Supervisors and Middle Managers," pp. 54-58 in John Langford (ed.), *Fear and Ferment: Public Sector Management Today.* Montreal: The Institute of Public Administration of Canada.

Davis, Doryn and Allen, Richard (1979). "The Evolution of a MIS in an Outpatient Mental Health Institute." *Administation in Mental Health* 6:3, 225-39.

deGraff, Hein (1987). "Computers in the Dutch Social Services." *Computer Applications in Social Work and Allied Professions* 3:4, 15-19.

deGroot, Leo, Gripton, James and Liker, Paul (1987). "The Digital Social Worker: Microcomputers in Clinical Social Work Practice." Calgary: University of Calgary, Faculty of Social Welfare. Mimeo.

De Montigny, Gerald A.J. (1980). "The Social Organization of Social Workers' Practice: A Marxist Analysis." Unpublished M.A. thesis, University of Toronto.

Dermer, Jerry (1977). "Evaluation of Family Services Agency Information Systems." Mimeo.

Dery, David (1977). "The Bureaucratic Organization of Information Technology: Computers, Information Systems and Welfare Management." Unpublished Ph.D. thesis, University of California, Berkeley.

Dickson, G.W. and Simmons, John K. (1970). "The Behavioural Side of MIS: Some Aspects of the 'People Problem.'" *Business Horizons* 13 (August), 69-71.

Donahue, Jack M., Angell, Elizabeth *et al.* (1978). "The Social Service Information System," pp. 481-92 in Simon Slavin (ed.), *Social Administration: The Management of the Social Services.* New York: The Haworth Press.

du Feu, D. (1982). "Computers and Social Workers: The Reception of a Computerized Client Record System in Social Services Fieldwork District Offices." Unpublished Ph.D. thesis, Edinburgh University, Edinburgh, Scotland.

Eason, D.D. and Bjorn-Anderson, Neils (1980). "Myths and Realities of Information Systems Contributing to Organizational Rationality," pp. 97-110 in Abbe Mowshowitz (ed.), *Human Choice and Computers,* Vol. 2. Amsterdam: North Holland Publishing.

Ehlers, W.H., Austin, N.J. and Prothers, J.C. (1976). *Administration for the Human Services: An Introductory Programmed Text.* New York: Harper & Row.

Ein-Dor, Philip and Seger, Eli (1978). "Organizational Context and the Success of Management Information Systems." *Management Science* 24:10, 1631-41.

Ellul, Jacques (1968). *The Technological System.* New York: Vintage Books.

Etzioni, Amatai (1960). "Two Approaches to Organization Analysis: A Critique and a Suggestion." *Administrative Science Quarterly* 5, 257-78.

Farber, John M. and Sime, K.C. (1979). "A Computerized Department Information System." Mimeo.

Federation of Jewish Philanthropies of New York (1985). *Computerization in the Human Services: Proceedings of a Study Tour of a Delegation from Israel's Ministry of Labour and Social Affairs.* New York: Federation of Jewish Philanthropies Management Assistance Program.

Fein, Edith (1975). "A Data System for an Agency." *Social Work* 20:1, 21-24.

Flaherty, David H. (1982). "The Challenge of New Information Technology to Personal Privacy: A Canadian Perspective." *Proceedings from a Workshop, Microelectronics — Information Technology and Canadian Society.* Queen's University, Kingston, Ontario, May 5-7.

Fuller, Theron K. (1970). "Computer Utility in Social Work." *Social Casework* 51 (December), 606-11.

Gandy, John (1987). "The Impact of Computer Technology on 'People Processing' amd 'People Changing' Social Welfare Organizations." Paper delivered at First International Convention of Human Technology Applications, Birmingham, England, September 8-11.

―――― and Djao, Angela (1987a). "Staff Resistance to Computerization Information Systems in Social Welfare Organizations: Some Tentative Findings." *SPAN — Canadian Review of Social Policy* nos. 16-17, 59-65.

―――― (1987b). "Les reactions du Personnel à l'introduction et à l'utilisation de l'informatique dans les organismes de service social." *L'Information dans les Services Sociaux* 26:1, 33-53.

Geiss, Gunther R. and Viswanathan, Narayan (eds.) (1986). *The Human Edge: Information Technology and Helping People.* New York: The Haworth Press, Inc.

Glastonbury, Bryan (1985). *Computers in Social Work.* Practical Social Work Series. London: Macmillan Publishers Ltd.

―――― (1986). "Managing the Social Services Computer System: Some Problems and Pitfalls." *Computer Applications in Social Work and Allied Professions* 3:1, 10-13.

Globerman, Steven (1981). *The Adoption of Computer Technology in Selected Canadian Service Industries: Case Studies of Automation in University Libraries, Hospitals, Grocery Retailing and Wholesaling, and Department and Variety Stores.* Ottawa: The Economic Council of Canada.

Golstein, Howard (1973). *Social Work Practice: A Unitary Approach.* Columbia, South Carolina: University of South Carolina Press.

Goodfriend, Shirley (1979). "The Introduction and Utilization of a Computer Based Program Monitoring System in a Comprehensive Child Welfare Agency." Unpublished Ph.D. thesis, University of California, Berkeley.

Gorry, G. Anthony and Morton, Michael S. Scott (1971). "A Framework for Management: Information Systems." *Sloan Management Review* 13:1, 55-70.

Gotlieb, C.C. and Borodin, A. (1973). *Social Issues in Computing.* New York: Academic Press.

Griest, John H., Klein, Margoir H. *et al.* (1977). "Computer Measures of Patient Progress in Psycho-therapy." *Psychiatry Digest* 38:9, 23-32.

Gripton, James (n.d.) "Microcomputers and Word Processors: Their Contribution to Clinical Social Work Practice." Mimeo.

Gruber, Murray (1974). "Total Administration." *Social Work* 19:5, 625-36.

Grusec, Ted (1987). "Office Automation Trials in the Federal Government: Lessons for Managers," pp. 48-54 in John Langford (ed.), *Fear and Ferment: Public Sector Management Today*. Montreal: Institute of Public Administration of Canada.

Hammer, Allen L. and Hile, Matthew G. (1985). "Factors in Clinicians' Resistance to Automation in Mental Health." *Computers in Human Services* 1:3 (Fall), 1-25.

Hanbery, Glyn W., Sorensen, James E. and Kucie, A. Ronald (1982). "Management Information Systems and Human Service Resource Management." *Administration in Social Work* 5:3-4, 27-42.

Hardin, William G., Jr. (1970). "Human Relations and Automation." *Advanced Management Journal* 35:3, 43-48.

Harrison, W. David (1980). "Role Strain and Burnout in Child-Protective Services Workers." *Social Service Review* 54:1, 31-44.

Hasenfeld, Yeheskel (1972). "People-Processing Organizations: An Exchange Approach." *American Sociological Review* 37 (June), 256-63.

——— and English, R.A. (1974). *Human Service Organizations*. Ann Arbor: University of Michigan Press.

——— (1980). "Implementation of Change in Human Service Organizations: A Political Economy Perspective." *Social Service Review* 54:4, 508-20.

Herzlinger, Regina (1977). "Why Data Systems in Non-Profit Organizations Fail." *Harvard Business Review* 55:1, 81-86.

Hill, Gareth S. (1974). *Ethical Practices in the Computerization of Client Data: Implications for Social Work Practice and Record Keeping*. Washington, D.C.: National Association of Social Workers.

Holbrook, Terry (1986). "Computer Technology — 1984 and Beyond." *Journal of Sociology and Social Welfare* 13:1, 98-114.

Holland, Thomas P. (1977). "Management Information Systems for Human Services Programs." Paper prepared for the Evaluative Research Training Workshop, Faculty of Social Work, University of Regina, Canada.

Hoos, Ida (1960). "When the Computer Takes Over the Office." *Harvard Business Review* 38, 102-12.

———, I.R. (1972). *System Analysis in Public Policy: A Critique*. Berkeley: University of California Press.

Hoshino, George (1982). "Computers: Tool of Management and Social Work Practice." *Administration in Social Work* 5:3-4, 5-10.

——— and McDonald, Thomas P. (1975). "Agencies in the Computer Age." *Social Work* 20:1, 10-14.

Huckabay, Loucine, Anderson, Nancy *et al.* (1979). "Cognitive, Affective, and Transfer of Learning Consequences of Computer Assisted Instruction." *Nursing Research* 28:4, 228-33.

Institute for Research on Public Policy (1986). *International Symposium on the Impact of New Information Technologies on the Work Place*. Montreal: The Institute for Research on Public Policy.

Jaffe, Eliezer D. (1979). "Computers in Child Placement Planning." *Social Work*

25:5, 380-85.

Johnson, Deborah and Snapper, John (1985). *Ethical Issues in the Use of Computers*. Belmont, California: Wadsworth Publishing Co.

Jonasson, Sven (1980). "Computerization and Human and Social Requirements," pp. 53-70 in Abbe Mowshowitz (ed.), *Human Choice and Computers*, Vol. 2. Amsterdam: North Holland Publishing.

Jones, Kathleen, Brown, John and Bradshaw, Jonathan (1978). *Issues in Social Policy*. London: Routledge and Kegan Paul.

Jones, T.E. (1980). *Options for the Future: A Comparative Analysis of Policy Oriented Forecasts*. New York: Praeger Publishers.

Karger, Howard (1986). "The De-Skilling of Social Workers: An Examination of the Impact of the Industrial Model of Production on the Delivery of Social Services." *Journal of Sociology and Social Welfare* 13:1, 115-29.

Kates, Joseph (1982). "Perspectives on the Computer Age." *Proceedings from a Forum: The Social Impacts of Computerization*. University of Waterloo, January 14-16.

Kling, Rob (1976). *Automated Information Systems in Public Policymaking*. Irvine, California: Public Policy Research Organization, University of California.

_____ (1978). "Automated Welfare Client-Tracking and Service Integration: The Political Economy of Computing." *Communications of the ACM* 21:6 (June), 484-93.

_____ (1980a). "Social Issues and Impacts of Computing: From Arena to Discipline," pp. 25-46 in Abbe Mowshowitz (ed.), *Human Choice and Computers*, Vol. 2. Amsterdam: North Holland Publishing.

_____ (1980b). "Report of Working Group: Research of Social Issues and Impacts of Computing," pp. 47-52 in Abbe Mowshowitz (ed.), *Human Choice and Computers*, Vol. 2. Amsterdam: North Holland Publishing.

_____ (1980c). "Social Analyses of Computing: Theoretical Perspectives in Recent Empirical Research." *Computing Surveys* 12:1 (March), 61-110.

Kraemer, Kenneth L. (1976). *Local Government, Information Systems, and Technology Transfer. Evaluating Some Common Assertions about Transfer of Computer Applications*. University of California, Irvine, Public Policy Research Organization.

_____ and Dutton, William H. (1979). "The Interests Served by Technological Reform: The Case of Computing." *Administration and Society* 11:1, 80-105.

Kucic, A. Ronald, Sorensen, James and Hanbery, Glyn (1983). "Computer Selection for Human Service Organizations." *Administration In Social Work* 7:1, 43-75.

Kumar, Krishan (1978). *Prophecy and Progress: The Sociology of Industrial and Post Industrial Society*. Harmondsworth, England: Penguin Books.

LaMendola, W. (1976). "Management Information System Development for General Social Services." Unpublished doctoral dissertation, University of Minnesota, Minneapolis.

_____ (1985). "The Future of Human Service Information Technology: An Essay on the Number 42." *Computers in Human Services* 1:1 (Spring), 35-49.

Lenk, Klaus (1980). "Computer Use in Public Administation: Implications for the Citizen," pp. 193-212 in Abbe Mowshowitz (ed.), *Human Choice and Computers*, Vol. 2. Amsterdam: North Holland Publishing.

Levi, Linda (1985). "State of Computerization of the Jewish Federation Agency Network." New York: Federation of Jewish Philanthropies of New York. Mimeo.

Lewis, Harold (1978). "Management in the Non-Profit Social Service Organization," pp. 7-14 in Simon Slavin (ed.), *Social Administration: The Management of the Social Services*. New York: The Haworth Press.

Lowe, Burt H. and Sugarman, Barry (1978). "Design Considerations for Community Mental Health Management Information Systems." *Community Mental Health Journal* 14:3, 216-23.

Lucas, Henry C., Jr. (1975). "Performance and the Use of an Information System." *Management Science* 21:8, 908-19.

Luse, F. Dean (1980). "Use of Computer Simulation in Social Welfare Management." *Administration in Social Work* 4:3.

Mann, Louella (1986). "Social Service Delivery Systems: The Impact of Technology and Organizational Structure." *Journal of Sociology and Social Welfare* 13:1, 157-70.

Mannheim, Karl (1958). *Ideology and Utopia*. New York: Harvest Books.

Mason, Richard O. and Mitroff, Ian I. (1973). "A Program for Research on Management Information Systems." *Management Science* 19:5, 475-87.

McCurdy, W.B. (1976). "Commentary." *Social Casework* 57:7, 438-44.

McLuhan, Marshall (1965). *Understanding Media*. New York: McGraw-Hill.

Menzies, Heather (1981). *Women and the Chip: Case Studies in the Effects of Informatics on Employment in Canada*. Montreal: Institute for Research on Public Policy.

_____ (1982). *Computers on the Job*. Toronto: James Lorimer and Company.

Minahan, Anne (1981). "Social Workers and the Future." *Social Work* 26:5, 363-64.

Ministry of Community and Social Services (1978). *Consultation Paper: Information Systems Development for Children's Services in Ontario*. Toronto: Ministry of Community and Social Services, Children's Services Division.

Mowshowitz, Abbe (1976). *The Conquest of Will — Information Processing in Human Affairs*. Don Mills: Addison-Wesley Publishing.

_____ (1979). "Social Issues in Computing: Problem Definition and Research Strategy," pp. 336-50 in *Human Context for Science and Technology*. Ottawa: Social Science and Humanities Research Council of Canada.

_____ (1980a). "Ethics and Cultural Integration in a Computerized World," pp. 251-69 in Abbe Mowshowitz (ed.), *Human Choice and Computers*, Vol. 2. Amsterdam: North Holland Publishing.

_____ (1980b). "Afterthoughts and Reflections," pp. 291-99 in Abbe Mowshowitz (ed.), *Human Choice and Computers*, Vol. 2. Amsterdam: North Holland Publishing.

Mullis, Scott (1978). "Management Applications to the Welfare System," pp. 43-51 in Simon Slavin (ed.), *Social Administration: The Management of the Social Services*. New York: The Haworth Press.

Mutschler, Elizabeth and Cnaan, Ram A. (1985). "Success and Failure of Computerized Information Systems: Two Case Studies in Human Service Agencies." *Administration in Social Work* 9:1 (Spring), 67-79.

National Conference on Social Welfare (1976). *Expanding Management Technology and Professional Accountability in Social Service Programs.* Washington, D.C.: National Conference on Social Welfare.

National Institute for Social Work (1982). *Social Workers: Their Role and Task.* London: Bedford Square Press.

Neilson, Robert E. (1987). "Results of Human Services Systems Survey." *Computer Use in Social Services Network.* 7:1, 4-10.

Newman, Edward and Turem, Jerry (1978). "The Crisis of Accountability," pp. 310-25 in S. Slavin (ed.), *Social Administration: The Management of the Social Services.* New York: The Haworth Press.

Newson, Janice A. (1980). "New Perspectives on Occupational Studies with Reference to the Professions." Paper presented at Canadian Sociology and Anthropology Association Meeting, University of Quebec, Montreal, June 3-7.

Niece, D., Snider, L. and Zureik, E. (1982). "Issues in the Analysis of Information Based Societies." *Proceedings from a Workshop, Microelectronics — Information Technology and Canadian Society.* Queen's University, Kingston, May 5-7.

Noah, James C. (1978). "Information Systems in Human Services: Misconceptions, Deceptions and Ethics." *Administration in Mental Health* 5:2, 99-111.

Noble, John H., Jr. (1971). "Protecting the Public's Privacy in Computerized Health and Welfare Systems." *Social Work* 16:1, 35-41.

Nolan, R.L. (1979). "Managing the Crises in Data Processing." *Harvard Business Review* 57 (March-April), 115-26.

Nutter, R. (1983). "Information Systems and Social Work Practitioners." *The Social Worker* 51:1, 3-7.

Office of Technology Assessment (1981). "Computer Based National Information Systems." *Computers and Society* 11:4, 3-11.

——— (1982). "An Assessment of Alternatives for a National Computerized Criminal History System." *Computers and Society* 12:3, 14-25.

Ottley, Pennie and Kempson, Elaine (1982). *Computer Benefits? Guidelines for Local Information and Advice Centers.* London: National Consumer Council.

Papert, Seymour A. (1980). "Computers and Learning," pp. 73-86 in Michael L. Dertouzos and Joel Moses (eds.), *The Computer Age: A Twenty-Year View.* Cambridge, Mass.: M.I.T. Press.

Patti, R. (1978). "The New Scientific Management: Systems Management for Social Welfare," pp. 345-59 in S. Slavin (ed.), *Social Administration: The Management of the Social Services.* New York: The Haworth Press.

Peitchinis, Stephen G. (1982). "Microelectronic Technology and Employment: Micro and Macro Effects." *Proceedings from a Workshop, Microelectronics — Information Technology and Canadian Society.* Queen's University, Kingston, May 5-7.

Pettingill, Peter Garfield (1983). "A Design for a Randomized Trial to Assess the Effect of a Computerized Information System on Services Delivered by Children's Mental Health Centres in Ontario." Unpublished M.Sc. thesis, McMaster University.

Phillips, Bruce A., Dimsdale, Bernard and Taft, Ethel (1982). "An Information System for the Social Casework Agency: A Model and Case Study." *Administration in Social Work* 5:3-4, 129-44.

Poertner, John and Rapp, Charles A. (1980). "Information System Design in Foster

Care." *Social Work* 22:2, 114-19.

Pounds, W.F. (1969). "The Process of Problem Finding." *Industrial Management Review* 11:1, 1-20.

Quinn, Robert E. (1976). "Impacts of a Computerized Information System in the Integration and Coordination of Human Services." *Public Administration Review* 36:2, 166-74.

_____ and Greenberg, Myron (1973). *Computer Information Systems for Human Services: An Impact Analysis.* Cincinnati, Ohio: Information Systems Center.

_____, Walker, Donald B. *et al.* (1973). *Development of a Computer Based Information System for Social Service Agencies.* Cincinnati, Ohio: Information Systems Center.

Rapp, Charles A. (1984). "Information, Performance, and the Human Service Manager of the 1980s: Beyond 'Housekeeping.'" *Administration in Social Work* 8:2 (Summer), 69-79.

Reamer, Frederic G. (1986). "The Use of Modern Technology in Social Work: Ethical Dilemmas." *Social Work* 31:6 (November-December), 469-71.

Reid, William J. (1974). "Developments in the Use of Organized Data." *Social Work* 19:5, 585-93.

Rode, Roderick (1986). "Computer Innovation in Social Services." Unpublished Master of Social Welfare thesis, Faculty of Social Welfare, University of Calgary.

Rogers, Everett and Kincaid, D. Lawrence (1981). *Communication Networks: Toward a New Paradigm for Research.* New York: The Free Press.

Rubin, Elliot R. (1976). "The Implementation of an Effective Computer System." *Social Casework* 57 (July), 433-45.

Sarri, R.C. and Hasenfeld, Y., eds. (1978). *The Management of Human Services.* New York: Columbia University Press.

Schoech, Dick (1979). "A Microcomputer Based Human Service Information System." *Administration in Social Work* 3:4, 423-40.

_____ and Arangio, T. (1979). "Computers in the Human Services." *Social Work* 24:2, 96-102.

_____ and Schkade, Lawrence L. (1980a). "Computers Helping Caseworkers: Decision Support Systems." *Child Welfare* 59:9 (November), 566-75.

_____ (1980b). "What Human Services Can Learn from Business about Computerization." *Public Welfare* 38:3, 18-27.

_____ (1981). "Human Service Workers as the Primary Information System User." Mimeo.

_____ (1982). *Computer Use in Human Services: A Guide to Information Management.* New York: Human Sciences Press.

_____ and Mayers, Raymond S. (1982). "Strategies for Information Systems Development." *Administration in Social Work* 5:3-4, 11-26.

Sharron, Howard (1984). "The Ghost in the Machine." *Social Work Today* 15:21, 14-17.

Siporin, Max (1975). *Introduction to Social Work Practice.* New York: Macmillan Publishing Co., Inc.

Sircar, Sumit, Schkade, Lawrence L. and Schoech, Dick (1983). "The Data Base Management System Alternative for Computing in the Human Services." *Administration in Social Work* 7:1, 51-62.

Skinner, Harvey A. and Allen, Barbara A. (1983). "Does the Computer Make a Difference? Computerized Versus Face-to-Face Versus Self-Report Assessment of Alcohol, Drug and Tobacco Use." *Journal of Consulting and Clinical Psychology* 51:2, 267-75.

Staff Association of the Children's Aid Society of Metropolitan Toronto (1978). *A Brief to the Commission on Freedom of Information and Individual Privacy.* Toronto: Children's Aid Society of Metropolitan Toronto.

Sullivan, Richard J. (1980). "Human Issues in Computerized Social Services." *Child Welfare* 59:7, 401-406.

Tepperman, Lorne (1984). "Informatics and Society: Will There Be an 'Information Revolution'?" Paper presented at a symposium, Computers and Society, Ryerson Polytechnical Institute, Toronto, January 30.

Thies, James B. (1975). "Hospital Personnel and Computer Based Systems: A Study of Attitudes and Perceptions." *Hospital Administration* 20:1, 17-26.

Toffler, Alvin (1981). *The Third Wave.* New York: Bantam Books.

Trute, Barry, Tefft, Bruce and Scuse, David (1982). *An Overview of the Design and Implementation of the Manitoba Health Centres Information System: A Final Report.* Winnipeg: Manitoba Health Centres Project, School of Social Work, University of Manitoba.

Trute, B., Tonn, R. and Ford, G. (n.d.). *Privacy and Computerized Health Information in Community Health Centres and District Health Systems.* Working Papers: Health Centres Information System. Winnipeg: University of Manitoba.

———— (n.d.). *Human Factors in Establishing and Maintaining a Computerized Health Information System.* Working Papers: Health Centres Information System. Winnipeg: University of Manitoba.

Turkle, Sherry (1980). "Computer as Rorschach." *Society* 17:2. Reprinted in Gary Gumpert and Robert Cathcart (eds.), *Inter/Media: Interpersonal Communication.* 2nd ed. New York: Oxford University Press, 1982.

Velasquez, Joan S. and Lynch, Mary M. (1982). "Computerized Information Systems: A Practice Orientation." *Administration in Social Work* 5:3-4, 113-28.

Vogel, Lynn Harold (1985). "Decision Support Systems in the Human Services: Discovering Limits to a Promising Technology." *Computers in Human Services* 1:1 (Spring), 67-80.

Walltersteiner, Ulrika (1982). "System Ergonomics: Enhancing the People-Technology Relationships in Offices," pp. 58-60 in John Langford (ed.), *Fear and Ferment: Public Sector Management Today.* Montreal: The Institute of Public Administration of Canada.

Walton, Richard E. (1982). "Social Choice in the Development of Advanced Information Technology." *Technology in Society* 4, 41-49.

Waterloo Public Interest Research Group (1982). *Proceedings from a Forum: The Social Impacts of Computerization.* University of Waterloo, January. Waterloo: University of Waterloo.

Weiner, Myron E. (1982). "Computers for Modern Human Services Management," pp. 286-330 in *Human Services Management: Analysis and Applications.* Homewood, Ill.: Dorsey.

Weirich, Thomas W. (1980). "The Design of Information Systems." pp. 142-56 in Felice D. Perlmutter and Simon Slavin (eds.), *Leadership in Social Adminis-*

tration. Philadelphia: Temple University Press.

Weissman, Harold H. (1977). "Clients, Staff, and Researchers: Their Role in Management Information Systems." *Administration in Social Work* 1:1 (Spring), 43-51.

———— (1983). "Accountability and Pseudo-Accountability: A Non-Linear Approach." *Social Service Review* 57:2, 323-36.

Welbourn, Anna (1980). "Management Tools and Social Service Delivery: A Contemporary Consideration." Mimeo.

Wilensky, Harold D. (1967). *Organizational Intelligence*. New York: Basic Books.

Williams, Robert (1983). "Thinking About Technological Change." *Perception* 6:4, 12-14.

Wilson, J.Q. (1966). "Innovation in Organizations: Notes Towards a Theory." pp. 193-219 in J.D. Thompson (ed.), *Approaches to Organizational Design*. Pittsburgh: University of Pittsburgh Press.

Yadav, Surya B. (1983). "Determining An Organization's Information Requirements: A State of the Art Survey." *Data Base* 14:3, 3-20.

Yin, Robert (1984). *Case Study Research Design and Methods*. Beverly Hills: Sage Publications.

Young, David W. (1974). "Management Information Systems in Child Care: An Agency Experience." *Child Welfare* 53 (February), 102-11.

Zuboff, Shoshana (1982). "New Methods of Computer-Mediated Work." *Harvard Business Review* 60 (September-October), 142-52.

INDEX